NEW LIGHT

ON DR. JOHNSON

NEW LIGHT
ON DR. JOHNSON

Essays on the Occasion of

his 250th Birthday

EDITED BY FREDERICK W. HILLES

New Haven: Yale University Press

1 9 5 9

Contents

Illustrations

Thomas Trotter's engraving, whatever its aesthetic merits, must be ranked as one of the most important likenesses of Johnson. It was taken from the life; it has more evidential value than handsomer portraits; and it is the parent of a large family of derivatives. Its place in this volume marks its rise from neglect to deserved attention.

Johnson sat to Trotter late in 1781 or early in 1782 at the request of George Kearsley, publisher of The Beauties of Johnson, *who intended the head for the frontispiece to Part II of the* Beauties. *Trotter made an engraving from his own drawing, and dated it 1 February 1782. At the last moment, George Steevens persuaded Kearsley to withdraw the portrait, as being "very ugly," and when the book appeared after some delay on 19 February it contained a head drawn by J. Harding.*

A few proofs of the rejected Trotter engraving were pulled for Johnson to give his friends. Kearsley held the plate until immediately after Johnson's death, when he had sudden need for a frontispiece to the Life of Johnson *by William Cooke, which was published on 30 December 1784. Trotter's original date was erased from the plate, the date 16 December 1784 substituted, and the engraving prefixed to Cooke's life in this form.*

Knowing the engraving only with the later date, Professor Tinker argued that Flaxman could not have used it for his Wedgwood medallion, though Flaxman's bill to Wedgwood includes the cost of a print used as a model. The availability of the Trotter engraving in 1782 and the close resemblance of the Wedgwood medallion to it clearly show that it served as the model for Flaxman, as it has for later and less distinguished artists.

H W L

Preface

Throughout the greater part of his life Johnson, like Bernard Shaw, deplored public notice of his birthday. To him the occasion was not a time for celebration; it was "an awful day," and more than once he was annoyed to discover that Boswell had brought it to the attention of those whom the two were visiting. "The return of my birthday, if I remember it, fills me with thoughts which it seems to be the general care of humanity to escape." The anniversary forced him to consider past and future. It reminded him that he had accomplished little and that he was one step nearer the terrors of death.

That Johnson's admirers today are celebrating his two hundred and fiftieth birthday suggests that in fact he managed to accomplish a good deal and that in a sense he has never died. Not only in his native Lichfield or his beloved London but in such widely separated places as Oslo in the north and the River Platte in the south, men and women now gather to toast his immortal memory. One such group, calling itself *The Johnsonians*, has since 1946 met annually in or near New York, and it is *The Johnsonians* who have seen fit to sponsor this volume.

To the undersigned has fallen the task of assembling the materials and of seeing them through the press. Throughout he has been ably assisted by the Messrs. Osborn and Liebert, chairmen respectively in 1958 and 1959. All the contributors are members, or honorary members, of *The Johnsonians*. Approximately half the volume consists of essays and commentaries that have never before been published. The others have existed as privately printed pamphlets or have been buried in bound volumes of periodicals, and of these almost all are here presented in a revised form.

Johnson himself would, at least in principle, have approved of this collection. "Pamphlets and small tracts," he wrote, are "a very important part of an English library." They are particularly valued by "those who aspire to the reputation of judicious collectors of books . . . because many advantages may be expected from the perusal of these small productions which are scarcely to be found in that of larger works." He adds that "our attempt to unite them in volumes cannot be thought either useless or unseasonable," since it may prevent "the loss of many pieces which deserve to be transmitted to another age."

It will be obvious that these pieces follow no common pattern. Some are long, some short; some biographical, some critical; some grave, some gay. But each in its way sheds new light on the subject. The adjective *new* may call to mind a remark Johnson made to Boswell soon after the two first met. "When I was a boy," he said, "I used always to choose the wrong side of a debate, because most ingenious things, that is to say, most new things, could be said upon it." Here Johnson was equating the new with the false, a charge that we hope cannot be levelled at this book. What is new in the following pages derives in part from materials that have only recently been unearthed, in part from a fresh reading of what Johnson wrote. Interest in Johnson's life and character is perennial. The fact that his writings are still being recreated by readers of the mid-twentieth century proves, as their author might have said with complacency, that they possess a vitality which has preserved them from putrefaction.

F W H

Acknowledgments

For permission to reprint certain essays we express our thanks to the editors and sponsors of the periodicals listed below.

Mr. Lewis' paper, in a slightly altered version, was first published in *The Virginia Quarterly Review*, xxv (1949), 66–73. Admittedly it sheds little "new light" on Johnson, but it is here included because it is the sole survivor of the early talks delivered before *The Johnsonians*. The essays by Mr. and Mrs. Hyde and Mr. Osborn have already appeared in shorter versions as pamphlets privately printed for members of *The Johnsonians*.

Originally an address to the Johnson Society of London, in 1941, Professor Nichol Smith's paper was published in *The Review of English Studies*, xix (1943), 44–50; it has been revised for this volume. Professor Butt's, an address to the Johnson Society this year, has been published in *The New Rambler*. Dr. Metzdorf's is a rewriting of a short article published in *The Harvard Library Bulletin*, iv (1950), 265–68. Professor Kolb's is here reprinted with minor alterations from *Modern Philology*, xlvii (1949), 24–31. Professor Quinlan's is reprinted from *The Pennsylvania Magazine of History and Biography*, lxxiii (1949), 34–44. Professor Clifford's is a revision of what was published in *The Columbia University Forum*, i (1958), 32–37. Professor Pottle's is a rewriting of his article in *Modern Language Notes*, lvi (1941), 325–29. Professor Abrams' is a shortened version of the article in *ELH*, ix (1942), 235–44. The greater part of Professor Bronson's was published in *ELH*, xiv (1947), 163–77, and in *Modern Language Notes,* LXXI (1956), 533–41. The other contributions are now first printed. Professor Wimsatt's was written as a lecture delivered in the Yale Library at the opening of an exhibition entitled "Johnson's Dictionary."

CUE TITLES

Diaries—Samuel Johnson, *Diaries, Prayers, and Annals,* ed. E. L. McAdam, Jr., with Donald and Mary Hyde, 1958.

Letters—*Letters of Samuel Johnson,* ed. R. W. Chapman, 3 vols., 1952.

Life—Boswell's *Life of Johnson,* ed. Hill–Powell, 6 vols., 1934–50.

Lives—Johnson's *Lives of the English Poets,* ed. G. B. Hill, 3 vols., 1905.

Miscellanies—*Johnsonian Miscellanies,* ed. G. B. Hill, 2 vols., 1897.

Poems—*The Poems of Samuel Johnson,* ed. D. Nichol Smith and E. L. McAdam, Jr., 1941.

Pope—Johnson's *Life of Pope* in Volume III of *Lives* above.

Private Papers—*Private Papers of James Boswell from Malahide Castle* (Isham Collection), ed. Geoffrey Scott and Frederick A. Pottle, 19 vols., 1929–36.

The Young Waterman

WILMARTH SHELDON LEWIS

When I was asked eleven years ago to talk to *The Johnsonians* at their annual dinner I of course accepted at once (what student of the eighteenth century has ever missed a chance to talk about Samuel Johnson?), but then I was left with the question, "What can I say to an audience that will answer 'Lily' at once if asked the name of Johnson's other cat and that knows the works of Derrick by heart?" The dinner was only three weeks off; I was away from Farmington, but I did have with me the copy of the *Life* I used in a Yale College course called "The Age of Johnson." It is the Oxford edition of 1904, a pleasant, handy, fat little book on India paper. Its blue binding is travel-worn: this copy went to Brazil by ship on my wedding trip and thence to Genoa and other cities; it has been to Australia by air and the islands of the South Pacific; it has sailed the seas and been

> hors'd
> Upon the sightless couriers of the air.

I determined to try the *Sortes Johnsonianae*. As I held the book it slowly opened at page 305 of Volume 1 and I read:

> On Saturday, July 30th, Dr Johnson and I took a sculler at the Temple-stairs, and set out for Greenwich. I asked him if he really thought a knowledge of the Greek and Latin languages an essential requisite to a good education. JOHNSON. "Most certainly, Sir; for those who know them have a very great advantage over those who do not. Nay, Sir, it is wonderful what a difference learning makes upon

1

people even in the common intercourse of life, which does not appear to be much connected with it." "And yet (said I) people go through the world very well, and carry on the business of life to good advantage, without learning." JOHNSON. "Why, Sir, that may be true in cases where learning cannot possibly be of any use; for instance, this boy rows us as well without learning, as if he could sing the song of Orpheus to the Argonauts, who were the first sailors." He then called to the boy, "What would you give, my lad, to know about the Argonauts?" "Sir (said the boy), I would give what I have." Johnson was much pleased with his answer, and we gave him a double fare. Dr Johnson then turning to me, "Sir (said he) a desire of knowledge is the natural feeling of mankind; and every human being, whose mind is not debauched, will be willing to give all that he has to get knowledge."

We landed at the Old Swan, and walked to Billingsgate, where we took oars, and moved smoothly along the silver Thames. It was a fine day. We were entertained with the immense number and variety of ships that were lying at anchor, and with the beautiful country on each side of the river.

Boswell introduced the subject of preaching and Methodism, and when they got to Greenwich he appropriately quoted the passage on "the seat which gave Eliza birth" from Johnson's *London*, a copy of which, by coincidence, he had in his pocket. They talked of the poetry of Buchanan, and presently came to "the business of the day," which was Johnson's advice as to Boswell's course of study at Utrecht. This advice Boswell did not, unfortunately, record fully. They stayed so long at Greenwich that the return up the river was by no means as pleasant as in the morning. Boswell shivered in the cold. "Why do you shiver?" Johnson asked, not at all pleased, as if Boswell's shivering "had been a paltry effeminacy." The day concluded at the Turk's Head with Boswell talking about his family and hereditary estate, which gave pleasure to both of the friends. At the end of the evening came the great announcement: when Boswell set out for Holland, Johnson would accompany him as far as Harwich. "I could not find words to express what I felt upon this unexpected and very great mark of his affectionate regard," Boswell concludes.

When I think over that pleasant summer's day there are three or four details in it which stand out. They are not the beauties of Buchanan, or the effectiveness of the Scotch clergy preaching the "discipline of regulated piety," nor the "silver Thames"—not a very original phrase? Boswell's failure to take notes on "the business of the day," Johnson's advice as to a course of study, is noteworthy, but I shall remember longer Boswell producing his copy of *London* at Greenwich, Johnson's annoyance at Boswell's shivering, and the young sculler who would give what he had to know about the Argonauts.

The great set-pieces—the meeting with Wilkes, the visit to the King's library—are not, I think, what give most of us who read in the *Life* as inclination leads us year after year our greatest delight. It is rather such a passage as the one I have read, with its many notes on a day's or evening's apparently desultory, accidental, and haphazard talk and companionship. Stress must be laid on the "apparently," as the production of his copy of *London* by Boswell proves. Mr. Tinker has shown that the trip to Greenwich was proposed by Johnson; and that Boswell wrote on the morning of the expedition that he would read Johnson's lines on Greenwich to him while they were there. To readers of the *Life*, Boswell's quotation appears as the apt response of a well-stocked mind, but we know that it was artful preparation. Did Johnson suspect it was? He must have seen through this rather clumsy device to please? It is not to be wondered at that when the novelty of such flattery had worn off, Johnson was gagged by it. But this was not the day when he said, "Sir, you have but two topics, yourself and me. I am sick of both." This was the 30th of July 1763, a benign and sunny day that closed with a chill and nipping breeze. What a contrast between the triumphant Boswell quoting the lines about Eliza's seat and the shivering young man crouching in the open boat on the return trip up the leaden Thames while his well-upholstered middle-aged friend snorted with contempt! "Paltry effeminacy!" Our sympathies are with the scorned.

But the high point of the day, I hope you'll agree, is neither of these passages, nor even the final, unexpected, and oh-so-welcome warmth of the elder man's promise to accompany the younger at the outset of his travels. When one reflects that they had met only seventy-five days earlier, that offer is, indeed, proof of the rapidity with which Boswell established his friendships; but the high moment of the day, I think, was provided by the young sculler who would have given what he had to know about the Argonauts. It is so dignified and so wistful that we long to know more about the speaker. Here he is in his scull pulling a not inconsiderable weight from the Temple-stairs to the Old Swan, a young waterman without a name. We know from the pictures of Scott and Canaletto that he is probably brightly dressed, perhaps with red or blue breeches, a white coat, and a red or black velvet cap. He is sturdy and he is earnest. Johnson and Boswell are sitting in the stern of the boat. The rhythmical movement of the boy strongly rowing has caught Johnson's attention. He likes this lad, whose face is not without intelligence, and he begins to talk for the boy's benefit: his explanation that the Argonauts were the first sailors was not made for Boswell's instruction. Then he brings the boy into

4

the conversation and he, in seven monosyllables, secures his place in the chronicle of the age.

What inspired that remarkable reply? How much had the boy understood of the conversation? He knew what sailors were, but "learning"? Did he perhaps suddenly receive what Homer calls "that divine prompting by which Zeus very often gives mankind an inkling of the truth," a communication which is readily received by simple minds? I think he did and I have grounds for thinking so. The pair before him must have seemed like persons from another world: the big man with the "loud voice and slow deliberate utterance" talked of strange matters with authority; what he said was so. He said that this learning which the first sailors had gave even the poor a great advantage in life; furthermore, it was something desirable in and for itself. So, when the question was unexpectedly put, the boy was ready with his answer: learning was worth all one had.

And now let us put the *Life* down and try to imagine what happened to the young waterman. How did he spend his double fare? In the ordinary pleasures of watermen? We prefer to think otherwise. I see him shyly entering a bookshop in the Poultry at the first opportunity, propelled to this audacity by the thought of gods and men. I see him emerging with a six-penny copy of Chapman's Homer—the assistant could make little out of his talk except that he wanted an old book about the sea. The boy hurried to his squalid waterside lodging, opened his book and—but, come to think of it, could he read? Alas, almost certainly he could not, and the question we were beginning to nourish, did he become a poet? was he a second John Taylor? is answered: we shall never find a volume of poems by James Blank, the Poetical Waterman, to put beside those of James Essex, the Poetical Bricklayer, James Wood-house, the Poetical Shoemaker, and Ann Yearsley, or Lactilla, the Poetical Milkmaid. Is it not, perhaps, just as well? We know what Johnson later said of Woodhouse: it was better to "furnish the man with good implements for his trade, than raise subscriptions for his poems."

Nevertheless, let us try again. The young waterman is rowing sturdily down the river: St Paul's looms behind us, All Hallows is on our left, the Old Swan stairs and Fishmonger's Hall are just ahead; what happened to him when his two fares clambered ashore to avoid "shooting the Bridge," and walked away to Billingsgate?

The memory of that short meeting lingered on in the boy's mind. We assume that he never sailed the wine-dark sea in a running ship, but did he perhaps win the race for Doggett's coat and badge—that agonizing race "rowed against the tide when the tide runs the strongest" between Chelsea and London Bridge in a single scull amid the river traffic and at the mercy of the flotsam and jetsam which, hidden by the waves, may smash the boat and sink its rower's hopes forever? If he won the race he received twenty guineas and enjoyed the protection of the Fishmongers Company the rest of his life. On its feast days he stood in a corner of the Hall, resplendent in his scarlet coat with the great silver badge bound about his left arm, for which service he was given a guinea. Yes, this is better, and I offer it for what it is worth to Johnsonian scholars, the keenest in the world. Gentlemen, let's see who is the first at Fishmonger's Hall!

And while you are about it, can you identify the youth with Tom Tugg who sang in Dibdin's *Waterman* of how he won the race for Doggett's coat and badge? If you can, it will add the needed touch of romance to his biography, his winning of Wilelmina:

> I row'd for the prize [Tom sings]
> To receive from those eyes
> A kind look, from those lips a sweet smile . . .

There wasn't a length between him and the next boat,

> But the Swan once in view,
>   My boat how it flew!
>   And verily b'lieve 'twas all thinking of you.

Married to Wilelmina and assured of lasting felicity, he perhaps became the father of sons who sang the song of Orpheus to their respected parent. You will want to know what happened to these sons. By the time you reach *their* sons you will have got the family to Eton and Christ Church, from whence it is an easy canter into Parliament, the upper ranks of the clergy, and the Grenadier Guards. When you have finished your researches you will yourself be old and full of honours and you will have demonstrated by your life and works how kind fate is to lads who love the classics.

Still, will your definitive biography of the young waterman mean more to posterity than Boswell's? On second thought, let us say Godspeed and farewell to the boy where Boswell left him, steadying his boat at the Old Swan stairs while the young man helped the big man lumber ashore. They bestowed upon him, quite accidentally and casually, the gift of immortality, and that should be enough for any man.

Johnson's Poems

DAVID NICHOL SMITH

The occasion of what I have now to say is the recent publication by the Clarendon Press of an edition of the poems of Samuel Johnson.[1] At no period since the days of Boswell has so much been added to our knowledge of Johnson as during the time while this edition has been in preparation. The Boswell papers have been brought from the obscurity of Malahide Castle by Colonel Isham. Most of the papers left by Mrs. Thrale—which are of great value to an editor of the poems—are now accessible, whether in the Rylands Library or the Huntington Library, and other manuscripts have trickled into the auction room. Poems of which the existence was unsuspected have been put up for sale, and have passed to America. One of these is the early "Feast of St. Simon and St. Jude," to which there is no parallel in the rest of Johnson's extant verse. In it he gave scope to poetic fervour in a way which he never allowed himself again. When I showed it to my friend Lascelles Abercrombie and asked him who was the author of this unknown poem he replied at once, "Why, Christopher Smart." It was a reasonable mistake. The poem is written in the stanza of the "Song to David," and it has a lift and a surge that remind us of that Song, which was not written till twenty years later.

> Thrice happy Saints—where do I rove?
> Where doth extatick fury move
> My rude unpolish'd song;
> Mine unharmonious verse profanes

1. This paper was originally an address to the Johnson Club, London, 11 Dec 1941.

9

Those names which in immortal strains
Angelick choirs have sung.

Henceforward Johnson was to hold his "extatick fury" in control. That he ever indulged it, even in his school days, *we* did not know. I say *we*, for there is good reason to believe that Boswell saw this poem and passed it over—passed it over in favour of other early pieces which gave a clearer indication of Johnson's mature manner.

Johnson's verse covers his whole life, from his school days till within a week of his death. His last poem bears the date 5 December 1784. Let us not lose sight of this, that on his death-bed he should have chosen to write verse, or rather wrote it without exercising any choice. We think of him as a prose man, and we are not wrong in so doing. But we must not forget the great number of occasions, throughout all his life, when his thoughts found their natural expression in verse. I believe it to be a common view that his greater poems—and *The Vanity of Human Wishes* is a very great poem which stands by itself in all our literature—were wrung fom this prose man with an effort, that his verse in general was produced by the methodical process of measuring syllables. Why he should have been moved to indulge in this process, what satisfaction he found in it that prose could not give, are questions which open up the wider question of the nature of poetry, and that need not detain us. We may follow the example that he set us in his *Life of Pope* and ask, if the greater passages of *The Vanity of Human Wishes* are not poetry, where is poetry to be found?

Some of us may be tempted to apply to him his own comments on the verses of Richard Bentley. We are told by Boswell, who was putting in his own words what he had heard from Langton, that Johnson one day gave high praise to Bentley's verses in Dodsley's *Collection* and recited them with his usual energy. Adam Smith, who was present, observed in his decisive professorial manner, "Very well—very well." Whereupon Johnson added, "Yes, they *are* very well, Sir; but you may observe in what manner they are well. They are the forcible verses of a man of a strong mind, but not accustomed to write verse."

Now that, I think, is what many people are disposed to say of his own. Yet the complete collection of his poems, as complete as it can at present be made, and arranged in the order in which they were written, shows that he dropped into verse all his life, humorously, or lightheartedly, or seriously, and at times gravely when he was deeply moved. There were thoughts and feelings which asked for utterance in verse and for which it was the only language.

When I recently ventured to express the opinion that the whole body of his poems affords us as true and vivid a picture of his mind as we gain from his prose, it was challenged, in the ease of conversation, by a friend who wondered if I had not been betrayed into an overstatement. But that is an opinion by which I am prepared to abide. Let us be frank with ourselves and admit that our picture of Johnson is usually derived from Boswell—that is, in the main, from the records of his talk. I do not think that many of us have derived it mainly from his prose writings. But in his poems, whether deliberate pieces or mere scraps of verse, we catch glimpses of facets which he did not mean to reveal in prose intended for the public; and this, I think, is not too bold a distinction, that he wrote his prose for the public, as most people do, and that in much of his verse he wrote for himself or for his closest friends. His minor pieces, which he never hoped to see printed, have more to tell us about himself than we might have expected.

But in order to get this picture at its truest, we have to read his Latin verse as well as his English. Latin was a living language to Johnson, and it was the language which he preferred for the expression of certain moods and feelings. His very last poem, written on his death-bed, was in Latin. When he has finished revising the *Dictionary* for its fourth edition and is musing on the drudgery which it has cost him, and the listlessness and depression which have followed, he writes in Latin. I quote from the expanded translation by Arthur Murphy:

> The listless will succeeds, that worst disease,
> The rack of indolence, the sluggish ease.
> Care grows on care, and o'er my aching brain
> Black Melancholy pours her morbid train.
> No kind relief, no lenitive at hand,
> I seek at midnight clubs the social band;
> But midnight clubs, where wit with noise conspires,
> Where Comus revels, and where wine inspires,
> Delight no more: I seek my lonely bed,
> And call on Sleep to sooth my languid head.
> But Sleep from these sad lids flies far away;
> I mourn all night, and dread the coming day.

Such a confession of his state of mind, such matter so intimately personal, Johnson could not have paraded before English readers. Or when on a visit to Lichfield late in life he recalls how in his happy childhood he was taught to swim by his father in a pool that was overhung with trees and I suspect became more umbrageous as he viewed it through the mists of memory, again Latin is necessarily his language. Poems about himself and his feelings he did not write in English. If we take all his English poems that most readily occur to us—*London, The Vanity of Human Wishes*, the verses to Sir John Lade and on the Death of Dr. Robert Levet, and the Prologues—in not one of them does he speak directly about himself, though personal experience sometimes lies clearly behind what he says.

Two cant words in modern criticism are "romantic" and

"classical"—cant words, I borrow his own phrase; but he did not apply it to them, for he did not recognize the distinction implied in these handy labels which may save the trouble of clear thinking. I should like to have heard him giving his views on these two words, so dear to critics for the last hundred years. Some of us to-day are far from sure what they mean. But assuming for the moment that there is a clear distinction between the "classical" and the "romantic," that impersonality is the prerogative of the one, and that the other takes under its wing the more intimate individual experiences with their evanescent shades of feeling, we shall then have to say that Johnson wrote his "romantic" poems in Latin and his "classical" poems in English. By any definition of the term that I know, some of his Latin poems are "romantic." But it is a term of which I wish that we were rid.

In his Latin there is a considerable body of verse which is represented in English only by that early piece to which I have already alluded, "Upon the Feast of St. Simon and St. Jude." He frequently expressed his dislike of religious poetry, and he wrote against it in the *Lives of the Poets*. "In sacred poetry who has succeeded?" he asks. "Let no pious ear be offended if I advance, in opposition to many authorities, that poetical devotion cannot often please." "From poetry the reader justly expects, and from good poetry always obtains, the enlargement of his comprehension and elevation of his fancy; but this is rarely to be hoped by Christians from metrical devotion." "It is sufficient for Watts to have done better than others what no man has done well." Johnson spoke from long experience both as writer and reader, for his own religious verses belong to widely separated periods of his life, though mainly to the time of the *Lives of the Poets*. We need not make any claims for them which he himself would not have made. Many of the pieces are based on collects, such as the death-bed verses. Their outstanding quality is their earnestness and intimate humility. What we need no longer ignore is that they are preserved for us in sufficient numbers to rank him as a religious poet, though a minor one. But they are all, after his school days, in Latin.

So far I have said little about his English poems. His slighter pieces, most of which have been preserved for us by Mrs. Thrale, we may be tempted to pass by, because they are slight. But they represent the gay and jovial side of his nature, which I rather think we should not know so well without them. At least one of them was written in "a fit of frolicsome gaiety." He was never quite so frolicsomely gay in the company of Boswell as in that of the witty, attractive, responsive, vexing Mrs. Thrale. He was completely at his ease with Boswell, but he always knew what Boswell was about, and he was less disposed to mere clever fun in Boswell's company, when the note-book was never far away, than in that of his less methodical and more occupied hostess. Baretti remarked on Johnson's power of improvisation; he can do it as well, he said, as any Italian of us all if he pleases. We should have known less about this power had Mrs. Thrale not jotted down her recollections at her leisure.

The verses on Mrs. Thrale's nephew, Sir John Lade—

> Long-expected one and twenty
> Ling'ring year at last is flown—

were written for Mrs. Thrale. On sending them to her he wrote: "I have enclosed a short song of congratulation, which you must not shew to any body. It is odd that it should come into any body's head. I hope you will read it with candour; it is, I believe, one of the authour's first essays in that way of writing, and a beginner is always to be treated with tenderness." Johnson was then over seventy. It has been suggested that A. E. Housman knew this poem, and was in some way indebted to it; but such evidence as I have seen is inconclusive.

14

His first and only elegy, "On The Death of Dr. Levet," was wrung from him a year or two later by his deep sense of personal loss. It is not a studied work, as our greater elegies are, and, unlike them, it confines itself strictly in its few stanzas to its simple and unpromising theme. Though not to be compared with them, it helps us to understand what Johnson looked for in an elegy, and failed to find in *Lycidas*. The sense of loss is shot through every line of this earnest record of the virtues of an awkward friend who had employed well "the single talent," and makes the whole poem glow with the warmth of natural sentiment. Of Collins, let me remind you, Johnson said that he did not sufficiently cultivate sentiment; of Dryden, that he studied rather than felt, and produced sentiments not such as Nature enforces, but meditation supplies. Again we have to say that what Johnson missed in the poems of others was not always lacking in his own. The elegiac note is to be heard also in his few epitaphs, a form of composition which first engaged his attention as a critic—his "Essay on Epitaphs" was his first critical essay—and for which he was eminently suited. When his epitaphs are mentioned, we think of the prose epitaph on Goldsmith in Westminster Abbey. We should not forget the verse epitaph on Claudy Phillips, the strolling musician.

But when all is said, Johnson owes his fame as a poet to *The Vanity of Human Wishes*. Probably no passage in it is better known than the character sketch of Charles XII of Sweden, and it was never more apposite than at the present day:

> Peace courts his hand, but spreads her charms in vain;
> "Think nothing gain'd," he cries, "till nought remain,
> On Moscow's walls till Gothic standards fly,
> And all be mine beneath the polar sky."
> The march begins in military state,

> And nations on his eye suspended wait;
> Stern Famine guards the solitary coast,
> And Winter barricades the realms of Frost.

The rest we know.

The most highly emotional passage in this poem paints the afflictions which await even on virtuous old age:

> Year chases year, decay pursues decay,
> Still drops some joy from with'ring life away;
> New forms arise, and diff'rent views engage,
> Superfluous lags the vet'ran on the stage,
> Till pitying Nature signs the last release,
> And bids afflicted worth retire to peace.

"The deep and pathetic morality of this poem," said Sir Walter Scott, "has often extracted tears from those whose eyes wander dry over pages professedly sentimental." We are told by Mrs. Thrale that the account of the life of the scholar in this poem extracted tears from Johnson's own eyes, that he "burst into a passion of tears," when one day at Streatham he came upon it afresh late in life.[1]

Let us recall Johnson's remark about Bentley, which some of his critics would apply to his own verses—"the forcible verses of a man of a strong mind, but not accustomed to write verse." We may now put the concluding phrase out of account; Johnson, though a prose man, was accustomed to write verse, and his heroic couplets, as in these passages which I have just quoted, have a resonant music of their own, distinct from the

---

1. Boswell was off his guard when he cited Johnson's character of Dryden to show that it gives "some touches of his own." He rounded off the citation with this unconsidered assertion: "It may indeed be observed, that in all the numerous writings of Johnson, whether in prose or verse, and even in his Tragedy, of which the subject is the distress of an unfortunate Princess, there is not a single passage that ever drew a tear" (*Life*, IV.45).

music of the verses of Dryden and Pope. There remains the question whether the "strong mind" dominates his verse to the overshadowing of the more obvious poetic qualities. Certainly we never feel the loosening of the intellectual grip in any of his poems. But no one who reads *The Vanity of Human Wishes* aright ever ends it, I believe, without being most of all impressed by its emotional quality. In this poem Johnson shows himself to be a master of pathos. The forces of intellect and emotion are displayed in perfect balance.

Johnson's Practice in the Poetical Imitation

JOHN BUTT

Boswell tells us that Johnson's poem *London* was published on the same morning of May 1738 as the first of the dialogues which Pope was later to call *An Epilogue to the Satires*. He appears to have been misinformed, since what records there are suggest that Pope's poem appeared three days later than Johnson's. But Boswell's legend, if that is what we must call it, is eminently happy, for the coincidence draws attention to a comparison, indeed a challenge, that Johnson's poem offers to Pope's. Three of Johnson's letters survive in which he discusses the publication of this poem with Edward Cave. They make no allusion to comparison or to challenge; but it can scarcely be doubted that Johnson knew what he was doing. Both in literary form and in physical appearance *London* courts comparison with Pope; in substance and in manner it differs sufficiently to challenge him.

The literary form Johnson had chosen was the imitation, and it was a form that was well established. It had sprung from the paraphrastic manner of translation widely admired in the mid-seventeenth century, and strongly advocated by Denham and Cowley. "If Virgil must needs speak English," Denham had said, in the preface to his *Destruction of Troy* in 1656, "it were fit he should speak not only as a Man of this Nation, but as a Man of this Age." There is the new policy of translation; and it is not a far cry from that to Oldham's determination, when rendering Horace's *Ars Poetica* in 1681, "to alter the scene from *Rome* to *London*, and to make use of *English* names of Men, Places, and Customs, where the Parallel would decently permit." Other poets were quick to take the hint. The last thirty years of the century can show numerous imitations, ranging from the loosest of paraphrases to modernized versions, like those of Dryden, which run more or less in parallel with their originals. Creech, the translator of Lucretius, reports that when beginning to render Horace in the early 1680's, he had been advised to "turn the *Satyrs* to our own Times," since "*Rome* was now rivall'd in her Vices; and Parallels for Hypocrisie, Profaneness, Avarice and the like were easie to be found." Creech resisted the temptation, but there were many poets who seized this opportunity. The finest examples belong to Johnson's lifetime. Between 1712 and 1714 Swift published imitations of two epistles and one satire of Horace, and Pope's splendid series of imitations, eleven in all, appeared in the five years preceding the publication of Johnson's *London*.

This then was the tradition that Johnson inherited at what appears to our later eyes as the very climax of its reputation. How much Johnson knew of the tradition at the beginning of his career is doubtful; in later years he was to show himself, as we should expect, sufficiently well informed: in the *Life of Pope* he says that this manner of imitation "was first practised in the reign of Charles the Second by Oldham and Rochester, at least [he continues] I remember no instances more ancient." But for his present purposes in 1738, it was sufficient that he knew what Pope had done. Pope had followed Swift in drawing attention to his originals by printing the Latin parallels, and Johnson follows this lead. He did not demand so much paper as Pope had done when he printed the Latin in his first folio editions on facing pages with the English. Johnson was content, in *London*, with the less obtrusive practice of Pope's collected octavos, where the Latin is relegated to the foot of the page; while in *The Vanity of Human Wishes*, only the line numbers of the original Latin were given.

20

There is one other aspect of this literary form in which it was sufficient that Johnson knew Pope's work without knowing the work of Pope's predecessors, and that is in the application of the form to political satire. Earlier poets had been attracted by the opportunities that the form offered for general satire upon the age, and it was in that tradition that Pope himself was at first content to work. A commendation of statesmen out of place in the first *Imitation* and a reflexion upon Walpole's Excise Bill in the second certainly showed where Pope's sympathies lay; but these early imitations could only be regarded as political satires in so far as the moral standards advocated were patently different from those professed by government supporters. They were indeed different; for Pope advocates the Horatian doctrine of contentment with a modest competence, while Walpole's government drew its support from the city merchants and the great Whig landlords, amongst whose virtues modesty was not included. But political satire of that kind, though honourable enough, does not bite. It is only in the later *Imitations* that Pope unmistakably directed this literary form to a political target. These are the ironic Epistle to Augustus, the imitation of the Sixth Epistle of the First Book in which he shows his contempt of moneyed interests and rigged elections, and the First Epistle of the First Book, addressed in reverential terms to the Government's arch enemy Bolingbroke, and attacking Court and City with such vigour that several writers in Government pay were put up to reply. All three poems were published within the twelve months preceding the publication of *London*, the first of them in May 1737, and the remaining two even nearer in time, namely in January and March 1738. Here then is the tradition in which Johnson began to publish. He was not merely the latest recruit to a group of anti-Government poets; he shows in this first publication that he has recognized the very latest development in the attack, the enlisting of a classical moralist in the political struggle. In the last few months Pope had enrolled Horace in the Tory party; Johnson now shows that Juvenal was a Tory champion as well.

But in spite of these similarities, so intentional and so well marked as to court comparison with Pope's work, there are almost equally marked differences in substance and in manner of attack. To have trespassed on Pope's ground by choosing another satire of Horace to imitate was no doubt unthinkable; but the choice of Juvenal seems to have been made with some deliberation, and though the choice was not confirmed so happily and frequently as Pope's had been, when confirmation came, eleven years later, it could not have been more authoritative. The choice of classical satirist by the two poets conditioned to some extent their manner of attack. Each, of course, is aided by parallels which might have been termed lucky if we had not been pretty sure that it was awareness of those very parallels that first directed the choice; and each poet is embarrassed, as Johnson himself was to point out in later years, by "an irreconcileable dissimilitude" between Roman images and English manners. But the attack is largely conditioned by the attitude of the original. Horace's doctrine of contentment, as I have already mentioned, was well suited to oppose the mercenariness and the display of a mercantile Government's supporters. Pope stands aside with Horace to pity the desperate itch for money that has infected the country:

> Here, Wisdom calls: "Seek Virtue first! be bold!
> As Gold to Silver, Virtue is to Gold."
> There, London's voice: "Get Mony, Mony still!
> And then let Virtue follow, if she will."
> This, this the saving doctrine, preach'd to all,
> From low St James's up to high St. Paul; ...
> Can they direct what measures to pursue,
> Who know themselves so little what to do?

> Alike in nothing but one Lust of Gold,
> Just half the land would buy, and half be sold:
> Their Country's wealth our mightier Misers drain,
> Or cross, to plunder Provinces, the Main:
> The rest, some farm the Poor-box, some the Pews;
> Some keep Assemblies, and wou'd keep the Stews;
> Some with fat Bucks on childless Dotards fawn;
> Some win rich Widows by their Chine and Brawn;
> While with the silent growth of ten per Cent,
> In Dirt and darkness hundreds stink content.

This humorous indictment was written, as Pope had remarked in his latest poem, not by

> one that Temperance advance
> Cramm'd to the throat with Ortolans:

but rather by one

> Extremely ready to resign
> All that may make me none of mine.
> South-sea Subscriptions take who please,
> Leave me but Liberty and Ease.
> 'Twas what I said to Craggs and Child,
> Who prais'd my Modesty, and smil'd.

It was written, in short, by a man conscious of his own superiority in breeding and conscious of that of the friends who grace his retreat; and Pope is normally content to frame his indictment in terms suited to conversation with friends such as these; though there are times when he will express a nobler disdain, as for example in a passage which saw the light three days after Johnson's *London*: Vice is riding in her triumphal car, and

> Our Youth, all liv'ry'd o'er with foreign Gold,
> Before her dance; behind her crawl the Old!

23

> See thronging Millions to the Pagod run,
> And offer Country, Parent, Wife, or Son!
> Hear her black Trumpet thro' the Land proclaim,
> That "Not to be corrupted is the Shame."

A little out of character, perhaps; not altogether suited to Horace's "polite, insinuating style"; but skilfully modulated from the strain of cultivated conversation with which this elder statesman of poets is entertaining his intellectual equals.

And how utterly inappropriate all this would have been from the lips of the young Samuel Johnson, unknown, with no influential friends, and with a radically different experience of life! In so far as he and Pope may be said to have belonged to the Tory party—the very phrase is anachronistic—they belonged, in modern parlance, to different wings. Both are agreed in their diagnosis: moral standards have been tainted by this widespread lust for money. Pope can condemn it from a position of modest competence, but Johnson hasn't got even that. His is the rancour of unrecognized merit, the indignation of one who scorns to learn the art of currying favour, and yet suffers by not practising it. The toady provides one of the commonplaces of satire. Pope had known plenty of them:

> One dedicates, in high Heroic prose,
> And ridicules beyond a hundred foes;
> One from all *Grubstreet* will my fame defend,
> And, more abusive, calls himself my friend.
> This prints my Letters, that expects a Bribe,
> And others roar aloud, "Subscribe, subscribe."

But Pope sits, surfeited, at the receiving end; Johnson, equally nauseated, stands aside to watch his competitors make their offering:

> Well may they venture on the mimick's art,
> Who play from morn to night a borrow'd part;

24

> Practis'd their master's notions to embrace,
> Repeat his maxims, and reflect his face;
> With ev'ry wild absurdity comply,
> And view each object with another's eye;
> To shake with laughter ere the jest they hear,
> To pour at will the counterfeited tear,
> And as their patron hints the cold or heat,
> To shake in dog-days, in December sweat.
> How when competitors like these contend
> Can surly virtue hope to fix a friend?

Of course Juvenal had taken the stance before him. But Juvenal was chosen in the first place because his stance was one that Johnson had already adopted. I think we may feel sure of this from observing those passages where Johnson adds his own emphasis, or insinuates a moral peculiarly applicable to the time. This "surly virtue" in that last couplet is Johnson's, not Juvenal's; and we may recall that Boswell noted its appropriateness and used it to describe Johnson's first response to Wilkes' ingratiating approaches at Dilly's famous dinner party. It is not difficult to appreciate Johnson's recognition that Juvenal's indignant resentment is much more appropriate for an unfriended young man than the polite insinuations of Horace. It suggests a radical zeal in attack, an "angryness" (if I may use a fashionable term), far removed from the cultivated reproaches of the elder statesman.

Unlike a translator, an imitator is not in duty bound to find a parallel for every phrase in his original. He may select. The extent to which Johnson exercised the privilege can be indicated roughly by measurements of length. In spite of the greater conciseness of the Latin language, *London* is 60 lines shorter than the original, and *The Vanity of Human Wishes* is about the same length as the tenth satire. Dryden, with every phrase on his conscience, needed 503 lines of English verse to render the 322 of the third satire, and 561 to render the 366 lines of the tenth. Even Oldham, who had set himself a task similar to Johnson's required 477 lines, 114 more than Johnson; and Pope exceeded his originals every time by amounts varying from 42 lines to 149. To some extent we may account for Johnson's brevity by the skill with which he packs his verse. That famous line, "Slow rises worth, by poverty depress'd," is the distillation of a line and a half in Juvenal:

> Haud facile emergunt, quorum virtutibus obstat
> Res angusta domi.

Six English words represent nine Latin ones. Both Oldham and Dryden come off poorly by comparison. Here is Oldham:

> 'Tis hard for any man to rise, that feels
> His virtue clogg'd with poverty at heels;

and Dryden:

> Rarely they rise by Virtues aid, who lie
> Plung'd in the depth of helpless Poverty;

and neither of them achieves Johnson's admirably sombre note. But the practice of conciseness will not fully account for the differences. Pope can be concise too: "Or," says Horace, "if so great a love of writing seize thee, be brave enough to speak the praises of unconquered Caesar, and you will carry off many prizes for your pains":

> Aut, si tantus amor scribendi te rapit, aude
> Caesaris invicti res dicere, multa laborum
> Praemia laturus.

Two lines and a half of Latin which Pope reduces to a couplet, and yet finds room to specify the prizes:

> Or if you needs must write, write Caesar's Praise:
> You'll gain at least a *Knighthood,* or the *Bays.*

No, the main difference lies in the treatment of parallels. Johnson was to complain in future years, as I have already mentioned, of the irreconcileable dissimilitude between Roman images and English manners; and in discovering parallels he was not nearly so successful as Oldham had been. As one of Oldham's nineteenth-century editors remarks of his performance, "the whole poem is interesting from its details of contemporary characteristics, and in this point of view more curious than the *London* of Johnson." An instance lies to hand in the episode of Orgilio, a wealthy man whose house is burnt down, rebuilt, and refurnished by gifts and public subscriptions. Johnson's footnote in the original edition observes that "this was by Hitch a Bookseller justly remarked to be no picture of modern manners, though it might be true at Rome." That does not deter Oldham, who exerts himself to provide modern instances of official notice taken of a calamity, and modern instances of appropriate gifts for refurnishing:

> But if the fire burn down some great man's house,
> All straight are interested in the loss;
> The court is straight in mourning sure enough,
> The act, commencement, and the term put off;
> Then we mischances of the town lament,
> And fasts are kept, like judgments to prevent.
> Out comes a brief immediately, with speed
> To gather charity as far as Tweed.
> Nay, while 'tis burning, some will send him in
> Timber, and stone to build his house again;
> Others choice furniture; some rare piece
> Of Rubens, or Vandyke presented is;
> There a rich suit of Mortlack tapestry,

A bed of damask or embroidery;
One gives a fine scrutoire, or cabinet,
Another a huge massy dish of plate,
Or bag of gold: thus he at length gets more
By kind misfortune than he had before;
And all suspect it for a laid design,
As if he did himself the fire begin.

Johnson's version is four lines shorter. In keeping with the political slant of his Imitation he represents the great man as an owner of parliamentary boroughs with a train of pensioners in his pay; but he does not compete with Oldham in decorating the scene with particular details. It will be noticed that he proceeds in a quite different manner:

Should heaven's just bolts Orgilio's wealth confound,
And spread his flaming palace on the ground,
Swift o'er the land the dismal rumour flies,
And publick mournings pacify the skies;
The laureat tribe in servile verse relate,
How virtue wars with persecuting fate;
With well-feign'd gratitude the pension'd band
Refund the plunder of the beggar'd land.
See! while he builds, the gaudy vassals come,
And crowd with sudden wealth the rising dome;
The price of boroughs and of souls restore,
And raise his treasures higher than before.
Now bless'd with all the baubles of the great,
The polish'd marble, and the shining plate,
Orgilio sees the golden pile aspire,
And hopes from angry heav'n another fire.

Instead of Oldham's five different instances of public recognition of the calamity, Johnson is satisfied with "publick mournings pacify the skies"; instead of enumerating the gifts which are lavished upon Orgilio, Johnson leaves them as "the baubles of the great." These are not the only examples of Johnson's dislike of unnecessary particularities. Both Oldham and Dryden enlarge upon the taunts and jests made at the expense of the poorly clothed citizen:

> If his apparel seem but overworn (says Oldham)
> His stocking out at heel, or breeches torn,
> One takes occasion his ripped shoe to flout,
> And swears 't has been at prison-gates hung out;
> Another shrewdly jeers his coarse cravat,
> Because himself wears point; a third his hat,
> And most unmercifully shows his wit,
> If it be old, or does not cock aright.

Dryden mentions "the torn Surtout" and "the tatter'd Vest,"

> The greasie Gown, sully'd with often turning,
> Gives a good hint, to say The Man's in Mourning:
> Or if the Shoo be ript, or patches put,
> He's wounded! see the Plaister on his Foot.

But Johnson leaves us to do our own particularising, to invent our own jests and taunts, from these bare directions:

> The sober trader at a tatter'd cloak,
> Wakes from his dream, and labours for a joke;
> With brisker air the silken courtiers gaze,
> And turn the varied taunt a thousand ways.

Again Oldham and Dryden enter into some detail on how to gain access to a noble patron; Dryden mentions the "tributary cracknels" which the page must be given and which he then proceeds to sell; Oldham speaks of the fees paid to porter, groom, and steward: "Why!" he exclaims, "You may see the

Tombs, and Tower for less." But Johnson reduces all this detail to a vignette:

> Where won by bribes, by flatteries implor'd,
> The groom retails the favours of his lord.

This is Johnson's habitual way; and wherever he had learnt it,
he had not learnt it from Pope. In this respect, Pope resembles
Oldham; he likes his detail, and he seizes any opportunity to
decorate Horace's text. Horace says that he is protected by his
very capacity for satire, like carrying a sword in its sheath; "so
why should I bother to draw it," he continues, "when I'm safe
from dangerous robbers." Pope cannot resist the chance of particularizing, and he enumerates some of the enemies from
which a good man needs protection:

> I only wear it in a Land of Hectors,
> Thieves, Supercargoes, Sharpers, and Directors.

Horace continues by declaring that he is a peace-loving fellow,
"but he who provokes me will weep for it." Pope sees even in
this the opportunity for a compliment to Louis XV's chief ad-
viser and for a cut at Walpole's sensitiveness to criticism; and
his version runs

> Peace is my dear Delight—not *Fleury*'s more:
> But touch me, and no Minister so sore.

And while Horace remarks merely "Some say that verses like
mine can be spun at the rate of a thousand a day," Pope glances
once more at his bête noir, the effeminate Lord Hervey:

> The Lines are weak, another's pleas'd to say,
> Lord *Fanny* spins a thousand such a Day.

A political satire without contemporary detail would be utterly
ineffective. Johnson recognized this, of course. It is scarcely
necessary to recall lines like these:

> Here let those reign, whom pensions can incite
> To vote a patriot black, a courtier white;
> Explain their country's dear-bought rights away,
> And plead for pirates in the face of day,

and a footnote explains that "the invasions of the Spaniards were defended in the houses of Parliament." "To vote a patriot black, a courtier white": it is a clever topical expansion of Juvenal's "maneant qui nigrum in candida vertunt," and the application is entirely in Pope's manner. There are many more. But in writing like that I am inclined to think that Johnson was writing against the grain. The whole bent of his genius was towards generalization, and as I have already suggested, that irreconcileable dissimilitude between Roman images and English manners did something to encourage him in his bent, even in *London*.

He could yield to it more fully in *The Vanity of Human Wishes*. The original was a philosophical satire not necessarily requiring illustration with contemporary detail. Johnson indeed chose two instances of very recent memory; when he wrote that "Swift expires a driv'ler and a show," he was describing in rather too highly coloured terms what had happened four years previously; and it was in the same year, 1745, that Charles VII, "the bold Bavarian," stole "to death from anguish and from shame." But the force of these examples is not derived from their contemporaneity. On the contrary, I expect that we are all of us aware of passages in the poem for which Johnson may have had some contemporary instance in mind, but for which we might supply instances from recent history. I read, for example, the fall of the defeated statesmen: "Hate dogs their flight, and insult mocks their end," and what I am reminded of are the scenes which attended the death of Mussolini. Indeed I am sometimes tempted to think that the mastery of *The Vanity of Human Wishes* consists in Johnson's power of lifting the particular to the universal. It is Pope's power too, and yet how differently they proceed may be seen from a comparison of their great characters. Pope's characters are composed of sharp little pictures: we see without question precisely what he would have us see: Atticus sitting attentive to his own applause; Bufo paying his bards with Port; the two puddings smoking on Sir Balaam's Sunday board; the tritons spewing to wash your face before dining with Timon. From this assembly of particulars a type emerges, even more clearly than it does in the best Theophrastan characters of the previous century. But Johnson's characters are different. They do not sit for their portraits against an appropriately furnished background. All but one are historical, not Theophrastan, and their life-stories are briefly told. Accordingly it is episodes and events which take the place of Pope's camera shots. But none of the episodes is vividly painted, and opportunities offered by the Latin are often rejected. Thus it is Dryden that describes the "young enthusiast" as

> So small an Elf, that when the days are foul,
> He and his Satchel must be borne to School;

it is Dryden that asks of Juvenal's Hannibal, Johnson's Charles XII:

> Ask what a Face belong'd to this high Fame;
> His Picture scarcely wou'd deserve a Frame:
> A Sign-Post Dawber wou'd disdain to paint
> The one Ey'd Heroe on his Elephant;

and, to take an example from outside the characters, it is Dryden that describes

> The Fearful Passenger, who Travels late,
> Charg'd with the Carriage of a Paltry Plate,
> Shakes at the Moonshine shadow of a Rush;
> And sees a Red-Coat rise from every Bush;

while Johnson merely tells us of the same traveller:

> Now fears in dire vicissitude invade,
> The rustling brake alarms, and quiv'ring shade,
> Nor light nor darkness bring his pain relief,
> One shews the plunder, and one hides the thief.

But while we may regret the absence in Johnson of that picturesqueness of imaginative detail which Popes shares with Dryden, and which they use to make vivid, to particularize, a situation of whose general truth they are convinced; we shall not fail to recognize the skill which Johnson shows in defining the general situation so accurately as to incite us to supply our own particular versions of it. All of us who teach must have reflected upon the dangers which attend Johnson's young scholar's career, as we have watched our most promising students grow up. "Nor Praise relax, nor Difficulty fright": praise should serve to encourage, and difficulty to challenge; but how often one has wondered whether the young man's character will be strong enough to respond to praise or to the difficulties with which one confronts him, and then Johnson's line comes echoing back across the centuries. The incitement which these generalizations offer to our experience might well provide an ample quarry for the essayist or the story-teller. Johnson himself might have treated us, in one of his more frolicsome *Ramblers*, to an expansion of that couplet about the nymphs,

> Who frown with vanity, who smile with art,
> And ask the latest fashion of the heart;

we can readily detect a tale suited to Crabbe in what follows:

> With distant voice neglected Virtue calls,
> Less heard and less, the faint remonstrance falls;
> Tir'd with contempt, she quits the slipp'ry reign,
> And Pride and Prudence take her seat in vain;

and what short-story writer should we entrust—is it Guy de Maupassant?—with the miser's last days?

> The still returning tale, and ling'ring jest,
> Perplex the fawning niece and pamper'd guest,
> While growing hopes scarce awe the gath'ring sneer,
> And scarce a legacy can bribe to hear;
> The watchful guests still hint the last offence,
> The daughter's petulance, the son's expence,
> Improve his heady rage with treach'rous skill,
> And mould his passions till they make his will.

We might do well to recall a phrase or two from Johnson's censure of the metaphysical poets. "The fault of Cowley, and perhaps of all the writers of the metaphysical race, is that of pursuing his thoughts to their last ramifications, by which he loses the grandeur of generality." It is just that "grandeur of generality" that Johnson has attained in these passages. The pursuit of his thoughts to their last ramifications is the challenge he leaves with his readers.

Johnson and Juvenal

MARY LASCELLES

To throw light on Johnson's two great poems by means of a comparison with the two satires of Juvenal which they were designed to recall is no new endeavour. Indeed, in respect of one of them, this good office of criticism has been performed afresh, and notably, within the last few years.[1] Nevertheless, taking heart from a characteristic remark of Johnson's—"Men more frequently require to be reminded than informed"[2]—I propose to lay the English alongside the Latin where significant likenesses and differences appear to me worth reconsideration, and to draw such general inferences as I may.

Of the place occupied by *London* and *The Vanity of Human Wishes* in the pattern of Johnson's life, it can be argued that with their publication he opened and closed his poetical career, though not his life as poet. When he assailed the citadel of English letters with his "imitation" of Juvenal's third satire, he was, in the current phrase, writing for bread and reputation—for such reputation at least as should ensure that more bread would be forthcoming; and this poem declared his intention. The assault was not unsuccessful: Pope is said to have spoken cordially of the new poet, and those who were in sympathy with its politics applauded the poem. When he published his "imitation" of the tenth satire, however, he was about to put to the proof his cherished vocation as tragic poet. In Johnson's own eyes, the reception of *Irene* did not vindicate this claim. He had

---

1. Henry Gifford, *"The Vanity of Human Wishes,"* *Review of English Studies*, new ser., VI (1955), 157–65.
2. *Rambler 2.*

had the taste of failure in his mouth for most of his forty years, and found it unmistakable. He seems to have put away his project for another tragedy, and never thereafter challenged public notice as a serious poet. Many years later, Mrs. Thrale was to record an occasion on which he had shown her some verses. " 'But Sir,' said I, 'this is not ridiculous at all.' 'Why no (replied he), why should I always write ridiculously?' "[3] True, the context may have prompted her to expect burlesque; but it is a curious exchange between the author of *The Vanity of Human Wishes* and a familiar friend.

My undertaking requires that I should characterize, however briefly and tentatively, the satires which Johnson is imitating and the eighteenth-century practice of imitation.

Juvenal's satires appear to be the work of an embittered and frightened man; a brilliant rhetorician; no philosopher; disappointed in respect of worldly ambition, professing to despise worldly success, perhaps despising himself. He was born about 60 A.D., probably in the small Italian town of Aquinum. Schooled in rhetoric, he looked for a splendid career, but was frustrated. Incurring the hostility of Domitian, he was exiled to Egypt. He returned after Domitian's death, and, under Hadrian's more liberal rule, published satires; but most of the illustrations (that is, references to particular persons and events) are drawn from the reign of terror in which he had grown up, and some from even earlier history. Perhaps he was still afraid to speak; perhaps the bitterness of that past experience would not be denied expression. By one of those strange turns that literary and social history may take, something in these nihilistic satires recommended them to Christian moralists, while the sombre phosphorescence of their style attracted writers and speakers.

Whether we ascribe to France the initial impulse, or allow

3. Piozzi, *Anecdotes* (1786), 66.

merely that French prestige lent momentum, the art of "imitating" an ancient author, as English poets were to practise it in the eighteenth century, seems traceable to John Oldham. He formulates it in the prose apology prefixed to *Some New Pieces* in 1681: he fears lest he may be censured for his boldness in offering a version of Horace's *Art of Poetry* (the first and biggest piece) after those of Ben Jonson and Roscommon; but "it was a Task impos'd upon me" and

> being prevail'd upon to make an Essay, I fell to thinking of some course, whereby I might serve myself of the Advantages, which those, that went before me, have either not minded, or scrupulously abridg'd themselves of. This I soon imagin'd was to be effected by putting *Horace* into a more modern dress, than hitherto he has appear'd in, that is, by making him speak, as if he were living, and writing now. I therefore resolv'd to alter the scene from *Rome* to *London*, and to make use of *English* names of Men, Places, and Customs, where the Parallel would decently permit, which, I conceiv'd, would give a kind of new Air to the Poem, and render it more agreeable to the Relish of the present Age.[4]

There is a difference between this and what Rochester had tried out some three years before; small, but sufficient to justify a claim on Oldham's behalf to originality. Rochester, in his *Allusion to the Tenth Satire of the First Book of Horace*, had taken a piece of coterie-writing, framed his opening to recall that of Horace, but thereafter followed an independent course, playing the game with English poets and pretenders, careless as to their correspondence with Horace's Romans. Oldham, on the other hand, kept as many of the original "men, places and

4. *Some New Pieces*, "by the Author of the *Satyrs upon the Jesuites*."

customs" as he altered, and, even in his alterations, aimed at finding recognizable equivalents. His experiment, therefore, may be said to have given rise to that train of "imitations," "allusions," and "paraphrases"[5] which leads eventually to *The Vanity of Human Wishes*.

Thus in Oldham's work we may fairly look for the inherent possibilities and limitations of this way of writing as these presented themselves to his English successors. It requires of the reader just so much familiarity with the original poem as will make him quick to recall, when adroitly prompted, some memorable passage; of the writer, a knack of analogy: the art, or trick, of awaking such recollections. Oldham scores by his boyish ingenuity and sense of fun—as when he makes Juvenal's *Sapientia* into "sound Divinity, and Sense," or substitutes this for the noise of ancient Rome:

> The restless Bells such Din in Steeples keep,
> That scarce the Dead can in their Church-yards sleep.[6]

To the writer who can avail himself fully of this interplay of likeness and difference, the imitation offers political opportunities, and risks. It allows him to direct attention towards the analogy between ancient and modern tyranny, or corruption; even, between dead and living perpetrators of such abuses; and to claim, with whatever inward trepidation, that his adversary will rather keep silence than admit, by reacting to insinuation, that the cap of Nero or Sejanus fits.

5. The terms seem to be used indifferently, but it will be convenient to keep to the one which has grown familiar: imitation.

When I wrote this essay, I had (quite inexcusably) overlooked an important article, *The 'Imitation' in English Poetry, Especially in Formal Satire, before the Age of Pope*, by Harold F. Brooks (*Review of English Studies*, April 1949); otherwise I should have qualified the claims to primacy made here on Oldham's behalf.

6. Oldham, *Poems and Translations* (1683), 42 (Juvenal's thirteenth satire, l.189), and 200 (Juvenal's third satire, ll.232 et seq.).

Johnson's choice of the third satire of Juvenal as a declaration of his poetic aspiration appears at first sight strange, for it had already been imitated by Oldham and translated (with an occasional preference of witty equivalence over exact correspondence) by Dryden, and Johnson knew both versions well; but the tale of editions called for, contrasted with that of the *Vanity*, shows *London* to have been congenial to the time: it vented popular indignation with the Whig policy towards Spain. Even in his first choice, moreover, we may catch sight of Johnson's preference for taking the well trodden way and walking in it with independent gait. The satire did not speak any the less forcibly to him because it had been long esteemed; and, sharing this esteem, he found encouragement to say something in his turn; for Dryden himself had, as he thought, caught the wit but missed the dignity of the original "The peculiarity of Juvenal," he was later to declare, "is a mixture of gaiety and stateliness, of pointed sentences and declamatory grandeur." One of these qualities was still to be recaptured. "It is therefore perhaps possible to give a better representation of that great satirist, even in those parts which Dryden himself has translated, some passages excepted, which will never be excelled."[7]

This, then, was Johnson's position: in imitating an ancient author, he was prepared to avail himself of the liberty which had already established itself among the conventions belonging to this literary newcomer; even to extend it. Thus he would tread freely in the footsteps of former imitators, diverting the course of the beaten track whenever his sense of the *intention* of their original required this of him. But how was this intention to be determined? Satire draws him to interpret by means of imitation; and to interpretation satire opposes certain difficulties, which the passage of time increases. It weathers queerly. I am not thinking of topical allusions; hard work and historical sense may come to terms with those. I mean irony. And what,

7. *Lives*, 1.447.

in the last analysis, is irony, but a tone of voice? It is for this *intonation* that the imitator must listen; and who will claim that he has caught the tones of a dead man's voice—dead for seventeen centuries? If we could but hear the *tone* of Juvenal's references, say, to the satisfaction of simple living, in the third satire, or the proper worship of the gods, in the tenth, all other difficulties would surely yield; particular allusions could be cleared up, or would cease to matter. It may have been something of this sort that Dryden had in mind when he recalled Barten Holyday's opinion that, while it was difficult to find "any" sense in Persius, with Juvenal the problem was to find "the best sense."[8]

If we try to characterize the kind of ironist with whom (I suppose) we have here to deal, we shall observe that, where he essays a self-portrait, he will represent himself as setting out gallantly, protected only by fool's motley, armed only with his dagger of lath, to assail the entrenched forces of society. To this it may fairly be retorted that disguise will hardly ensure protection if he gives such offence to powerful adversaries that they think it worth their while to silence him. Ambiguity is a far less effectual safeguard than luck or skill in timing: much can be risked when those in power cannot afford to notice his insinuations; nothing, when they cannot afford to ignore them. Thus we may suspect that some at least of the ambiguities which such an ironist attributes to the danger, and gallantry, of his undertaking are really shadows thrown by a conflict in his own mind. He both longs and fears to be understood, not merely by the little world of his friends—for their assent is given, not extorted at the point of his satire—but by the great world of hostile or indifferent readers. He longs to be understood, because otherwise he must confess himself ineffectual; he fears it, be-

8. "Original and Progress of Satire," *Essays of John Dryden*, ed. W. P. Ker (1926), ii.96.

cause understanding between the writer and the common reader proclaims an affinity which his satiric vision of mankind makes abhorrent to him. (He is indeed distinguishable from the generality of them in that he is by temperament more vulnerable than they; that is why his shafts go home only when he takes aim at fellow satirists.) This, then, is our deepest difficulty with the ironist: a man who does not wish to be taken at his word may not really have made up his mind how he wishes to be taken.

Juvenal's third satire assumes the form of a dialogue between friends—if that can be called a dialogue in which one does all the talking and the other nearly all the thinking. Umbritius, playing the part of Juvenal's well-wisher, takes leave of him with the advice: "Do as I am doing. Cut loose from Rome, and live by yourself in the country." But we are sensible of an unspoken commentary. This counsel to seek happiness elsewhere is not offered all at once. Juvenal is too able a rhetorician for that; he knows how to weave to and fro, obtaining a cumulative effect. Besides, he cannot afford to be very explicit about advice that he has no intention of taking himself. His real theme is not country pleasures but the mingled attraction and repulsion exercised by the great cosmopolitan city, and Umbritius' leave-taking is merely an occasion for a denunciation of all that displeases him in Roman life. The two men are represented as going together to the point of departure from Rome, the gate on the Appian Way. There, Umbritius urges his friend to follow his example; but in much of what he says ironic overtones can be heard: in his allusions, for example, to the insignificant, depopulated village where he means to settle, or the even more desolate regions which Juvenal ought to prefer to Rome's tawdry splendour. These wry hints are surely but the echo of Juvenal's own thoughts: of his inmost certainty that, if life in Rome is disagreeable, dangerous, degrading, outside Rome there is nothing to be called life, at all. A particular illustration of this pervasive tone may be discerned in the representation of the great gate as a scene of mere squalour: even an allusion to its legendary associations seems to point at the foreign squatters now encamped round it; for it was once the haunt of the Camenae—native spirits ousted, in the process of Hellenizing Rome, by the Muses; and the Camenae themselves are mentioned in a tone of strident flippancy. Like Housman, Juvenal will call up some half-belief which has charmed or comforted men, only to bring it down with a piece of well aimed ribald familiarity.

It is worth while to compare what Oldham and Johnson, and occasionally Dryden, make of this invitation to a country retreat. Catching part of Juvenal's intention, Oldham sets the scene for his Timon's departure at Mile End, and exploits the opportunity for grotesque description; but Johnson chooses Greenwich, and makes his Thales gaze reverently at Queen Elizabeth's birthplace. True, any Elizabethan reference is an occasion for girding at the supposed policy of appeasing Spain; this, however, is but one of a number of passages in which Johnson summons up the shade of past greatness, in a tone which carries none of the vibrations of irony. When we reach the description of that retreat which Umbritius (Timon, Thales) proposes for himself and his friend, a sharper difference appears. Juvenal names little hill towns (romantic, perhaps, to us, but for him uncouth, cold, and dull); towns in which, for the price of a Roman garret, you can have the best house there is, with a little patch of kitchen-garden—a *very* little patch: there will be room enough merely to raise the vegetables on which you will have to subsist, with a lizard for livestock. Dryden gives the sardonic climax of the passage in a brisk couplet:

> 'Tis somewhat to be lord of some small ground,
> In which a lizard may, at least, turn round.

Oldham, with the freedom of an imitator and the rough playfulness of English satiric tradition, expands quip into conceit:

> Had I the smallest Spot of Ground, which scarce
> Would Summer half a dozen Grashoppers,
> Not larger than my Grave, tho hence remote,
> Far as S. *Michaels Mount*, I would go to't,
> Dwell there content, and thank the Fates to boot.

But Johnson turns *hortulus* into a country estate, and Juvenal's sour acceptance of a countryman's life into a little pastoral. His invitation begins bravely:

> Could'st thou resign the park and play content,
> For the fair banks of Severn or of Trent;
> There might'st thou find some elegant retreat,
> Some hireling senator's deserted seat;
> And stretch thy prospects o'er the smiling land,
> For less than rent the dungeons of the Strand.

The climax bears out this promise:

> There ev'ry bush with nature's musick rings,
> There ev'ry breeze bears health upon its wings;
> On all thy hours security shall smile,
> And bless thine evening walk and morning toil.

Here indeed is *stateliness*. Professor Nichol Smith comments that this is a piece of idealization which can never have expressed Johnson's real feelings about the country, associated as that was with the "disappointment and failure" of his early years; what he had always believed in his heart about pastoral bliss was to find utterance in his dry enumeration of the rural delights Savage expected in Wales. It is with great hesitation that I differ, and urge the significance of that allusion to Trent and Severn. Johnson was always fascinated by water: it was the thing he noticed in landscape—alike with eye and ear; it gave him imagery, when he wanted to convey a sense of deep contentment. Lichfield, moreover, was, and is, a little country town built round a confluence of springs and streams feeding the Trent. He had spent the best part of thirty years there; they had not been happy years, but the beginning of his struggle to establish himself in London may well have been worse. The poem as a whole suggests that he was suffering from revulsion against his new surroundings.

In such a mood, he might perhaps miss the irony in Juvenal's tale of country pleasures, yet find the denunciation of Rome (to which they had been a merely conventional foil) heartily congenial. Rome, Juvenal says, is not fit for a decent man to live in. Poverty hurts a man nowhere so much as in Rome; and only the man who is without decency or scruple can be anything but poor there. Prosperity in Rome comes to the blackmailer, the rich man's slave, the immigrant, never to the freeborn Roman—thus he aligns humanity. Besides, to dwell in Rome is to suffer countless evils, whether of mischance—stench, fire, traffic; or of malice—at the hands of the cut-throat, the bravo, and the sot. And all these press most heavily on the poor man. (He means the man like himself, of limited means and disappointed ambitions.) These complaints are not set out in logical progression; the argument would hardly bear it. They are so ordered that, except in one passage (the diatribe against foreigners, where personal bitterness prevails), attention is kept always in motion.

Congenial though the general import of his original may be, the imitator of an ancient satire must here and there find its particulars intractable. Difference of time and place may lend enchantment to other literary forms, but a considerable part of satirical complaint has to do with the immediate: with the sting of to-day's vexation, or the sourness of yesterday's hope;

with foul weather here and now. Thus, while there will be, in any great satire, passages which time cannot tarnish—passages that only await recharging with personal experience and the passionate affirmation "I know—I have been there myself"— there must necessarily be others from which the force, the very meaning, has ebbed. Success in imitation will therefore be the reward of insight and boldness: the good imitator will keep no lumber—what he cannot either take as it stands or transform by a turn of his wit he will throw out. Some of Juvenal's grievances are peculiar to his world: those, for example, that relate to slavery and its ramified consequences. Here Johnson's firmness appears. Whereas Oldham had encumbered himself with all the references (direct or oblique) to the particulars of Roman life in his original, *he* cuts out those which refuse to be translated into English terms. He reduces Juvenal's 322 lines to 263; but those figures fail to show how much he eliminates; for, where he chooses to keep a passage, he will sometimes expand, contracting others to make room. He has two principal ways of reducing his original: by silent omission of what is inapplicable, and what is gross; and by drawing a number of details to a head under a succinct generalization—notably in a single couplet:

> Fate never wounds more deep the gen'rous heart
> Than when a blockhead's insult points the dart.

There are indeed parts of Juvenal's imprecation which go home, anywhere, in any age: his evocation of the impenetrable indifference on the face of a big city, or the slights which must be endured by a man conscious of his own powers and promise amidst a society quite unaware that it needs, or he brings, anything of consequence. Johnson knew all about this. On a plinth of personal experience, he set the monumental line

SLOW RISES WORTH, BY POVERTY DEPRESS'D.

45

Compared with this, even Dryden's climax is weak:

> Rarely they rise by virtue's aid, who lie
> Plung'd in the depth of helpless poverty—

and Oldham's, amateurish:

> 'Tis hard for any Man to rise, that feels
> His Virtue clog'd with Poverty at Heels.

Between those passages which have become ineffectual, however, and those which need little more than vigorous translation, lie others which can be thrust home only by a skilful shift of aim: for example, Juvenal's gibes at the people with whom he, a Roman born, had to rub shoulders in an imperial city which was drawing provincials and foreigners, like wasps to a good plum crop. Here, Johnson's course is less clear, his sense of direction less sure. True, London was attracting men from other countries. The magnet, however, was not luxury but liberty: the freedom of the press sought by thinkers and writers. Then again, some of Juvenal's taunts might suit Johnson's London, but not Johnson. He *was* a provincial, his shabby clothes no more conspicuous than his Staffordshire speech. He obliterated the provincial; and Oldham showed him a way of dealing with Juvenal's abuse of foreigners—which was a pity; but it must in fairness be said that, when he converted the "hungry Greekling" into a Frenchman, the result was caricature rather than calumny: Juvenal's graver charges had been left out.

Johnson's *London* has not the brilliance of its original, because it lacks the lightning flash of its irony. It has not the sparkle of Oldham's best passages, for want of his high spirits. But it says what Johnson believed Juvenal to mean, and says it with unflinching consistency.

Juvenal's tenth satire is built on quite another plan than his

46

third, and Johnson's treatment tends to widen the division. The poet proposes to show the range of human futility and wrong-headedness as it must appear to the spirit of a philosopher, unconfined by bounds of space or time: the whole habitable world, past as well as present. His chosen symbol, repeated with variations throughout the poem, is the image of a man who would seem to have obtained what he asks of the gods —and is by so much the more wretched. This affords opportunity for two sorts of satiric picture: crowd scenes and portraits, not necessarily distinct; some of the portraits are, like the face of Chaucer's condemned man, distinguishable only by a significant trait from other faces in the crowd. These portraits may be historical (Sejanus, Hannibal, Xerxes), or typical (the old man who has outlived all that makes life worth living, the children whose ambitious parents obtain for them an unhappy eminence); and there are some betwixt and between: the would-be orator who is such a dunce that he misses the fame and escapes the fate of Cicero and Demosthenes.

Accepting this framework, Johnson handles what it contains even more independently than he had that of the third satire. His poem is, almost to a line, the same length as Juvenal's, but the proportions, and therefore the emphasis, are different. He leaves out what displeases him, and develops what he retains, as hitherto; and he avails himself of the full liberty traditional in imitation with regard to the illustrations: he substitutes Wolsey for Sejanus, Charles XII of Sweden for Hannibal, and the scholar's fate for that of the orator. Even where he keeps the man, or the type, he changes the tone; and he proceeds to a conclusion far removed from Juvenal's.

The most notable of the illustrations must suffice for comparison, and those that are least altered will best serve to open it. Johnson allows the figure of Xerxes to stand, as emblem of imperial vainglory. Juvenal has surely been betrayed here by his hatred of Greeks, or his profession of ironist, or both. He cannot mention the power and splendour of the Persian host without qualifying the impression of magnitude, even as it emerges, by hinting that Herodotus is a liar: the Greeks boasted that they had brought down a mighty tyrant—but, who knows? Thus he gives only the collapse of a half-mythical giant, the subject of tall stories—anticlimax proper to satire; Johnson, with tragic rather than satiric insight, the fall of a prince, powerful indeed, but himself the victim of tall talk, the talk of flatterers:

> Attendant Flatt'ry counts his myriads o'er,
> Till counted myriads sooth his pride no more.

Charles XII, taking Hannibal's place, runs true alike to the central purpose of both poems and to Johnson's lifelong conviction that war must be assessed in terms of its cost in human misery—together with the hope that it may be abolished by satirizing military ambition.[9] Yet, though they have so much in common, Johnson draws away from Juvenal even here. The Hannibal of the tenth satire is a bogey to frighten children: his campaigns are enumerated with a suggestion of grotesque bustle; each forced march brings him nearer his unpitied end. In exile, a "mighty suppliant"—the epithet is loaded with irony—he must suffer at the whim of a petty oriental tyrant and at last become the theme of schoolboys learning the rudiments of rhetoric. "Swedish Charles" had seized Johnson's imagination; he had written, and intended to write further, upon him. The passage given to him in the *Vanity* shows that no garish theatrical colours would have relieved the end of Johnson's tragedy:

> His fall was destin'd to a barren strand,
> A petty fortress, and a dubious hand;
> He left the name, at which the world grew pale,
> To point a moral, or adorn a tale.

9. He would find warrant for this in the writings of Prior and Swift.

The mood is not only sombre but stern. Nevertheless I hear no echo of the triumphant spite discernible in Juvenal's conclusion:

> i demens et saevas curre per Alpes,
> ut pueris placeas et declamatio fias.

If this is a true distinction, we may fairly ask: had Johnson taken to heart Armado's reproof to the sportive gallants—Hector "the sweet war-man is dead and rotten; sweet chucks, beat not the bones of the buried; when he breathed, he was a man"?

With the third of these historical transformations, we enter a country of the imagination where such Shakespearean analogies are clearly permissible: here is not simply Sejanus into Wolsey, but, as attentive readers have long observed, Sejanus into Shakespeare's Wolsey. The two passages invite particular comparison. Juvenal's approach to the fall of Sejanus is tactically unsurpassable. He makes eavesdroppers of us: we listen sometimes to the nobles, sometimes to the populace, sometimes to the poet himself; we overhear fragments of whispered or muttered talk, scraps of eye-witness reports—rumours, hints, allusions, in the voices of those concerned in the final crash. This it is (the voices suggest) to be an emperor's favourite; yet who would have the resolution to refuse, or strength to abide the consequences of refusal? By comparison, Johnson's tale of Wolsey's fall is unimpressive: it proceeds as simple narration, in the single voice of the poet, and the tone of that voice is grave, compassionate, devoid of irony. The climax is reached in a question which carries no sultry reverberations:

> Speak thou, whose thoughts at humble peace repine,
> Shall Wolsey's wealth, with Wolsey's end be thine?
> Or liv'st thou now, with safer pride content,
> The wisest justice on the banks of Trent?

I have given the last line as Johnson revised it in 1755. When he changed the "richest landlord" of 1749 into the "wisest justice," on the banks of his own Trent, he was ostensibly bringing the terms of the question nearer to Juvenal's "Would you rather be the man who was dragged just now through the streets, or a petty official in a provincial town, charged only with paltry decisions?" But it is the tone which tells what answer is expected, and in tone the new version is even further from its original than the old.

The most significant of these comparisons is that between illustrations which carry personal overtones, for both poets. Juvenal gets his knife into the orator early in his poem; he turns it round in lines 114 to 132. The quip of which the first passage consists is caught by Dryden in a flippant triplet:

> With laurels some have fatally been crown'd;
> Some, who the depths of eloquence have found,
> In that unnavigable stream were drown'd.

Johnson changes it into another key by the single word he chooses for the orator's fate—*impeachment*—a word of grave connotation through more than a century of English history. It is by his variation on Juvenal's second and fuller passage, however, that we may measure the difference between the orator of the one and the scholar of the other. Eloquence was the goal of Roman education; yet who, Juvenal asks, would not rather fail abjectly as a speaker than excel as Cicero and Demosthenes excelled, and end as they ended? Johnson's argument bears away in another direction. The scholar whom he substitutes for Juvenal's orator cherishes hopes which are not represented as ignoble, nor even unreasonable; yet the foregone conclusion is disappointment. Two possible courses are traced for him: first, the plain, hard way of ill-success. Here Johnson draws as near as ever he will come (in English) to speaking of himself. Slowly, ineffaceably, the image forms before our mind's eye: a man conscious of intellectual power, ambitious of excellence, who—even if he is not thwarted of his aim by sloth, sickness, melancholy—will share the 'doom of man' and also know his own peculiar unfulfilment:

> Deign on the passing world to turn thine eyes,
> And pause awhile from letters, to be wise.

From this sombre self-portrait, and self-admonition, he reverts to Juvenal's theme of the consequences of success, but still with a difference. His subject is now the scholar who wins recognition, and even high office, only to fall, like Laud. Some objections have been raised to Johnson's choice of illustrious victim. It cannot indeed be quite dissociated from his royalist and Anglican sympathies, and his Oxford piety. But the force of this passage consists in the use rather than the choice of illustration: the meaning is to be inferred from the conclusion, and is not constricted by such sympathies or antipathies as Laud may excite. Why, asks Juvenal sardonically, had not Cicero and Demosthenes sense enough to remain obscure, and safe? This, however, is the turn given to his apostrophe in *The Vanity of Human Wishes*:

> Mark'd out by dangerous parts he meets the shock,
> And fatal Learning leads him to the block:
> Around his tomb let Art and Genius weep,
> But hear his death, ye blockheads, hear and sleep.

It is not the fallen man who must meet the final challenge, as Johnson frames it.

This brief notice of divergent trends in some of the illustrations may serve to indicate a sort of *undertow*; but, if we are to understand the force of that big tide which is swinging Johnson's poem away to another conclusion than Juvenal's, we must now take Dryden for pilot. Johnson so valued his critical opinions that they became part of his own thought. (In *The Lives of the Poets* they are sometimes delivered as axioms.) He would, I surmise, have been prepared to maintain that Dryden was more faithful to Juvenal as critic than translator, and Dryden had said: "Juvenal excels in the tragical satire, as Horace does in the comical."[1] This epithet "tragical" must presumably relate not to literary form but to the presence of some element in a work of literature; such an element as we may recognize intuitively, afterwards bringing critical analysis to the task of verifying intuition. Lacking space for such analysis, I venture to offer a rough and ready test by which we may decide whether or no this tragic element is present in a particular composition. The people of tragedy are playing for high stakes; and it is real money. (Contrariwise, in comedy the winners hand over their gains, and the losers are released from their forfeits, even as the end breaks that spell which held us together in imagination's magic circle.) Now, if we set side by side Juvenal's and Johnson's monumental effigies of the fools of hope and vainglory, we shall observe that, while both mark the end of the man who asks too much of life, Juvenal implies that to ask at all is folly, because life has nothing to give. He will not allow his victims even the credit of playing a poor hand with style, for they stand to lose nothing but worthless counters. But Johnson's response to the man who plays high and loses all is the Shakespearean—that is, the tragic—response. Shakespeare will often communicate to us the meaning of some event, in the tragedies, by an observation put into the mouth of a secondary character who understands what is happening to the principals. Thus Charmian, when she has inherited from the dead Enobarbus this office of interpretation, intimates the significance of the final defeat at sea:

1. "Original and Progress of Satire," ii.96.

> The soul and body rive not more in parting
> Than greatness going off.

This sense of a greatness whose authenticity is manifest in the very agony of *going off* underlies Johnson's treatment of downfall and defeat. We may discern it even in the terrible picture of old age, which he shortens and, at the last, tempers by changing Juvenal's repulsive dotard among a crowd of parasites into a solitary figure, not without dignity:

> Superfluous lags the vet'ran on the stage.

All this must be borne in mind, that we may understand the explicitly Christian conclusion which Johnson imposes on his original. Can this be, as critics have alleged, a merely conventional *coda*? Juvenal has introduced his sole positive recommendation, the Stoic ideal of self-sufficiency, with a gesture of mock reverence towards the gods. They discern better than the suppliant what is good for him. (This is not to claim much for their sagacity.) When a man prays for wife or child, they alone know what he is getting. And (he continues), if you must force yourself on their notice with sacrifices, why, offer those delicious little sausages made from a white piglet, and ask only for a sound mind in a healthy body—no more than you can give yourself. Dryden's distrust of priestcraft leads him to overplay his hand a little here:

> Yet, not to rob the priests of pious gain,
> That altars be not wholly built in vain;
> Forgive the gods the rest, and stand confin'd
> To health of body, and content of mind.

He did not find all that in Juvenal; but he has come very close to Juvenal's superstitious man, with his cunning insurance policy of small offerings—a worshipper whose ingratiating air would discredit any divinity.

53

Johnson approaches the final question—"What may we then implore?"—without ironic overtones, as might have been expected; but, beyond expectation, he proceeds to amplify the answer. We are indeed to ask for

> a healthful mind,
> Obedient passions, and a will resign'd—

but, transcending all that this implies of philosophical equanimity, we are to pray

> For love, which scarce collective man can fill;
> For patience sov'reign o'er transmuted ill;
> For faith, that panting for a happier seat,
> Counts death kind Nature's signal of retreat...

Not only is this in accord with a vein of thinking that runs through all Johnson's works (clearest in *Rasselas*); it is consistent with the course of his argument in this poem.

For Juvenal, it is a bitter jest that man, being finite, must forever project his desires into infinitude. His eye rests always on the end; and for him *Respice finem* signifies: Look whether the end does not cancel all. But for Johnson this projection of our dream of fulfilment beyond the horizon is the proof of our immortality.

It appears that we may have to reckon with more sorts of irony than one. Whereas the ironist points the difference between what we are and what we would be thought, life admits of more various and subtle divergences than his art takes cognizance of. Thus, what becomes of us is separated from what we would attain not only by the distance between our pretensions and our powers, but also by that between fair expectation and the unforeseeable event. An onlooker endowed with sensibility will recognize these ironies inherent in our condition. If he is a writer, he may seek to express them. Two such were

among Johnson's favourite authors. It is a countenance not unlike his that Robert Burton sometimes turns upon the field of
error. Sir Thomas Browne invokes illustrious victims in the
very tones of the *Vanity*: "Though the funeral pyre of Patro-
clus took up an hundred foot, a piece of an old boat burnt
Pompey."[2] This is not satiric irony, generated by a quarrel with
life; it is tragic irony, learnt in the contemplation of life. The
awe and pity with which Johnson contemplates the spectacle
of human unfulfilment makes of *The Vanity of Human Wishes*
a great tragic poem. It is surely by an irony of circumstance that
it was published in the year which saw the eclipse of his hopes
as a tragic poet.

2. *Urn Burial*, iii.

Johnson at Drury Lane

ROBERT F. METZDORF

Johnson has been presented in many roles and (as this volume bears witness) continues to interest many people in different ways. But of all his protean appearances perhaps one of the least familiar is as Johnson the Playwright—Johnson as the author of a successful tragedy in 1749. The role was thirteen years developing—years of creation, frustration, and final fulfilment. After nine nights in Drury Lane, this particular facet of Johnson's career was rounded off, and he never again appeared as a playwright.[1]

When *Irene* was produced at Drury Lane on 6 February 1749, public reaction was immediate, though not profound. The triumph was a short one, but it captured the attention of the town. London's theatrical and literary circles had long known that Johnson had a play ready for the boards, but not until David Garrick produced it, under the stage title of *Mahomet and Irene*, was there a chance for public appraisal of this maiden dramatic effort.

After the play was produced, several commendatory accounts appeared in journals, and an anonymous pamphlet entitled *An Essay on Tragedy* (using the play as a springboard) was published by Ralph Griffiths on 8 March 1749. The advertisement for another critique appeared in the 21 February 1749 issue of the *General Advertiser*, as David Nichol Smith pointed out in *Essays and Studies* in 1929. The critique itself, however, remained unknown until quite recently, when four copies were

---

1. This essay depends heavily upon David Nichol Smith's introduction to *Irene*, in *Poems*.

located, one in the Harvard College Library, another in the collection of Mr. and Mrs. Donald F. Hyde, one in the library of Mr. H. W. Liebert, and the fourth in the collection of Professor Chauncey Brewster Tinker.

This addition to Johnsoniana is a small quarto of 20 pages (collating [ ]² B–C⁴, with C4 blank). The half-title, printed between double rules, reads "A criticism on *Mahomet* and *Irene*." The title-page reads:

> A / criticism / on / *Mahomet* and *Irene*. / In a / letter / to / the author. / [double rule] / [2-line quotation: — I seek occasions, court abuse, / To shew my parts, and signalize my muse. / Oldham.] / [double rule] / London: / Printed and sold by *W. Reeve*, in *Fleet-* / *street*; and *A. Dodd*, opposite St. *Cle-* / *ment's* church, in the *Strand*. 1749. / Price six-pence.

A brief account of the background is essential before the contents of the pamphlet can be understood. Johnson probably began his five-act tragedy in 1736.[2] He had borrowed a copy of Richard Knolles's *The General Historie of the Turkes* in Lichfield, and reworked the story of a fair Greek captive and her Ottoman oppressors. The year 1453 marked the fall of Constantinople and of the lovely Irene, who later met her death at the hands of her Turkish conqueror. Four earlier English dramatists had written treatments of the subject before Johnson (if one includes a lost play by George Peele), and at least six prose versions in various languages (beginning with Bandello's in 1554) had appeared, as Nichol Smith pointed out.[3]

Johnson read part of his unfinished play to Gilbert Walmsley in 1736; Walmsley urged him to finish it and have it produced. He had "great hopes" that Johnson would "turn out a

2. *Life*, I.100.
3. *Poems*, 237.

fine tragedy-writer."[4] Johnson took the uncompleted tragedy to London when he and Garrick set off for the metropolis in March 1737. According to Boswell the play was finished in Lichfield during the summer of 1737.[5]

In the autumn of 1737 Sam and Tetty Johnson moved to London. The school at Edial had failed; Lichfield offered few or no attractive prospects of employment: but now Johnson had something to sell and he also apparently hoped for employment under Edward Cave. "His tragedy being by this time, as he thought, completely finished and fit for the stage, he was very desirous that it should be brought forward. Mr. Peter Garrick told me, that Johnson and he went together to the Fountain tavern, and read it over."[6] The play was offered to Charles Fleetwood, patentee of Drury Lane from 1734 to 1745, only to be refused, "probably because it was not patronized by some man of high rank," as Boswell speculated.[7]

Not much happened for some time afterwards. A letter to his wife, written on 31 January 1740, shows that Johnson was still attempting to get the play on the boards, as his friend Gilbert Walmsley had urged him to do in 1736; but though Fleetwood appeared to be succumbing to David Garrick's arguments in favor of the tragedy, and the other players at Drury Lane thought well of the piece, nothing came of the matter. Even so, Johnson wrote of the play: "I hope it will at length reward me for my perplexities."[8]

Edward Cave, the publisher of the *Gentleman's Magazine* and Johnson's good friend and employer, had become interested in furthering the fortunes of the drama; Cave knew of

4. *Life*, I.102.
5. *Ibid.*, 107.
6. *Ibid.*, 111.
7. *Ibid.*
8. *Letters* 12.

the work as early as 1738. On 9 September he wrote to Thomas Birch, suggesting that the Society for the Encouragement of Learning subsidize the printing of the play. He also added that Fleetwood (the villain of the situation) had promised to produce the drama the previous season.[9]

Still nothing happened. As Nichol Smith observed, "Johnson was evidently abandoning hope of ever seeing the play on the stage, and was resigned to get what money he could for it by publication."[1] The manuscript was offered to the bookseller John Gray—and refused; but Johnson's attraction to the theatre was not entirely dampened. It is probable that he intended in the summer of 1742 to write a tragedy on the career of Charles XII of Sweden, for he wrote to John Taylor on 10 August 1742: "I propose to get Charles of Sweden ready for this winter, and shall therefore, as I imagine be much engaged for some Months with the Dramatic Writers into whom I have scarcely looked for many years. Keep Irene close, You may send it back at your leisure."[2] So far as we know, *Irene* remains Johnson's sole attempt at writing for the stage; the story of Charles XII was utilized in *The Vanity of Human Wishes*, but no dramatic treatment of the subject by Johnson is known to exist.

Six years later fortune smiled on the frustrated playwright. David Garrick, his friend and former student, became manager of Drury Lane in the autumn of 1747 and announced that he intended to produce Johnson's *Irene*. Nothing was done the first season, but Garrick took the manuscript in hand and produced the tragedy—thirteen years after its inception—on 6 February 1749.

It was not an easy task. Johnson, out of the pride of authorship and from long affection for his drama, objected strenu-

9. *Poems*, 240.
1. *Ibid.*
2. *Letters* 17; *Poems*, 26.

ously when Garrick suggested changes in the play, and it was only after the intercession of John Taylor that Johnson finally allowed Garrick to make any cuts, rearrangements, or rewording.[3] Garrick evidently went to some pains to produce what he hoped would be a hit: Sir John Hawkins noted the lavish costuming of the play, and Aaron Hill (whose *Merope* was brought forward at Drury Lane immediately after *Irene*, and who was thus in a sense one of Johnson's rival dramatists) also commented on the expense which Garrick had incurred.[4] The leading members of the Drury Lane company appeared in the principal roles of *Irene*—Mrs. Cibber, Mrs. Pritchard, Barry, and Garrick himself. Everything seems to have been done to ensure a successful production. Eked out at the end of the run by such audience-catchers as Scotch and Savoyard dances, as well as curtain-raisers, the play ran for nine evenings, and Johnson received almost £200 as his share of the profits (in addition to another £100 from Robert Dodsley for the copyright, with rights to one edition reserved for the author). But the play was not a popular one; it was never revived and soon came to be regarded only as a closet drama.

A run of nine performances was rather unusual for a play of that period, but one may attribute Johnson's good fortune as much to the efforts of Garrick and his troupe as to any inherent dramatic excellence of the play itself. Even Boswell agreed that *Irene* "did not please the publick."[5] Johnson himself had no inflated ideas regarding the worth of his drama; he denounced a man named Pot who had termed it the best play of the age, and Boswell records that on one occasion the author left a room in which a reading of *Irene* was going on—"I

3. *Life*, 1.196.

4. Sir John Hawkins, *Life of Johnson* (2d ed., 1785), 199; and *Poems*, 241–42.

5. *Life*, 1.197.

thought it had been better," was his unusually subdued comment.[6]

Lack of variety in characterization and timidity of expression are the two weaknesses most commonly charged against *Irene*; the unknown critic who wrote *A Criticism of Mahomet and Irene* seized on these faults, and also remarked others which he did not hesitate to expose.

The pamphlet is written in a rather colloquial style, in the form of a letter to the author. "You must not wonder that your Tragedy of *Irene* engross'd, for some Months before its Appearance, the Conversation of the Town, and every one was big with Expectation of seeing a Piece plann'd, and wrote up to the highest Pitch of a Dramatic Performance," the critic begins. (This indicates that Garrick and his associates, as well as Johnson and his other friends, had been assiduous in advertising the drama by word of mouth.) The whole town is disappointed, the critic continues, but instead of talking behind Johnson's back, as others are doing, he will marshal the weak points one by one, in public.

The first matter to which the pamphleteer objects is that strange men—the Greek hero and his friend Leontius—are introduced into a Turkish seraglio. He questions the geographical propriety of Johnson's scene (answer can be made that Johnson did not call it a seraglio, but indicated a sea-side, or Bosphorus-side, garden of a recently captured Greek palace). The critic also maintains that it is ridiculous to suppose that a large body of the enemy could penetrate the guards of the Turkish army, and approach so near to the emperor without being discovered.

This would, on the face of it, appear to be more of a criticism of Mahomet's security system than of Johnson's sense of realism, but there may be some justice in cavilling at the portrayal

6. *Life*, IV.5, and n. 1: "If Pot says so, Pot lies!"

of such a state of affairs on the stage. It is unlikely, however, that many playgoers would have noticed anything anomalous in the situation: to introduce such a criticism calls up the whole question of credibility in the theatre. Johnson, at least, must have thought he was well within his rights in constructing the play as he did.

The next point is that the sultan, Mahomet, is badly drawn: he is too precipitate in offering first Aspasia, and then Irene, the crown of Turkey (dramatic necessity for telescoping narration is the only defence that can be offered).

A burlesque of the action follows, with a rather heavy-handed spoofing of some of the more inflated passages. Clearly, the critic was no friend of the heroic tradition in drama. The characterizations of Mahomet and Abdalla are special targets for the sarcasm of the reviewer: "and whatever *Mahomet* may think of his Passion, *Abdalla*'s is as much above him for Fire, high Flights, and precipitate [*sic*] Designs, as Champaign, in its Effect, is above the Operations of Small Beer."

The *coup de grâce* is reserved for the manner of representing the heroine's death. Garrick proposed to have her strangled on stage, by means of a bow-string, in the high Turkish tradition. But when this was attempted at the first performance the audience stopped the play with shouts of "Murder! Murder!" and Irene (Mrs. Pritchard) was at length led offstage to be dispatched. The critic alludes to this opening-night event in this passage:

> I doubt not, but some of our *Conoisseurs* expected, according to the old Story, to have seen her Head Taken off by *Mahomet*, at one stroke of his Scymitar; which, when perform'd to the Height of Expectation, cou'd have been but a Pantomime Trick, and beneath the Dignity of a Tragedy; unless you cou'd suppose, the Hero was bred a Butcher.—As to the Trick, perhaps, some of our tender

hearted Countrymen, wou'd have eas'd that Objection, by having her Head cut off in good Earnest, and so have had the Pleasure of a new *Irene* every Night.[7]

A special censure was given to Sir William Yonge's rather free epilogue for the play. "It is its own Satire, and he that has a mind to Burlesque it, has nothing to do but to Copy it."

There still remains the mystery of the authorship of this pamphlet. One would like to be able to attribute it to Fielding, or to some other famous contemporary, but there are no specific clues to warrant such an ascription, and flights of fancy are uncalled for. No reference to the pamphlet has been found in correspondence or diaries of the period, and until some such discovery is made, the critic remains completely anonymous. All that can be claimed for the piece is that it reflects at least one man's opinion of Samuel Johnson's only attempt to write for the London play-going public.

Johnson had one month earlier (on 9 January 1749) captivated the town with his poem *The Vanity of Human Wishes.* Perhaps he was not unhappy as he sat in a box at Drury Lane in his new scarlet waistcoat and gold-laced hat (was Tetty with him, and what did she wear?), and heard his thirteen-year-old *Irene* exposed to the gibes of the London wits. He is not known to have responded publicly to the anonymous critic; if he read the pamphlet, it is probable that he went on feeling, as he later told Boswell, "like the Monument."[8]

7. A diary owned at one time by Mrs. Garrick contained the following entries: "Feb. 6, 1749. Irene. Written by Mr. Johnson—went off very well for 4 Acts, the 5th Hiss'd generally. Feb. 7. Ditto. 5th Act hiss'd again" (*Poems*, 241).

8. *Life*, I.199–200. The simile of the Monument echoes a line in Johnson's prologue to *Irene*: "Unmov'd tho' Witlings sneer and Rivals rail . . ."

Johnson's Dictionary

April 15, 1955

W. K. WIMSATT, JR.

Samuel Johnson's *Dictionary of the English Language* was published in two folio volumes by a combination of London booksellers on April 15 just 200 years ago. It is a big book—big enough to furnish materials for a number of different studies. Today I wish to talk about it[1] both as a certain kind of lexicographic feat and in virtue of that as a record and revelation of a certain mind and personality. On account of the latter bias it is inevitable that I shall not say everything of a technical and philological nature that it is possible to say about the Dictionary; it is even likely that I shall neglect some of the main things that historians of lexicography and the English language might wish to hear said.

What kind of bigness does Johnson's Dictionary have? We discover, perhaps with some surprise, that it was not the biggest English dictionary of its era in the sense of listing and defining more words than any other. Johnson's Dictionary lists about 40,000 words. But the folio *Dictionarium* of Nathan Bailey (Johnson's nearly immediate predecessor and one of his finding tools in his own work) had in the edition of 1730 listed about 48,000 words and in that of 1736, about 60,000. The re-

1. Parallels to several parts of the paper and further documentation are to be found in my *Philosophic Words* (1948), and in my articles and notes on Johnson's Dictionary appearing in the *Times Literary Supplement* (1946), *Review of English Studies* (1947), *Modern Language Review* (1948), *ELH* (1948), *Johnsonian News Letter* (1950), and *Studies in Philology* (1951).

vision of Bailey by Joseph Nicol Scott which appeared in 1755 as a rival to Johnson's second edition, went as high as about 65,000 words. There are other respects too in which Johnson's Dictionary was less extraordinary for its era than one might have thought. And these respects the scholars of the neutralizing and levelling habit of mind have recently been adducing with some gusto. It may not be altogether clear, for instance, that Johnson's selection of the words that make up his 40,000 was more judicious—that is, more prophetic of English linguistic development or more influential on that development —than the lists of Bailey or other contemporaries. And it must all along have been fairly obvious that Johnson was not the first to write a history of the English language, or a grammar, or a preface to a dictionary, and that his efforts under the first two of these heads were even somewhat perfunctory. His etymological notions were unlearned by modern standards, and in places even comic. His attempts to discourage some words by applying a kind of linguistic weed-killer, or notation of censure, were not very successful; even in his Preface he reports his loss of faith in that campaign. Johnson was not the first to write definitions of English words nor the first to subdivide and number his definitions. In short, and to use the phrasing of the recent scholarship, Johnson wrote his Dictionary in an age when "many men, at work on different undertakings, were thinking in similar ways." And both in his history and grammar and in his Plan and Preface, and presumably in all the rest of the work, he proceeded under the handicap of being rather "fully ... aware of tradition."[2]

2. Gwin J. Kolb and James H. Sledd, "Johnson's *Dictionary* and Lexicographical Tradition," *Modern Philology*, L (1953), 184. Shortly after the present paper was read, Professors Kolb and Sledd published *Dr. Johnson's Dictionary, Essays in the Biography of a Book* (1955), in which the article here cited reappeared as the first chapter.

A single respect remains in which Johnson must be credited with a large measure of originality. He was the first English dictionary-maker to collect and insert substantial illustrations of his meanings—authorities or testimonies from the wealth of documents in which the English language had been achieved and preserved. With respect to the use of authorities, simply considered, it is true, however, that certain anticipations of Johnson's method may be pointed out. These appear on the Continent, in Italian, French, Spanish, and Portuguese dictionaries, and especially in the revised *Vocabolario* of the Italian Accademia della Crusca issued in 1729. And once again we have our warning from the recent scholars. It would be "hardly wise" to view Johnson's Dictionary as the first English dictionary of its kind, a conspicuous transcendence of all earlier English dictionaries in the feature of its quoted authorities, the fulfilment of a demand which Englishmen had been voicing for nearly two hundred years. We are only "wise" if we try to see Johnson's Dictionary in an international perspective and to assimilate it as far as possible to Italian and French models. For Johnson's "announced intention" was to "rival the academies." That is, he refers several times to both the Italian and French academies in his Plan and in his Preface, and this is important—even though the authorities who composed the French Academy were content to rest on their authority and furnished their *Dictionnaire* with no illustrations.[3] But I am not sure I understand this line of argument.

I remain content to argue that Johnson's Dictionary has an extraordinary character and enjoys a unique position in virtue of its numerous, varied, and substantial illustrative passages and the framing of these by his discriminations and definitions. There are four contemporary accounts, including Johnson's own in his Preface, of how he made his Dictionary. The biog-

3. Kolb and Sledd, "Johnson's *Dictionary*," pp. 173–74, 184, 193.

rapher Hawkins says that Johnson began with a copy of Bailey's folio, using it as a list of words in which he interleaved definitions and illustrations when they had been discovered in his various authorities. Boswell's statement that words were "partly taken from other dictionaries, and partly supplied by [Johnson] himself," that they were "written down with spaces left between," and that Johnson then filled in the etymologies and definitions, seems a safe enough account of a certain phase of the work. But Boswell is not very clear about the authorities, seeming actually to suppose that these were copied by the printers of Johnson's Dictionary directly from the books which Johnson had marked with his black lead pencil. Later Bishop Percy in a reminiscence of talks with Johnson gives a more plausible testimony. As Johnson "himself expressly described" the matter:

> He began his task by devoting his first care to a diligent perusal of all such English writers as were most correct in their language, and under every sentence which he meant to quote, he drew a line, and noted in the margin the first letter of the word under which it was to occur. He then delivered these books to his clerks, who transcribed each sentence on a separate slip of paper, and arranged the same under the word referred to. By these means he collected the several words and their different significations; and when the whole arrangement was alphabetically formed, he gave the definitions of their meanings, and collected their etymologies from . . . writers on the subject.[4]

Here is a report which has the accent of substantial truth. Johnson himself in his Preface reported that "the deficiency of dic-

4. ". . . taken from the third edition of Dr. Robert Anderson's *Life of Johnson,* published in 1815. . . . recorded by Percy, in 1805, in an interleaved copy of the second edition" (*Miscellanies,* II.208, 214).

tionaries was immediately apparent." "When they were exhausted" (and I take this to mean: when a brief skirmish had revealed their almost total unfitness for his purpose), "what was yet wanting must be sought by fortuitous and unguided excursions into books, and gleaned as industry should find, or chance should offer it, in the boundless chaos of a living speech." Let us set to one side any thought about the mechanical difficulties which we may well suppose would have arisen through the attempt to interleave Johnson's copious illustrations in Bailey's one-volume folio—and set aside also any speculations about the actual assemblage of copy in the eighty large notebooks which are mentioned by Boswell in another place. The idea that is essential to a comprehension of Johnson's feat is that he read his authorities, at least in large part, first.[5] He embarked on a huge program of reading English poetry, drama, prose essays, history, biography, science, and arts. He then arranged his collection of words alphabetically, matched the list thus obtained against other dictionaries, mainly Bailey, and wrote in some words that he had missed—the occasional words that appear in the Dictionary with only the tag *Dict.* or *Bailey* or *Ainsworth* or *Phillips* appended. The one thing it is absurd to suppose Johnson did is that he began working through Bailey or any other dictionary alphabetically, departing on excursions through English literature for each illustration as the need arose. This, as Bishop Percy remarks, "would have taken the whole life of any individual." Try to imagine Johnson at his task of single-handed reading for the Dictionary, and you will see, or feel, that the essential and operative principles in the enterprise were precisely his

5. "Johnson has four Amanuenses still employ'd in his English Dictionary; but their Business will soon be over; for they have almost transcrib'd the Authorities" (Thomas Birch to Philip Yorke, 6 Aug. 1748, British Museum, Add. MS 35, 397, fol. 140. Courtesy Professor James L. Clifford).

own great powers as a reader—his strength and tenacity, his initial familiarity with English usage, his comprehension of what his plan implied, and his continuing and cumulative capacity to remember what he had already done and what he had yet to do. Imagine yourself half-way through Johnson's program of reading for the Dictionary, arriving at the page of Bacon's *Natural History* which lies open in the exhibition outside this room today. (See accompanying illustration.) Which of the words and passages on the page would you mark in black lead pencil for your amanuenses to copy? Which would you pass over? By what norms would you make your selection? How many minutes would you need to reach your decisions on one page? It is my impression on reading the tentative, brief, and scattered remarks on authorities which Johnson makes in his Plan of a Dictionary, published in 1747, that at that date he had barely begun his reading, or perhaps had not yet begun it at all. His elaborate and eloquent reflections on the topic in his Preface (written seven years later) testify to the magnitude, the novelty, and the richness of the experience when he actually encountered it, as well as to its supreme importance for the making of the Dictionary.

> I therefore extracted from philosophers principles of science; from historians remarkable facts; from chymists complete processes; from divines striking exhortations; and from poets beautiful descriptions.

> If the language of theology were extracted from *Hooker* and the translation of the Bible; the terms of natural knowledge from *Bacon*; the phrases of policy, war, and navigation from *Raleigh*; the dialect of poetry and fiction from *Spenser* and *Sidney*; and the diction of common life from *Shakespeare*, few ideas would be lost to mankind, for want of English words, in which they might be expressed.

70

for though it should be wholly rejected, yet that negative is more pregnant of direction, than an indefinite; as ashes are more generative than dust.

XXVII. *Of seeming wise.*

IT hath been an opinion, that the *French* are wiser than they seem; and the *Spaniards* seem wiser than they are. But howsoever it be between nations, certainly it is so between man and man. For as the Apostle saith of godliness, *having a shew of godliness, but denying the power thereof*; so certainly there are in points of wisdom and sufficiency, that do nothing or little very solemnly; *magno conatu nugas.* It is a ridiculous thing, and fit for a satyr to persons of judgment, to see what shifts these formalists have, and what prospectives to make superficies to seem body that hath depth and bulk. Some are so close and reserved, as they will not shew their wares but by a dark light; and seem always to keep back somewhat; and when they know within themselves, they speak of that they do not well know, would nevertheless seem to others, to know of that which they may not well speak. Some help themselves with countenance and gesture, and are wise by signs; as *Cicero* saith of *Piso*, that when he answered him, he fetched one of his brows up to his forehead, and bent the other down to his chin: *respondes, altero ad frontem sublato, altero ad mentum depresso supercilio, crudelitatem tibi non placere.* Some think to bear it by speaking a great word, and being peremptory; and go on, and take by admittance that which they cannot make good. Some, whatsoever is beyond their reach, will seem to despise or make light of it as impertinent or curious; and so would have their ignorance seem judgment. Some are never without a difference, and commonly by amusing men with a subtilty, blanch the matter; of whom *A. Gellius* saith, *hominem delirum, qui verborum minutiis rerum frangit pondera.* Of which kind also, *Plato* in his *Protagoras* bringeth in *Prodicus* in scorn, and maketh him make a speech that consisteth of distinctions from the beginning to the end. Generally such men in all deliberations find ease to be of the negative side, and affect a credit to object and foretel difficulties: for when propositions are denied, there is an end of them; but if they be allowed, it requireth a new work: which false point of wisdom is the bane of business. To conclude, there is no decaying merchant, or inward beggar, hath so many tricks to uphold the credit of their wealth, as these empty persons have to maintain the credit of their sufficiency. Seeming wise men may make shift to get opinion; but let no man chuse them for employment, for certainly you were better take for business a man somewhat absurd, than over-formal.

XXVIII. *Of friendship.*

IT had been hard for him that spake it, to have put more truth and untruth together, in few words, than in that speech; whosoever is delighted in solitude, is either a wild beast, or a god. For it is most true, that a natural and secret hatred, and aversation towards society, in any man, hath somewhat of the savage beast: but it is most untrue, that it should have any character at all of the divine nature, except it proceed, not out of a pleasure in solitude, but out of a love and desire to sequester a man's self for a higher conversation: such as is found to have been falsely and feignedly, in some of the heathen; as *Epimenides* the *Candian*, *Numa* the *Roman*, *Empedocles* the *Sicilian*, and *Apollonius* of *Tyana*; and truly and really, in divers of the ancient hermits, and holy fathers of the church. But little do men perceive

VOL. III.   U u

The chief glory of every people arises from its authors . . . I shall not think my employments useless or ignoble . . . if my labours afford light to the repositories of science, and add celebrity to *Bacon*, to *Hooker*, to *Milton*, and to *Boyle*.

Johnson's reading of the authorities first was a shrewd, an energetic, a daring stroke. The most conspicuous result was that he got the Dictionary done. Look for a moment at Johnson's Dictionary as a practical and economic venture, a piece of bookmaker's engineering, and you find it a signal instance of that sanity, perspective, balance, and sense of proportion for which Johnson's whole career is so notable. Consider the meaning of his complacent statement to Boswell: "I knew very well what I was undertaking—and very well how to do it —and have done it very well." Or of the somewhat too confident boast, in midstream, about the single Englishman and three years against forty Frenchmen and forty years. One of Johnson's humble amanuenses, a Scot named Macbean, later began to compile a geographical dictionary, provoking from Johnson the comment: "I have lost all hopes of his ever doing anything properly, since I found he gave as much labour to Capua as to Rome." Johnson's own way was exactly the opposite. It is true that as the work proceeded he had to make certain retrenchments. One of these, as he complains in his Preface, was the "detruncation" and even the complete sacrifice of numerous flowers of expression which were part of his original collection. Another was the minimizing and slighting of references which begins in the Dictionary, so obviously, after the letter A. But on the whole Johnson set out with a strategy admirably fitted to his aims and to the mechanics of research which were at his disposal, a workable set of rules, well calculated to bring a single master reader and a staff of amanuenses in nine years to the conclusion of even so large a task. The job was done with economy of effort, confidence, rapidity. If it was also in some senses haphazard, incomplete, even careless, any other policy, under the conditions which governed the enterprise, would have been quixotic. Johnson had the good sense to see that, given the generosity of his major vision, some deficiencies were inevitable. He had the courage to proceed without scruple.

And here I think it may be appropriate if I insert a few words in recognition of those London booksellers who were Johnson's immediate patrons in the Dictionary project and who made it possible not only that a Dictionary, but that this particular kind of Dictionary, should be compiled. W. Strahan, J. and P. Knapton, T. and T. Longman, C. Hitch and L. Hawes, A. Millar, and R. and J. Dodsley (thus runs the roster on the title page of the first edition)—with their business addresses in New Street, in the Strand, at the Crown in Ludgate Street, at the Ship and at the Red Lion in Paternoster Row, at Tully's Head in Pall Mall—these sponsors of the Dictionary were in their own way members of an English academy, and in their alliance with Johnson, who supplied the learning of the academy, they contrast with the continental academies in a manner closely tied in with the spirit of sturdy eccentricity which the English during that age were cultivating with so much satisfaction. What a literary academy might have done for England was to be recited more than a century later by Matthew Arnold in his anachronistic essay on "The Literary Influence of Academies." The reason why there was never an English academy is somewhat violently betrayed by Johnson himself in his Dictionary Preface. "If an academy should be established for the cultivation of our style," he begins to speculate—, but immediately adds: "which I, who can never wish to see dependence multiplied, hope the spirit of *English* liberty will hinder or destroy." "The edicts of an English

Academy," he wrote later, in his *Life of Roscommon*, "would probably be read by many, only that they might be sure to disobey them."

Johnson seems to have had a strong sense of the personal character of his undertaking, his personal proprietorship. Let me pursue for a few moments one of the most traditional themes of Johnsonian Dictionary celebration—that of the numerous whimsical and licentious manifestations of his personality which the lexicographer permitted himself. Here again of course I encounter the frown of the levellers, who want to tell me that even in Johnson's day dictionary-making was a sober thing, that the lexicographer had "few opportunities for originality, few temptations to eccentricity, and every inducement to follow the beaten track."[6] But here again I would urge Johnson's sense of proportion, his insight into the nature of the specific thing he was doing, and its real decorum. A century and a half later, if he had been one of the staff working on the new *Oxford English Dictionary on Historical Principles*, certain things might not have been possible. Modern scholarship sometimes seems to want to read Johnson as if he had been a member of such a staff. An elaborate article in *PMLA* was once devoted to arguing that Johnson's account of "oats" in the Dictionary was not a joke on the Scots (because the joke has sources, and because such trifling would have been out of place in a philological monument). But Johnson himself said later that he "meant to vex them." And in his own Dictionary, I ask, why not? Boswell alludes to Johnson's "capricious and humorous indulgence" of his own "opinions" and "prejudices." Johnson's Scotch critic Lexiphanes Campbell said it was a "very facetious dictionary"—"witty," "personal," "po-

6. Sledd and Kolb, "Johnson's Definitions of *Whig* and *Tory*," *PMLA*, LXVII (1952), 882.

litical," "national," and "patriotical," "in a word, everything
but what it ought to be." A long list of the curiosities in the
Dictionary—the jests against Whig, patron, dedicator, favourite, pension, or excise, the audacities, delinquencies, loyalties,
and mellow moments—have long ago become common property, to be looked up, if we forget them, in Courtney's *Bibliography*, in Hill's footnotes to Boswell, in the more neglected
Leisure Moments in Gough Square by Alfred Stringer. A few
other matters of this sort I believe I myself may have been the
first to discover, and as news of such discoveries does not travel
very fast, I may still share with the shade of Johnson some kind
of proprietorship.

Under the head of satire and insult, for instance, Johnson
would not only write a definition of "oats" that said something
about horses in England and men in Scotland, but he would
cut up a metaphysical satire by John Cleveland, *The Rebel
Scot*, and insert twenty-seven pieces of it in his Dictionary, at
least thirteen of them good, cleanly pointed anti-Scot jibes, the
more amusing, or annoying, perhaps, because planted mostly
under quite innocent words. Thus, under *proselyte* and again
under *twilight*.

> He that saw hell in's melancholy dream,
> And in the *twilight* of his phancy's theme,
> Scar'd from his sins, repented in a fright,
> Had he view'd Scotland, had turn'd *proselyte*.

Or consider the case of Lord Bolingbroke. Bolingbroke had
written deistic essays and at his death had left "half a crown"
to a "beggarly Scotchman" to publish them. Bolingbroke used
Gallicisms. And it has been often noticed that his name appears coupled with a linguistic censure under the word *Galli-
cism* in the Dictionary. But other ways occurred to Johnson
too. Thus under the word *irony* he would write simply: "A

mode of speech in which the meaning is contrary to the words: as, *Bolingbroke was a holy man.*" And under the word *sophistically,* he would take a friendly passage in a letter from Swift to Pope, something about the difference between Swift's poverty and Bolingbroke's wealth: "I must observe that my Lord Bolingbroke, from the effects of his kindness to me, argues most sophistically. The fall from a million to a hundred thousand pounds is not so great, as from eight hundred pounds a year to one." Johnson would take this and trim it down to four words, which it seems safe to say few readers have ever understood as *not* referring to philosophic or political argument. "*Sophistically*: With fallacious subtilty."

Bolingbroke argues most sophistically.— Swift

In the 18th century Horace Walpole could write: "It would have been a very extraordinary work if he had inserted all the words he has coined himself, but he had unluckily excluded himself, as he confined his authorities to our Standard authors." We of course know better than that. We know that Johnson would quote himself in the Dictionary, sometimes overtly, sometimes under cover of the tag "anonymous." In a spurt of curiosity a few years ago I counted altogether forty-eight of these self-quotations.[7] Some of them show Johnson's memory at work in the characteristically free way of a poet, as when a line quoted from *Irene*[8] does not follow the printed text nor yet the manuscript now in the British Museum, but is a tidying up of the latter. And at least some of the quotations marked "anonymous" I should suppose to represent a real mo-

7. Professor William R. Keast, in *Notes & Queries,* new ser., II (1955), 392–93, and III (1956), 262, adds three more. The same writer's "The Two *Clarissas* in Johnson's *Dictionary*," *Studies in Philology,* LIV (1957), 429–39, is one of the most curious revelations yet made concerning Johnson's use of a contemporary source.

8. Mouldring arches, and *disjointed* columns.

ment of uncertainty on Johnson's part as to their authorship. As a kind of support and complement to this theory, let me adduce the couplet quoted under the word *island* from Pope's *Essay on Man*:

> Some safer world in depths of woods embrac'd,
> Some happier *island* in the wat'ry waste,

to which Johnson affixes his own name: *Johnson*. Certain phrases—something about a "secret island in the boundless main," "some happier place"—in two passages of Johnson's *London* (a poem quoted twice by title and five times anonymously in the Dictionary) do a great deal, it seems to me, to promote the suspicion that in that quotation from Pope over Johnson's name the sympathy between the minds of the two poets was for a moment perfect. Let me insist that for me this notion has not the faintest derogatory implication.

But what I shall call the "best" instance of Johnson's self-quotation in the Dictionary is a different sort of thing. The word *dissipate* in the Dictionary is unique in that under it Johnson quotes himself two times. And behind that juncture a person with a pinch of good will may read the following story: In the spring of 1738 appeared Johnson's *London*. Here, following his Juvenalian model, he produces the "injured" and complaining character Thales, who is about to leave London for the rural retirement of Wales and bids farewell to a sympathetic friend. A little more than a year later it must indeed have seemed a curious parallel (as if, to use the sceptical words of Boswell, "the event had been foreseen") when Johnson himself said a fond farewell to his friend the down-at-heels and chronically injured poet Richard Savage as the latter was about to set out toward a last and unsuccessful attempt at readjustment in the retirement of Wales. Savage "parted" from Johnson "with tears in his eyes." Johnson himself wrote a *Life of Savage* a few years later and tells us that circumstance. In the Dictionary under the transitive verb *dissipate*, sense 2, "To scatter the attention," Johnson quotes:

> This slavery to his passions produced a life irregular and *dissipated.*
> —*Savage's Life.*

And immediately below, under sense 3, "To spend a fortune," he quotes:

> The wherry that contains
> Of *dissipated* wealth the poor remains.
> —*London.*

I suggest that in this collocation of materials we have Johnson's casually erected and semi-private testimony to the fact that in what was for him a peculiarly poignant instance, life had been the realization of poetic vision.

Certain other examples of softer sentiment in the Dictionary are very well known. Let me conclude this section of my paper by quoting two of them, with some attempt at a gloss upon the second. Both touch the theme of home-coming. Under *Grubstreet*, after the abrasive definition:

> originally the name of a street in Moorfields in London, much inhabited by writers of small histories, dictionaries, and temporary poems; whence any mean production is called *grubstreet,*

he throws in two lines of Greek from the *Palatine Anthology*, which mean approximately:

> Hail! Ithaca! after struggles and after bitter trials,
> Gladly do I approach thy threshold.

Then there is the word *lich*, a dead body, and *Lichfield*. . . . ("The earth that's nature's mother is her tomb; What is her burying grave that is her womb.") A strong blend of interest attaches to the very etymology and history of the name, and upon these Johnson dwells for a moment, before the sudden intrusion of a Latin apostrophe which leaps to the paradoxically united opposite of feeling.

> *Lich*, a dead carcase, whence *lichwake*, the time or act of watching by the dead; *lichgate*, the gate through which the dead are carried to the grave, *Lichfield*, the field of the dead, a city in Staffordshire, so named from martyred Christians. *Salve magna parens.*

But it is now time to shift our attention and attempt to say something about certain more essential features of the Dictionary, the peculiar and richly interesting texture of its illustrations and definitions as these appear from page to page, from A to Z. One main principle to be observed is that Johnson regularly chose passages not only because they were good examples of certain meanings but because they were in themselves interesting. In his Plan he had promised "such sentences as, besides their immediate use, may give pleasure or instruction, by conveying some elegance of language, or some precept of prudence or piety." After the abbreviations and eliminations which in the course of his work had been forced upon him, he reflected in his Preface that he had yet "spared" some passages which might "relieve the labour of verbal searches, and intersperse with verdure and flowers the dusty desarts of barren philology." This policy was noted and censured as a lexicographical fault by his American successor Noah Webster. It may not be an economical pattern of lexicography. But the very objection of Webster serves to point up the difference between the Dictionary of Johnson and all others.

Johnson's Dictionary—as a reader knowing the character and literary taste of the author might indeed have hoped—is, for one thing, embellished by numerous aphorisms, anecdotes, thumbnail dramas, biographical glimpses, drawn from Bacon, for instance, from Shakespeare, from Ben Jonson, from Knolles, from Camden, from L'Estrange, from Swift.

> As a cock was turning up a dunghill, he espied a dia-mond: Well (says he) this sparkling foolery now to a *lapidary* would have been the making of him; but, as to any use of mine, a barley-corn had been worth forty on't.
> —L'Estrange

> And must they all be hang'd that swear and lie?
> .... Every one.
> .... Who must hang them?
> .... Why, the honest men.
> .... Then the liars and *Swearers* are fools; for there are liars and *Swearers* enow to beat the honest men, and hang them up.
> —Shakespeare

> Thou hast most traitorously corrupted the youth of the realm in erecting a *Grammar School.*
> —Shakespeare

> A philosopher being asked in what a wise man differed from a fool? answered, send them both *naked* to those who know them not, and you shall perceive.
> —Bacon

> Hope is a good *breakfast*, but it is a bad supper.
> —Bacon

> Sir Henry Wotton used to say, that criticks were like *brushers* of noblemen's clothes.
> —Bacon

> Cromartie after fourscore went to his country-house to live *thriftily*, and save up money to spend at London.
> —Swift

79

> An old lord of Leicestershire amused himself with mending *pitchforks* and spades for his tenants gratis.
>
> —Swift

(Johnson's marked copy of Bacon's *Apophthegms* and *Ornamenta Rationalia* shows that he originally selected many more examples of this kind than actually appear in the Dictionary after his retrenchments.)

Again, Johnson's Dictionary is generously planted with miniature expressions of literary theory and of critical judgement—from Sidney's *Defense*, from Ben Jonson's *Timber* (a work otherwise largely neglected during the eighteenth century), from Dryden, from Swift, from Addison—the shapers of the English critical tradition before the time of Johnson himself.

> Spenser, in *affecting* the ancients, writ no language; yet I would have him read for his matter, but as Virgil read Ennius.
>
> —Jonson

> After Chaucer there was a Spenser, a Harrington, a Fairfax, before Waller and Denham were in being; and our numbers were in their *nonage* 'till these last appeared.
>
> —Dryden

> *Nineteen* in twenty of perplexing words might be changed into easy ones, such as occur to ordinary men.
>
> —Swift

> Since phrases used in conversation contract meanness by passing through the mouths of the vulgar, a poet should guard himself against the *idiomatick* ways of speaking.
>
> —Addison

Again, the Dictionary is fortified on almost every page by morality and religion—by passages from the whole range of

the Old and New Testaments, from the sermons of South,
Sprat, Tillotson, Bentley, Atterbury, and other divines, from
such devotional manuals as *The Decay of Piety* and *The Government of the Tongue*.

> *Slothfulness* casteth into a deep sleep, and an idle soul
> shall suffer hunger.
> —Proverbs, XIX, 15

> Let atheists and *sensualists* satisfy themselves as they are
> able; the former of which will find, that, as long as reason
> keeps her ground, religion neither can nor will lose hers.
> —South

And once again, the Dictionary is a magazine of contemporary science—though it has to be admitted that here one
encounters certain rather severe limitations. The technical
articles, extracted from Chambers' *Cyclopedia* and from various other lexica, seem to be inserted somewhat at random and,
though often curiously associated with other details, are not
on the whole among the Dictionary's clearest triumphs. Under
the word *electricity*, for example, there is in addition to a
brief, out-of-date technical definition also a short original
essay in which Johnson sketches the recent rise of electrical
theory, from the beginnings by Stephen Gray (the Charter-
house inmate who had been a friend of Johnson's friend the
blind poetess Anna Williams) up to the wave of activity with
lightning rods stimulated by Cave's publication in 1751 of
Franklin's *Experiments and Observations*. Much comes out
if we look into the background of that Dictionary entry. But
it is one of the Dictionary's personal revelations, rather than
a part of any systematic effort at science.

The most impressive scientific feature of the Dictionary is
the wealth of illustrations drawn from the prose of the seven-
teenth- and eighteenth-century physical, chemical, mechan-

ical, and medical essayists—from Bacon, for instance, from Browne, Boyle, Newton, Ray, Derham, Arbuthnot, Cheyne, and a crowd of others. The first volume of the Dictionary, from A to K, contains about 10,000 illustrations from such authors, which is about one in five of all the illustrations in the volume. Some of these passages, falling even in Johnson's day under the head of fantastic science (science fiction), are part of the lighter side of Dictionary reading.

> Bellerophon's horse, fram'd of iron, and placed between two loadstones with wings expanded, hung *pendulous* in the air.
> —Browne's *Vulgar Errors*

> That cold country where discourse doth freeze in the air all winter, and may be heard in the next summer, or at a great *thaw*.
> —Wilkins' [*Mathematical Magic*]

But, to speak more broadly, Johnson's numerous scientific illustrations show us a world of physical "philosophy" in conjunction with a great variety of other things—with poetry, with history, with moral philosophy and religion, with the homeliest parts of everyday life. Look up the word *digger*, for instance, in Johnson's Dictionary, and you find Robert Boyle in the mines studying the effect of the atmosphere on candles. Look up *druggist*, and Boyle is in a shop buying nitre; look up *drugster*, and the same scientist appears again, buying turpentine; look up *distiller*, and he sends for spirit of salt. Look up some of the many concrete and makeshift expressions for shades of sensory experience which were beginning to expand the English vocabulary in that era—*brownish, bluishness, greenish*, for instance—and you find Boyle, Newton, or the geologist Woodward.

One of the most persistent strains of higher meaning which

run through the Dictionary is the union of the scientific and religious. Six mighty works of the physicotheological school, Ray's *Wonders of God in the Creation*, Grew's *Cosmologia Sacra*, Derham's *Physico-Theology*, Burnet's *History of the Earth*, Bentley's *Sermons on the Boyle Foundation*, Cheyne's *Philosophical Principles*, and works of a similar tenor like More's *Antidote against Atheism* and Hale's *Primitive Origination of Mankind*, provided Johnson with succinct arguments for insertion under the most widely varied, concrete, and commonplace words.

> The reason of the motion of the balance is by the motion of the next wheel, and that by the motion of the next, and that by the motion of the *fusee*, and that by the motion of the spring; the whole frame of the watch carries a reasonableness in it, the passive impression of the intellectual idea that was in the artist.
>
> —Hale

> The wise author of nature hath provided on the rump two glandules, which the bird catches hold upon with her bill, and squeezes out an oily pap or *liniment*, fit for the inunction of the feathers.
>
> —Ray

Johnson's Dictionary is an eighteenth-century tabloid *speculum*—a *Speculum Historiale, Naturale,* and *Doctrinale.* As John Ray had seen the wonders of God everywhere in the Creation, Johnson's readers found the same wonders everywhere in the variegated realm of discourse of which his Dictionary was the alphabetized reflection.

I have heard it argued that Johnson's reading for the Dictionary is hardly to be counted as first-rate reading, that it would not have made the kind of impression on his mind that we can consider an influence. To this I would object the principle—for which I feel sure the psychologists must have a name —that casual attentiveness, the tension of some fairly easy routine job, is often very productive of side discoveries and inspirations. Not drowsy boredom and not the clenched effort of a conscious frontal assault on a difficult puzzle, but the mind running easily alert—turning a stick on a lathe and thinking a variety of thoughts, looking for words in a book and noticing all sorts of passages *en route*. This comes strictly under the head of Johnson's intellectual biography.

One very nice report on this side of his biography has recently appeared—perhaps the only pointed instance so far. A good many of the scientific arguments concerning the possibility of "volant or flying automata" that make up Johnson's "Dissertation on the Art of Flying," chapter vi of *Rasselas*, appear to be derived from one of the most venerable scientific sources of the Dictionary, Bishop John Wilkins' *Mathematical Magick: Or the Wonders That May Be Perform'd by Mechanical Geometry*, published first in 1648.[9] Other instances I think might be more or less readily developed. Such essays in the *Rambler* and *Idler* as those on the English historians, the history of translations, the sufficiency of the English language, exhibit fairly clear evidence of Dictionary reading. How many passages in Johnson's *Lives of the Poets*, published twenty-five years after the Dictionary, were drawn not from new reading but from the capacious storage of his memory? A great deal of research into his conversations and later writings might be undertaken and might not yield conclusive results. But it seems at least clearly on the side of plausibility to speak of Johnson's long labor on the Dictionary, from his thirty-seventh to his forty-sixth year, as one of the great episodes, the last great epi-

9. See below, pp. 91–106. The phrase "volant or flying automata" is from Wilkins' definition in Bk. II, chapter vi, quoted by Johnson in the Dictionary s.v. *volant*. Chapter vi of *Rasselas* speaks of the "structure of all volant animals."

sode, in the formation of his mind. From this he emerged the terrifying arbiter and universal cham of the mature years with which we are most familiar.

But to return to the Dictionary: It seems to me that at least three main principles have to be borne in mind in order to appreciate the most seriously original character of Johnson's performance. That character is essentially a literary and imaginative character, and the principles are: (1) that his discriminations of meanings and definitions grow out of and are determined empirically by the materials gathered from his actual reading; (2) that these discriminations and definitions, at their best and most interesting, which comes often enough, are metaphorically structured; (3) that there is often a close relation in the Dictionary between metaphor and the scientific or "philosophic" materials to which we have been alluding.

The metaphoric principle in Johnson's Dictionary may be more or less implicit and elliptical in places, and it may spread out into various broadly associative patterns. Consider, for example, the elaborately rounded treatment of the word *swan*, where a natural and historical account from Dom Augustin Calmet's *Historical, Critical, Geographical and Etymological Dictionary of the Holy Bible* is followed by three quotations from Shakespeare:

And I will make thee think thy swan a crow,

a comment from Peacham on the drawing of the swan, a quotation from Dryden, and a concluding description from Locke of "the idea which an Englishman signifies by the name swan." Or consider such words as *lentil* and *thigh*, where the treatment moves in only two examples from the realm of Miller's *Gardeners Dictionary* and Quincy's *Lexicon Physico-Medicum* to the "ground full of lentils" in II Samuel and Jacob's thigh out of joint in Genesis. I persuade myself, however, to pass over a number of variations on my theme—curious matters concerning science and everyday life in that age of Boyle, Newton, and Arbuthnot, or science and burlesque in that age of Scriblerus —and to conclude my argument with a brief emphasis upon the kind of arrangements which appear in the Dictionary under words of the scientific or "philosophic" vocabulary itself—the big Latinate abstractions which were so congenial to Johnson as a prose stylist. I estimate that he includes about 3,000 of these in the Dictionary. Under the letter A we are likely to find the most explicit and full examples of almost any character of the Dictionary we may be discussing. We are taking then a somewhat select, but not unfair, example when we look at the word *accelerate* and note that it has a primary physical sense ("It is generally applied to matter, and used chiefly in philosophical language"), and that this sense is illustrated by five quotations, from the scientific writings of Bacon, Glanville, Newton, and Arbuthnot, and from the philosophic poet James Thomson. It has a secondary sense (". . . it is sometimes used on other occasions"), and this sense is illustrated from Bacon's *History of Henry VII* and from Isaac Watts's *Improvement of the Mind*. Or take the word *adhesion*. The definition of sense 1 of this word embodies a special distinction:

> 1. The act or state of sticking to something. *Adhesion* is generally used in the natural, and *adherence* in the metaphysical sense: as, *the adhesion of iron to the magnet*; and *adherence of a client to his patron*.

An illustration from Boyle and one from Locke refer to the adhesion of particles of matter; one from Prior is more widely applied:

> —Prove that all things, on occasion,
> Love union, and desire adhesion.

Then the definition of the second sense, which has already been indicated:

> 2. It is sometimes taken, like *adherence*, figuratively, for firmness in an opinion, or steadiness in a practice.

> The same want of sincerity, the same adhesion to vice, and aversion from goodness, will be equally a reason for the rejecting any proof whatsoever.
> —Atterbury.

The relation between such Dictionary materials and Johnson's own mind and character as a prose stylist may be specially illustrated in the fact that of the thirty-five Dictionary quotations which he acknowledges to be from his own writing, eleven are for the metaphoric or psychological meaning of philosophic words. The word *dissipate* which we have already seen illustrated from Johnson in its second and third meanings (psychological and social) has of course also a first meaning, physical and scientific, illustrated from the geologist Woodward, the botanist Ray, and the poet Thomson. The word *transmute*, to take another example, after being illustrated in its alchemical sense from Raleigh and Ray, has a line from the *Vanity of Human Wishes*:

> Patience, sov'reign o'er *transmuted* ill.

Johnson remembers his own work to complete a metaphoric pattern with an example which his original excursions into English literature have by chance failed to provide.

In a few other instances, he apparently cannot remember the example from his own writing, or perhaps has not *yet* written it. The prime Johnsonian words *fugacity, suavity,* and *volatility* are illustrated in the Dictionary under their physical senses from Boyle, Browne, and Bacon, but under their second or psychological senses there is an absence of illustration which cannot better be filled than by turning to Johnson's main creative writing of the Dictionary years, the *Rambler*. Here we find that poets lament "the fugacity of pleasure," good humour is defined as "a constant and perennial . . . suavity of disposition," and the author speculates "whether a secret has not some subtle volatility."

Both in his Plan of a Dictionary and his Preface Johnson lays some stress on the liability of scientific terms to undergo the metaphoric process.

> As by the cultivation of various sciences a language is amplified, it will be more furnished with words deflected from their original sense; the geometrician will talk of a courtier's zenith, or the eccentrick of a wild hero, and the physician of sanguine expectations and phlegmatick delays.

We may say—or at least we shall not be challenged by modern linguistics if we do say—that metaphor through the ages shows a characteristic direction of reference, from the physical towards the social, psychological, and spiritual. And this was one of the main assumptions upon which Johnson the dictionary-maker proceeded. Where his predecessor Nathan Bailey and others, in accord with their technical bent and in a way that emphasized only the more recent chronology of word histories, made the philosophic or physically scientific meaning, when they gave it, a special instance of a more general meaning, Johnson, as Latinist, etymologist, and literary philosopher, conceived a more remote history of words and a basically correct order of physical or "primitive" and of psychological or secondary meanings. In his Preface he explains that there are even some words (for instance, *ardour* and *flagrant*) where, in the absence of any known examples of the "primitive" meaning, he has extrapolated or supposed that meaning from known examples of the secondary.

88

The metaphoric movement of language from physical to psychological need not, of course, be specially related in all cases to scientific ideas or words. But there were good enough reasons why a certain special relation between metaphor and science did prevail during the age of Johnson.[1] During the period when most of the sources of the Dictionary were written—and indeed for a considerable time before that—the preferred vision of the physical universe had been a scientific one, and its language was the language of scientific experiment and speculation, that is, "philosophic diction." Many of the most novel and ample opportunities for metaphor arose during this period out of the very words by which science was altering the known contours of ordinary physical reality and the trend of any educated man's thoughts about that reality. The very Latinism of the vocabulary enhanced it with deep etymological vistas and luminous intimations of meaning. And this went well with a scientifically thoughtful and ambitious way of looking at things. Again, this scientific way was a way mainly oriented upon and endlessly repetitive of the Galilean and Cartesian philosophy—that radical division, and hence complete, if rather chilly, reflection, between the outer and the inner of human experience, matter and spirit. The scientific image of the universe was an image that required and promoted a special idiom of mechanical and chemical metaphor for the analysis of the spirit, the introspections of the moral and religious mind.

I have been arguing, in brief, that the history of science and

1. In his Plan of a Dictionary Johnson uses the word *arrive* and, perhaps by an accident in the composition and transcription of drafts of the *Plan*—cf. W. R. Keast, *Philological Quarterly*, xxxiii (1954), 341–46—also the word *ground* in his main account of the relation between "primitive" and metaphoric meanings. The examples are synthetic, however, and when these nonphilosophic words actually make their way into the Dictionary, though the treatment is ample and informative, neither the definitions nor the examples lay any stress on a metaphoric pattern.

of scientific words in English for the century and a half before he wrote his Dictionary provided Johnson with one of his best opportunities, perhaps his best opportunity, for illustrating the metaphoric structure of language, that he took this opportunity, and that his general interest in metaphor and his capacity for dealing with it were among a few main reasons why he wrote the first English Dictionary that gives a lively reflection of the modern English language. In this feat he became a champion among English lexicographers in his day and for some days to come, and at least a noteworthy figure on the broader horizon of international lexicography.

Johnson's "Dissertation On Flying"

GWIN J. KOLB

Though the "Dissertation on the Art of Flying" has always been one of the best-known chapters in *Rasselas,* an analysis of its structure in relation to certain sections of John Wilkins' *Mathematical Magick* (1648)[1] throws some new light on Johnson's probable method of constructing the larger part of the chapter.

Earlier in the work, it will be recalled, Rasselas, fired by the hope of leaving the "happy valley," has concluded his search for an opening through which to escape. For the narrative to proceed, however, he must be led to engage in another attempt at flight, and, since he has exhausted his own resources, another agent must obviously be introduced to provide the means of the second attempt. The agent Johnson selects is the "artist" who in chapter VI proposes to the prince the possibility of building a contrivance for flying. But if Rasselas, discouraged and rather sceptical as a result of his failure, is to take the artist's scheme seriously, then the latter must be represented as an unusually skilful "mechanist." And so Johnson not only states that the artist is a man famous for "his knowledge of the mechanick powers" but also lists specific examples of his mechanical ability. Furthermore, when Rasselas visits him, the workman is engaged in building a novel vehicle of locomotion —a "sailing chariot"—which further demonstrates his ingenuity as a craftsman.

1. All quotations in this paper refer to the text of the work published as a part of Wilkins' *Mathematical and Philosophical Works* (1708).

91

When the prince urges the completion of the chariot, the artist, desirous of "higher honours," broaches the notion of the "swifter migration of wings." Rasselas, although interested in the suggestion and impressed by what the artist has "already performed," is nevertheless doubtful, and he therefore advances a series of objections, to each of which the artist makes a reply. Arranged in a logical sequence, these objections include (1) a general argument based on the belief that the earth is the proper element of man, (2) the fact that the limitation of human limbs prevents a flight of any consequence, and (3) the difficulty of respiration in the upper regions. Though prompt and glib, the artist's answers are not always pertinent: in response to the first he offers the analogy of swimming; against the second he urges the gradual suspension of the law of gravity; as to the third he remarks only that "nothing . . . will ever be attempted, if all possible objections must be first overcome."

After this series of objections and answers, the artist declares his intention of beginning the "wings" immediately, and he secures from Rasselas a promise not to divulge the "art" to anyone. During the process of construction the prince observes the work from time to time. Then, when the wings are finished, the artist makes his leap and, dropping into the lake, is pulled to land by the prince. Thus ends Rasselas' second scheme for escaping from the "happy valley."

From Johnson's "Dissertation" one may turn to another quite different work, certain parts of which become unusually interesting when examined in relation to chapter VI in *Rasselas*. John Wilkins' *Mathematical Magick: or the Wonders That May Be Perform'd by Mechanical Geometry*, although not among the most popular sources of quotations, is still quoted frequently enough in the first edition of the *Dictionary* to indicate clearly Johnson's familiarity with it; it supplies, for example, illustrative passages for the meanings of at least two of the important words ("contrivances" and "volant") used in the

"Dissertation."[2] The work is divided into two "books": (1) "Archimedes, or, Mechanical Powers," consisting of twenty chapters on such "mechanick faculties" as the balance, "leaver," wheel, etc.; and (2) "Dædalus: or, Mechanical Motions," containing fifteen chapters treating of the "divers kinds of Automata," the art of flying, perpetual motion, etc. Of these fifteen chapters, only the first eight need be considered here, and only five—I, II, VI, VII, VIII—treated in any detail.

In chapter I of "Dædalus," entitled "The divers kinds of Automata, or Self-Movers," etc.,[3] Wilkins first distinguishes the various "automata" into two kinds: (1) "Those that are moved by something which is extrinsical unto their own Frame; as Mills, by Water or Wind," and (2) "Those that receive their Motion from something" belonging "to the Frame it self; as Clocks, Watches," etc.[4] Selecting "mills" as the more common examples of the first class of "self-movers," he considers, initially, "Water-Mills" and, second, "wind-mills," which, if often "more convenient" than the former, are to the same purpose. After indicating several of their rarer uses, he turns, finally, to a "digression concerning wind-guns," which concludes the chapter.

Chapter II, labeled "Of a Sailing Chariot,"[5] records earlier instances of the use of "sailing chariots," includes sketches of two chariots, and contains Wilkins' treatment of the chief difficulty hindering the unlimited use of such a vehicle.

2. See n. 7, below. An examination of approximately every other letter in the first edition of the *Dictionary* reveals at least 105 quotations from *Mathematical Magick*, including passages from all five chapters discussed in this paper.

3. The complete title of the chapter is *"The divers kinds of Automata, or Self-movers. Of Mills, and the Contrivance of several Motions by rarify'd Air. A brief Digression concerning Wind-guns."*

4. P. 86. References to *Mathematical Magick* cited hereafter as "Dædalus."

5. The complete title is *"Of a Sailing Chariot, that may without Horses be driven on the Land by the Wind, as Ships are on the Sea."*

The next three chapters in "Dædalus" are concerned, respectively, with "Fixed Automata," "Moveable and Gradient Automata," and an "Ark for Submarine Navigations."[6] With chapter VI (entitled "Of the Volant Automata," etc.), however, Wilkins begins a three-chapter sequence dealing with various aspects of the art of flying. In this chapter he defines "volant Automata,"[7] presents previous opinions concerning this kind of "self-movers," and offers hints for the construction of the wings of the contrivances. Then, after advancing the notion that "it is possible also for a Man to fly himself," he mentions several of the difficulties obstructing aerial experiments.

Chapters VII and VIII are entitled "Concerning the Art of Flying," and "A Resolution of the two chief Difficulties that seem to oppose the Possibility of a flying Chariot" and consist of an account of the "several ways whereby" flying "hath been, or may be attempted." These ways include flying (1) "By Spirits, or Angels," (2) "By the help of Fowls," (3) "By Wings fastned immediately to the Body," and (4) "By a Flying Chariot."[8] Chapter VII contains Wilkins' discussion of each of them, flight by wings receiving most of his attention.

The "resolution," in chapter VIII, of the primary difficulties

6. The full titles of these chapters are: (1) *"Concerning the fixed* Automata, *Clocks, Spheres, representing the Heavenly Motions: The several Excellencies that are most commendable in such kind of Contrivances"*; (2) *"Of the Moveable and Gradient* Automata, *representing the Motions, of Living Creatures, various Sounds, of Birds, or Beasts, and some of them Articulate"*; (3) *"Concerning the Possibility of Framing an Ark for submarine Navigations. The Difficulties and Conveniences of such a Contrivance."*

7. This definition, which Johnson quotes—with the omission of a few words—in the *Dictionary* as illustrating one of the meanings of "volant," is: "The *volant*, or flying *Automata*, are such Mechanical Contrivances as have a Self-motion, whereby they are carried aloft in the open Air like the flight of Birds" ("Dædalus," 112).

8. *Ibid.*, 116.

94

opposing the possibility of a flying chariot involves, according to Wilkins, answering these "two *Quæries*": (1) "Whether an Engine of such Capacity and Weight, may be supported by so thin and light a Body as the Air?" and (2) "Whether the Strength of the Persons within it, may be sufficient for the Motion of it?"[9] The greater part of the chapter consists, therefore, of his examination of these two (and additional) questions. Later he considers the various probable uses and conveniences of a flying chariot, among them the fact that it could transport a man anywhere in the world. In the last paragraphs of the chapter, Wilkins returns to a discussion of some of the "particulars" which require attention "for the perfecting of such a flying Chariot."[1]

Certain obvious similarities between the "Dissertation" and parts of "Dædalus" will have become clear from this account of the earlier work. With one exception, however, no one, apparently, has noted these resemblances.[2] In his "Johnson on Ballooning and Flight,"[3] H. E. Hodgson remarks that Johnson "probably borrowed from Wilkins' earlier *Discourse concerning the Art of Flying* (1648)" the notion "of the decreasing power of the earth's attraction at great heights" (65). But, clearly, the similarities between Johnson and Wilkins are more numerous than Hodgson indicates; and thus a detailed examination of the narrative in the "Dissertation"—viewed in the light of certain sections of "Dædalus"—will, it is suggested, amount to at least a plausible, if admittedly partial, reconstruction of the way in which Johnson built chapter vi in *Rasselas*.

9. *Ibid.*, 122.

1. *Ibid.*, 128.

2. Professor Marjorie Nicolson's *Voyages to the Moon* (1948) treats both the "Dissertation" and Wilkins' numerous observations on flying, but makes no attempt to connect them (93–98, 113–16, 133–34, and *passim*).

3. *London Mercury*, x (1924), 63–72.

At the beginning of the chapter, Johnson, who has presumably already decided upon the general "flying" scheme of Rasselas' second attempt to escape from the "happy valley" (a hint for which may or may not have come from Wilkins), sets out—as mentioned above—to make the mechanical skill of the would-be flier convincing enough for the discouraged, but still determined, prince to take an active interest in the artist's plan for flight. And the results of his effort seem to be due, in part at least, to the discriminating use of material included in chapters I and II of "Dædalus." Discussing the activities of the workman "who had contrived," for the inhabitants of the "happy valley," "many engines both of use and recreation," Johnson lists these specific inventions:

> By a wheel, which the stream turned, he forced the water into a tower, whence it was distributed to all the apartments of the palace. He erected a pavillion in the garden, around which he kept the air always cool by artificial showers. One of the groves . . . was ventilated by fans, to which the rivulet that run through it gave a constant motion; and instruments of soft musick were placed at proper distances, of which some played by the impulse of the wind, and some by the power of the stream.

Finally, as an even stronger proof of the artist's ingenuity, he represents him as engaged in building a "sailing chariot," an unusual vehicle, at the moment of Rasselas' visit. And the prince, upon examination, perceives the contrivance to be "practicable" at least "upon a level surface."[4]

4. In her *Voyages to the Moon* (133) Professor Nicolson states that Rasselas found the mechanic "engaged in building a flying machine." She adds: "Although the term used by Johnson is 'sailing chariot,' this invention, too, belongs, as later description shows, to the history of artificial wings." The context of the chapter, however, makes it clear that the "sailing chariot" being built by the artist is not a flying machine but a vehicle designed for travelling only on land.

96

In chapter I of "Dædalus," Wilkins, referring to the various services performed by water-mills, remarks: "Herein doth the Skill of an Artificer chiefly consist, in the Application of these common Motions unto various and beneficial Ends; making them serviceable, not only for the Grinding of Corn, but for the ... *elevating of Water*, or the like."[5] He makes no mention of the "artificial showers" produced by Johnson's clever artist, but in the succeeding account of wind-mills (cf. Johnson's "ventilated by fans") he describes a "Musical Instrument invented by *Cornelius Dreble*; which being set in the Sunshine, would of it self render a soft and pleasant Harmony; but being removed into the Shade, would presently become silent."[6] Again, somewhat later, when considering the several uses of circular "sails" to be placed in the chimney and turned by the motion of the ascending air, he suggests the possibility of using them "for the Chiming of Bells, or other musical Devices; and there cannot be any more pleasant Contrivance for continual and cheap Musick."[7] Afterwards comes the "digression concerning Wind-Guns."

Next, Wilkins turns to a discussion, in chapter II, of a "sailing chariot," which can be driven by sails on land. He proposes as the "chief doubt" of the practicability of such a contrivance the question of whether "every little Ruggedness or Unevenness of the Ground, will not cause such a jolting of the Chariot, as to hinder the Motion of its Sails."[8] But this problem, Wilkins thinks, is "capable of several Remedies," and he closes the chapter by wondering "why none of our Gentry who live near great Plains, and smooth Champions, have attempted any thing to

5. "Dædalus," 86–87. Italics mine.
6. *Ibid.*, 87.
7. *Ibid.*, 89.
8. *Ibid.*, 95. Johnson quotes this passage in the *Dictionary* under "to jolt."

this Purpose."[9] Then follow the three chapters on other kinds of "automata."

Granted, then, that the similarity between the first two paragraphs of the "Dissertation" and the first two chapters in "Dædalus" may be more than mere coincidence, one may speculate briefly about some of the reasons for Johnson's inclusion or omission of material in Wilkins. In the first place, he would not want to use all the notions found in (say) the first five chapters of "Dædalus" simply because he is to be primarily concerned with the attempt at flight in the "Dissertation" and consequently needs only to present the artist as a very clever contriver of "engines." Moreover, in the choice of suggestions he would, one may suppose, be guided by the principle of what would be suitable to the general character of the "happy valley." For instance, to mention "wind-guns" as one of the workman's inventions would be clearly inappropriate to the peacefulness of the valley. Again, since the inmates already possess all the ordinary comforts of life, certain of the remaining notions in Wilkins seem more apropos than others for Johnson's particular purpose; e.g., to conceive of the artist as constructing elaborate musical instruments is a more appropriate example of his ingenuity than to picture him building a spit turned by "sails" for the roasting of meat. In some such way, it seems reasonable to assume, Johnson proceeded until he had actually composed the beginning of the "Dissertation."

Next, the artist, flattered by the prince's remarks concerning the sailing chariot and wishing "to gain yet higher honours," advances the idea of flying. And Rasselas, interested but conscious of his own failure to discover a means of escape from the valley, quite logically "enquire[s] further" before he allows his "hope to afflict him by disappointment." He objects, therefore, that "every animal has his element assigned him; the birds have

9. *Ibid.*, 96.

the air, and man and beasts the earth." " 'So, replied the mechanist, fishes have the water, in which yet beasts can swim by nature, and men by art. He that can swim needs not despair to fly: to swim is to fly in a grosser fluid, and to fly is to swim in a subtler.' " By proportioning the " 'power of resistance to the different density of the matter through which we are to pass,' " he declares, a man " 'will be necessarily upborn by the air,' " provided that he " 'can renew any impulse upon it, faster than the air can recede from the pressure.' "

" 'But,' " returns the prince, passing to his second objection, " 'the exercise of swimming . . . is very laborious; the strongest limbs are soon wearied; I am afraid the act of flying will be yet more violent, and wings will be of no great use, unless we can fly further than we can swim.' " In reply the artist admits that " 'the labour of rising from the ground . . . will be great, as we see it in the heavier domestick fowls; but,' " he asserts, " 'as we mount higher, the earth's attraction, and the body's gravity, will be gradually diminished, till we shall arrive at a region where the man will float in the air without any tendency to fall: no care will then be necessary, but to move forwards, which the gentlest impulse will effect.' "

Turning again to "Dædalus," one finds in chapter VI (on "volant automata"), after the suggestion that man can fly himself, a paragraph dealing with the various "Impediments" to aerial experiments. Eusebius expressed one of these, says Wilkins, when he spoke of "the necessity" with which

> every thing is confined by the Laws of Nature, and the Decrees of Providence, so that nothing can go out of that way unto which naturally it is designed; as a Fish cannot reside on the Land, nor a Man in the Water, or aloft in the Air; [he] infers, that therefore none will venture upon any such vain Attempt, as passing in the Air, . . . unless his Brain be a little crazed with the Humour of Melancholy;

99

whereupon he advises, that we should not in any Particular, endeavour to transgress the Bounds of Nature, . . . and since we are destitute of Wings, not to imitate the Flight of Birds.[1]

Later, in his answer (chapter VIII) to the question of whether a heavy chariot can "be supported by so thin and light a Body as the Air," he remarks, "It is this [difficulty] must add a Glory to the Invention," and declares that just as a "Kite" is able to "swim up and down in the Air" at will, so men, by "long Practice," will be able to do likewise in a flying chariot. Furthermore, Wilkins argues, in terms similar to those of the artist:

> As it is in those Bodies which are carried on the Water, tho' they be never so big or so ponderous . . . yet they will always swim on the Top, if they be but any thing lighter than so much Water as is equal to them in Bigness; So likewise is it in the Bodies that are carried in the Air. It is not their Greatness . . . that can hinder their being supported in that light Element, if we suppose them to be extended unto a proportionable Space of Air.[2]

Earlier, also, in chapter VII, in the discussion of the problems involved in flying by wings, he admits that, because of the inevitable weariness resulting from the extended motions of a man's arms, human flight would be "but short and slow, answerable . . . to the *Flight of such Domestick Fowl as are most conversant on the Ground.*"[3] His solution to the problem is the

1. "Dædalus," 115. Italics mine.
2. *Ibid.*, 124.
3. *Ibid.*, 121. Italics mine. In chapter XIV of *The Discovery of a New World* (given, incidentally, as a reference in chapter VIII of "Dædalus"), a work included, like *Mathematical Magick*, in the 1708 ed. of Wilkins' *Mathematical and Philosophical Works*, is a passage closer to Rasselas' second objection and the "domestick fowl" remark of the artist. Dis-

conjecture that the legs, instead of the arms, might be used to effect the motion of the wings; "by which means a Man should (as it were) walk or climb up into the Air."[4] Again, in his treatment of the second "chief doubt" about flying, in chapter VIII —that of whether the passengers' strength will be sufficient to move the chariot—he states that "the main Difficulty and Labour of it will be in the raising of it from the Ground; near unto which, the Earths attractive Vigor is of greatest Efficacy. . . . When once it is aloft in the Air, the Motion of it will be easie."[5] And on the same page he asserts that, though the motion of the chariot "may be difficult at the first," yet it will "still be easier" as the flying machine "ascends higher, till at length it shall become utterly devoid of Gravity, when the least Strength will be able to bestow upon it a swift Motion"—as, he notes, he has "proved more at large in another Discourse."[6]

---

cussing the possibility of flying to the moon, Wilkins says: " 'Tis usually observed, that amongst the variety of Birds, those which do most converse upon the Earth, and are swiftest in their running . . . together with all Domestical Fowl, are less able for flight than others which are for the most part upon the Wing. . . . And therefore we may well think, that Man being not naturally endowed with any such Condition as may enable him for this Motion; and being necessarily tied to a more especial Residence on the Earth, must needs be slower than any Fowl, or less able to hold out. Thus it is also in Swimming; which Art though it be grown to a good eminence, yet he that is best skilled in it, is not able either for continuance, or swiftness to equal a Fish, because he is not naturally appointed to it. So that though a Man could fly, yet he would be so slow in it, and so quickly weary, that he could never think to reach so great a Journey as it is to the Moon" (116).

4. "Dædalus," 121.

5. *Ibid.*, 125–26.

6. *Ibid.*, 126. The "discourse" is *The Discovery of a New World* (see n. 3, above); the passage referred to reads, in part: "If a Man were above the Sphere of this Magnetical Virtue which proceeds from the Earth, he might there stand as firmly in the open Air, as he can now upon the Ground: And not only so, but he may also move with a far greater Swiftness, than any living Creatures here below; because then he is without all Gravity,

In the "Dissertation," the artist, after explaining his conception of the law of gravity to Rasselas, imagines the "pleasure" with which "a philosopher, furnished with wings, and hovering in the sky, would see the earth, and all it's inhabitants, rolling beneath him, and presenting to him successively, by it's diurnal motion, all the countries within the same parallel." While acknowledging the benefits of flying, the prince, eager but still sceptical, voices his third objection. " 'I am afraid,' " he says, " 'that no man will be able to breathe in these regions of speculation and tranquility,' " and he cites the difficulty of respiration "upon lofty mountains." The artist, brushing aside this doubt, declares that, with Rasselas' approval, he will "try the first flight" himself, and adds: " 'I have considered the structure of all volant animals, and find the folding continuity of the bat's wings most easily accommodated to the human form. Upon this model I shall begin my task to morrow.' "

As indicated in the earlier general description of "Dædalus," Wilkins, like Johnson's artist, also considers the various possible uses of a flying contrivance. Among these is the fact that "it would be serviceable . . . for the Conveyance of a Man to any remote Place of this Earth."[7] "For," he points out, "when once it was elevated for some few Miles, so as to be above that Orb of Magnetick Virtue, which is carried about by the Earth's *diurnal Revolution*, it might then be . . . directed" anywhere in the world. "If the Place which we intended," he continues, "were *under the same Parallel, why then the Earth's Revolution once in Twenty four Hours, would bring it to be under us*; so that it would be but descending in a straight Line, and we might presently be there."[8] Moreover, he observes, "the

---

being not attracted any way; and so consequently will not be liable to such Impediments as may in the least manner resist that kind of Motion which he shall apply himself unto" (122).

7. "Dædalus," 127.
8. *Ibid.* Italics mine.

upper Parts of the World are always quiet and serene" and travelers would thus "be perfectly freed from all Inconveniences of Ways or Weather...."[9] Again, like Rasselas, Wilkins in chapter VIII refers to the "Doubts" concerning "the extream Thinness" (and also coldness) of the "Æthereal Air" which—as in the case of whether heavy bodies can be supported in thin air—he has "resolved" in another "Discourse."[1] Finally, in the last paragraphs of the chapter, he discusses further some of the "particulars" which must be considered in the construction of a flying machine. And he suggests that a person attempting "any Thing to this Purpose"

> should first *make Enquiry what kind of Wings would be most useful to this End; those of a Bat being most easily imitable, and perhaps Nature did by them purposely intend some Intimation to direct us in such Experiments;* that Creature being not properly a Bird, because not amongst the *Ovipara,* to imply that other kind of Creatures are capable of Flying as well as Birds; and if any should attempt it, that would be the best Pattern for Imitation.[2]

Assuming, then, that these numerous similarities between parts of the "Dissertation" and certain passages in "Dædalus" indicate a more or less direct borrowing from the earlier work, one may again consider briefly the reasons for Johnson's distinctive use of the material. For one thing, Rasselas has been discouraged by his own failure to find a means of exit from the

9. *Ibid.*, 128.

1. *The Discovery of a New World*, 130–31, where Wilkins presents both problems; regarding the thinness of the air, he mentions that it may "make [the air] unfit for Expiration"; for, he notes, "in some Mountains (as *Aristotle* tells us of *Olympus*, and out of him *St. Austin*) the Air be so thin, that Men cannot draw their Breath, unless it were through some moistned Spunges..." (130).

2. "Dædalus," 129. Italics mine.

valley and thus quite appropriately determines "to enquire further" before giving his approval to a very unusual experiment in transportation. And in what more suitable manner, Johnson might well ask himself, could the prince express his doubt than by raising a series of objections to the possibility of flying. Thus he could select from "Dædalus" three notions which together would form a logical, almost exhaustive, progression in the "Dissertation": i.e., (1) man cannot fly; (2) granted man can fly, he cannot fly far; and (3) granted man can fly far, he cannot breathe in the ether. On the other hand, the artist must answer Rasselas' criticisms, or else the flying attempt will not be made. Again "Dædalus" could supply the basis of these answers, which (since, for all their assurance, they are not real refutations of the prince's objections), when viewed in the light of the dismal failure of the flying experiment, help to create the ironical effect produced by the chapter as a whole. Similarly, the artist's glowing anticipation of the pleasures of air travel presents a striking contrast to the result of his actual leap. Once again "Dædalus" could provide the hint for this neat addition. Finally, at the end of the objection–reply exchange, the artist could naturally be expected to reveal to the still hesitant Rasselas something about his specific plan for building the wings. And, again, Wilkins had discussed in some detail the advisability of modelling one's wings on those of the bat.

Following the artist's revelation of the proposed model for his wings, he and Rasselas discuss the need for secrecy concerning the flying project. The prince promises to tell no one of the "art." He visits "the work from time to time" and "remarked many ingenious contrivances to facilitate motion, and unite levity with strength." At last, when the wings are finished, the maker appears "furnished for flight on a little promontory." After waving "his pinions a while," he "leaped from his stand,

and . . . dropped into the lake," from which "the prince drew him to land, half dead with terrour and vexation."

Since "Dædalus" contains no passages paralleling the discussion between Rasselas and the artist about the possible evil uses of a flying contrivance, their remarks must, for present purposes, be referred entirely to Johnson's own invention. But, toward the conclusion of chapter VIII, Wilkins mentions *"special Contrivances, whereby the Strength of these Wings may be severally applied,* either to ascent, descent, progressive, or a turning Motion; all which, and divers the like Enquiries can only be resolved by particular Experiments."[3] Earlier, too, in the same chapter he recommends that the flying chariot take "its first Rise from some Mountain or other high Place."[4] And in discussing the previous efforts of artists attempting flight by wings, he attributes their almost universal failure to "their want of Experience, and too much Fear, which must needs possess Men in such dangerous and strange Attempts."[5]

Controlled only by the data noted above, speculation about Johnson's procedure in composing roughly the last third of the "Dissertation" must be considerably less precise than the previous attempts at reconstruction. First of all, the paragraph on the need for secrecy concerning the flying machine—while forming an effective contrast to the artist's earlier rosy description of the delights of flying—cannot be paralleled by any of Wilkins' remarks on flying. Next, of Rasselas' periodic inspections of the wings under construction, one may say only that they are specific evidence of his continued interest in the ex-

3. "Dædalus," 128. Italics mine. He continues: "[Flying] may at first perhaps seem perplexed with many Difficulties and Inconveniences, and yet . . . many things may be suggested to make it more facil and commodious" (128–29). In the *Dictionary* Johnson quotes this passage under "facile."

4. "Dædalus," 126.

5. *Ibid.,* 119.

periment and that the "ingenious contrivances" he observes during his visits provide a tangible basis upon which to found his hope for its success. And in "Dædalus," it will be remembered, are references to various kinds of contrivances by means of which particular problems of flight might, perhaps, be solved. As for the artist's jump from the promontory, one may suppose that Johnson, in order to produce the striking effect actually achieved, would have decided that the account of the flight should be relatively brief. Suggestions for the initiation of the experiment and the subsequent "terrour" of the projector were available in "Dædalus," and he may have drawn on them. In a single paragraph—the more forcible for its shortness—the flight begins and ends: the artist leaps into the air and drops into the lake. He is rescued—but Rasselas' hope of seeing the world via wings is lost.

Dr. Franklin Meets Dr. Johnson

MAURICE J. QUINLAN

While serving in London as agent for the American colonies, Benjamin Franklin met various prominent Englishmen. Several of his friends were also intimates of Dr. Samuel Johnson. Both men, for instance, knew William Strahan, the printer, John Hawkesworth, the writer, Dr. William Heberden, and that curious-minded and sociable Scot, James Boswell. Altogether Franklin spent about fifteen years in London between 1757 and 1775. Like Dr. Johnson, he was a member of various clubs, he enjoyed the company of women, and he believed in keeping friendship in repair by constantly broadening the circle of his intimates. Thus there is nothing strange in the fact that these two distinguished men shared many acquaintances, especially at a time when scholars and writers formed a rather distinct group. What has seemed remarkable to students of the period is that no one has been able to prove that Franklin and Johnson knew each other. Boswell, despite his fondness for bringing people together, never mentions an occasion when both were present, and neither Franklin nor Johnson ever refers to the other as an acquaintance. Because of the apparent lack of evidence in other sources, many have concluded that these two remarkable men were probably never in each other's company.

This opinion can now be rejected. Franklin and Johnson definitely did meet upon at least one occasion. In fact, they both held membership in an eighteenth-century society which, though almost forgotten, included several prominent Englishmen. The nature of this society, the meeting between Franklin and Johnson, and the part each played in the organization will be described in this essay.

The society to which Franklin and Johnson belonged was called the Associates of Dr. Bray. It was one of several semi-religious, benevolent organizations that came into existence during a century noted for its philanthropies. It differed from most societies of the time in that it was formed to perpetuate the work of one man. Its founder, the Reverend Thomas Bray (1656–1730), had become interested in the first of his philanthropic projects shortly after his appointment in 1695 to assist the governor of Maryland in the maintenance of clergymen in that colony. In selecting missionaries to serve abroad, Bray was disturbed to find that most of them were too poor to provide themselves with libraries. To supply them with religious literature, he began soliciting donations of books. After a short time in Maryland, he returned to England, where he undertook the ambitious project of supplying books not only to the colonial clergy, but also to many English parishes. So successful were these endeavours that during his lifetime he sent upwards of 34,000 books and tracts to America, besides establishing eighty-three catechetical libraries in Great Britain.[1]

Bray also became interested in a plan to educate and convert Negroes in the American colonies. This project won the support of Mr. Abel Tassin D'Allone, once secretary to William III. To help finance schools for Negroes, D'Allone established a fund of nine hundred pounds and made a further provision for this charity in his will. As administrator of this endowment, Bray saw the importance of naming responsible persons to carry on his work after his death. Hence, in 1723, he appointed a group known as "Dr. Bray's Associates for Founding Clerical Libraries and Supporting Negro Schools." The most distin-

1. *An Account of the Designs of the Associates of the Late Dr. Bray* (1767), 21.

guished of the early members was James Oglethorpe, founder of Georgia, whom Bray had met through their common interest in the plight of British prisoners.[2]

After Bray's death in 1730, the society continued to further his philanthropies. New members joined from time to time, but at no period did it become a large organization. In 1767 it had fifty-four members, about half of whom were clergymen. The Associates paid an annual fee of a guinea, and these dues, added to the income from invested funds and occasional contributions, enabled the society to conduct its charities on a modest scale.[3]

Rather full information about the Associates is found in two sources, the occasional printed reports and the manuscript Minute Books of the organization.[4] Monthly meetings were held at Mr. Bird's bookshop in Ave Mary Lane. Generally not more than eight or ten members were present. During the year 1760 the most regular attendants were Joseph Waring, who served as secretary, the Reverend John Berriman, the Reverend John Burton, Fellow of Eton College, and Benjamin Franklin.

Franklin's election to the society had occurred on 2 January 1760. At this meeting it was decided to fix the first Thursday of the month as the regular date for future gatherings. Before adjourning, however, the members agreed to hold a special session on 17 January to consider the founding of additional schools for Negroes, and the secretary was instructed to consult Mr. Franklin beforehand about the project.

2. Edgar L. Pennington, *Thomas Bray's Associates and Their Work among the Negroes* (Worcester, Mass., 1939).

3. *Account . . . of the Associates.*

4. The Minute Books are in the London Archives of the Society for the Propagation of the Gospel in Foreign Parts. Photofilm reproductions have been made for the Library of Congress. In this paper all references to meetings between Jan 1760 and 5 May 1768 are from Minute Book i. Later references are from Minute Book ii.

When the Associates convened on 17 January, Franklin was on hand. They had undoubtedly wanted him as a member because of his knowledge of America, and at this meeting he showed his familiarity with the situation in various colonies. Up to this time, the only Negro school supported by the society was one that had been established in Philadelphia in 1758. Franklin now proposed that the Associates found schools at Williamsburg, Virginia; in New York; and at Newport, Rhode Island. He also knew people in these communities who might serve to get the schools started. At Williamsburg, he suggested postmaster William Hunter; the Reverend Mr. Dawson, President of William and Mary College; and the minister of the local church. For New York he named the American Samuel Johnson, President of King's College; the Reverend Henry Barclay, rector of Trinity Church; and his assistant, the Reverend Samuel Auchmuty. At Newport he mentioned the Reverend Mr. Pollen. The other Associates at the meeting agreed to Franklin's suggestions and asked him to write to these Americans about the project.

Franklin attended the two following meetings of the society, on 7 February and 6 March. Upon the latter occasion the Associates paid him the honour of naming him their chairman for the ensuing year. He was not present on 6 April, however, when the Reverend John Burton, occupying the chair, "recommended Samuel Johnson, M.A., as a proper person to be an Associate." The others promptly cast a ballot unanimously electing Dr. Johnson to their society.

Although the Minutes of the next meeting record only routine business, historically it was the most important session of the Associates. For here at Mr. Bird's in Ave Mary Lane, on 1 May 1760, Benjamin Franklin and Dr. Johnson met. Possibly they had been in each other's company before this date. Very likely they saw each other on later occasions. But that they met at least once, on 1 May 1760, we may be certain.[5] Like most of the monthly meetings, this one was attended by only a few members. Altogether there were only eight present. Under these circumstances, it was inevitable that the two men should be introduced, if they had not met before. Furthermore, since they constituted two of a company of eight, they probably conversed with each other.

Unfortunately the secretary did not keep verbatim reports, and one can only speculate upon the nature of the discussion that may have ensued between these stalwart individualists. As the American Revolution would prove, their political views were in many respects irreconcilable. And if they had probed very deeply into each other's religious beliefs, the orthodox Dr. Johnson would have been disappointed to find that his American acquaintance was virtually a deist. Nevertheless, they shared many tastes—a seasoned delight in the conversation of others, a gusto for travelling and visiting new scenes, a curiosity that led each to perform scientific experiments. Both men were intellectual giants, towering above most of their contemporaries in wisdom, and excelling all but a few in understanding the culture of their own day. The fact that they were fellow members of a society dedicated to improving the lot of the Negro seems particularly significant. History has credited each with various accomplishments, but posterity will perhaps remember them longest for their strong and selfless humanitarianism.

The other Associates present on 1 May 1760 were the Reverend John Berriman, the Reverend Dr. John Burton, the Reverend John Waring, Joseph Waring, a Mr. Jones, and a Mr. Dixon. The most interesting item of business was the reading of a letter from Mr. Sturgeon, supervisor of the Negro school

5. The Minutes of each meeting are headed by the names of those who attended. Both Johnson and Franklin are so listed on 1 May 1760.

in Philadelphia. He wrote that eleven boys and twenty-four girls were enrolled. All were receiving instruction in reading and religion, and the girls were learning needlework. The Associates also heard a report on their lending library at Bampton, Westmorland, and, before adjourning, voted to establish a library at Landaff.

After this one appearance, Johnson never again attended a business session of the society, according to the Minutes. Nevertheless, he remained a subscriber, and, as we shall see, he later contributed substantially to its funds.

Although the meeting of 1 May 1760 was the only regular session of the society jointly attended by both men, Franklin and Johnson may have met again at one of the annual dinners of the Associates. The custom of holding an annual dinner was instituted in May 1761. The members dined at their own cost, usually at the Mitre Tavern in Fleet Street. Special invitations were issued to all subscribers. Although there is no record of the attendance, presumably these gatherings attracted a much larger representation than the monthly meetings. Franklin definitely attended some of the dinners, and Johnson, with his taste for sociability, would certainly have welcomed an occasion at which he could dine and discourse at large with various friends. If he was present at the dinner held in May 1761, for instance, he would have met, besides Franklin, two of his most esteemed intimates, William Strahan and Dr. William Heberden.[6]

Franklin continued to be a leading light in the organization.[7] Altogether he attended eight of the regular meetings in

6. At the regular meeting in June 1761 it was reported that Strahan had paid a guinea and that Dr. Heberden had given Franklin three guineas for the society at the dinner held in May.

7. For a detailed account of Franklin's part in the society see Richard I. Shelling, "Benjamin Franklin and the Dr. Bray Associates," *The Pennsylvania Magazine of History and Biography*, LXIII (1939), 282–93.

1760. He was present only five times the next year, but the Associates did not convene during the summer months, since he and Secretary Waring were both away from London. In March 1761 his fellow members named him their chairman for a second term. Meanwhile, the society received encouraging reports from America. Franklin's correspondents in Williamsburg, New York, and Newport responded to his appeal, and each of these communities eventually established a Negro school for about thirty children.

Franklin was now planning to return to Philadelphia for a visit. After presiding at the January and March meetings of the society, he attended no further sessions in 1762. In August he sailed for America, where he was to remain until the end of 1764. During this visit he devoted considerable time to inspecting post offices in different colonies. These trips gave him the opportunity to visit several of the Negro schools, and he faithfully reported his observations to the Associates in London. In a letter of 27 June 1763, he informed them that he had found the school at Williamsburg, Virginia, conducted in a satisfactory manner. He also expressed his intention of inspecting the schools in New York, at Newport, Rhode Island, and in Philadelphia.[8]

His next letter provides an interesting account of the Negro school in his home city. The report, as recorded in the Minutes of 2 February 1764, reads as follows:

> Read a letter from Benj^m Franklin, Esq., LLd. of Philadelphia dated Decr 17, 1763, wherein he says that He, Mr. Sturgeon, & some others visited the Negroe School and had the Children thoroughly examined. They appeared, He says, all to have made considerable Progress in reading for the Time they had respectively been at School & most of Them answered readily and well the Questions of the

8. Meeting of 6 Oct 1763.

113

Catechism. They Behaved very orderly, showed a proper Respect and ready Obedience to their Mistress & seemed very attentive to and a good deal affected by a serious Exhortation, with which Mr. Sturgeon concluded our Visit. I am on the whole pleased, says He, & from what I there saw have conceived a higher Opinion of the natural Capacities of the Black Race than I had ever before entertained. Their Apprehension seems as quick, their Memory as strong, and their Docility in every Respect equal to that of white Children.

Franklin returned to England in December 1764 but according to the Minutes did not attend a meeting of the society until 2 October 1766. His presence on this occasion had probably been specifically requested. In July the Associates had learned that the Reverend Mr. Abbot Upcher of Sudbury, Suffolk, had offered to invest a sum of money in lands in America and to allocate the income to the society's program of educating Negro children.[9] Naturally the other members would want Franklin's advice on such a matter. The Minutes do not reveal the specific nature of the discussion, but before adjourning the Associates asked Franklin to write to Upcher. Complying with this request, Franklin wrote the clergyman on 4 October 1766, "I think the best Province to make the Purchase in is Pennsylvania, where titles are generally clear." He particularly favored Philadelphia, and suggested that three Americans be empowered to purchase "Ground Rents within that City and other safe & profitable Estate in or near the same, as Bargains may offer."[1] When Franklin next appeared at a meeting, on 7 May

9. Upcher originally proposed investing 1,000 pounds with the understanding that the estate should be settled upon the Church in America when episcopacy was established there. From later Minutes it appears that this plan was changed. He actually gave the society 500 pounds, which remained in its possession.

1. Albert H. Smythe, ed., *The Writings of Benjamin Franklin* (1907), IV.463–64.

1767, negotiations with Upcher had reached such a point that the Associates now asked Franklin to proceed with the purchase of land in Pennsylvania. For one reason or another, however, the actual investment in an estate was delayed for several years.

Franklin was next present at the meetings of 7 January and 4 February 1768, when the Associates decided to support schools in Bermuda. But the routine business of determining where to found the next school, or where in England to send the next parcel of books, must have palled on anyone as busy as Franklin. Three years passed before he attended another meeting. That was held on 7 March 1771. The chief item on the calendar was the reading of a letter from the Reverend Mr. Lyttleton of Bermuda, who reported that "he had discharged the Mistress of the first School for having received a Company of Jugglers into her home."

More important business ensued when Franklin next appeared at the society. Apparently he had asked two American acquaintances to report on opportunities to purchase real estate in Philadelphia. One of these men was Edward Duffield; the other was Francis Hopkinson, who in a few years would become one of the signers of the Declaration of Independence. These gentlemen now recommended that the Associates buy a tract in the city of Philadelphia, having a frontage of 136 feet on Market Street and running along Ninth Street to a depth of 360 feet. With Franklin present, the members discussed this proposal at their meeting of 2 September 1773. They finally decided to purchase this plot of land, for which they eventually paid 575 pounds sterling.[2]

Franklin had now attended his last meeting of the society. In these busy days on the eve of the American Revolution, first things came first. When he left England in March 1775, he re-

2. The lot is later described as being bound by Market, Ninth, Filbert, and Tenth Streets. See Minutes, 19 May 1774, 1 Sep 1774, and 8 Jan 1787.

turned to America to help found a new nation. Even before the outbreak of the Revolution, the society's school at Fredericksburg, Virginia, had failed because of the opposition of the slave owners, and the school in New York had closed when the mistress died. With a war in progress, Dr. Bray's schools on the American mainland came to an end, although the schools in Bermuda continued for a while and the society later supported schools for Negroes in Nova Scotia. The Associates also experimented with the education of poor children at home, chiefly at Kingswood, Gloucestershire, and in the Scilly Islands, but these ventures never amounted to much.

Franklin still had one more service to perform for the society. At the conclusion of the American Revolution, Francis Hopkinson informed the Associates that their land in Philadelphia had lain idle for several years. In further correspondence he reported that the lot could be rented at favourable terms. The Associates finally agreed to this suggestion and empowered Hopkinson and Franklin to lease the plot. In acceptance of this appointment Franklin wrote the secretary the following letter:[3]

Philadelp.ª June 3, 1786

Sir,

I received duly the Letters you wrote to me of Oct. 4, 1785 and April 4th 1786. Being much occupyd I referrd the first to Mr. Hopkinson, who I suppose has written to you. This serves to acknowledge the Receipt of the Power of Attorney enabling us to lease the Ground belonging to the Associates, and to assure you that my best Assistance therein shall not be wanting.—With great Esteem for the Society, I am

Sir   Your most obedient
humble Servant
B. Franklin

3. Minutes, 11 Sep 1786.

Shortly thereafter, Hopkinson reported that he had divided the land in Philadelphia into lots. He had leased one of these with a twenty-five-foot frontage on Market Street for twenty-five pounds a year and expected, when the other lots were leased, that the entire tract would yield the Associates the annual sum of 250 pounds in American currency. The investment which Franklin had helped to negotiate proved in the end a profitable one.

During the American Revolution, Dr. Bray's society went through a period of stagnation. Meetings were infrequent, and sometimes only two or three members were present. The organization began to recover its vitality with the end of the war. General Oglethorpe, one of the original Associates appointed by Dr. Bray, had attended only one meeting between 1760 and 1783. Thereafter, however, this hale old warrior, who had been born in 1696, made up for his earlier delinquency by frequent participation. He made his last appearance at the society on 6 June 1785, three weeks before his death. As the older generation died off, new members took their places. Among the new subscribers were two of Johnson's younger friends, Bennet Langton, who joined on 7 July 1783, and the Reverend George Strahan, who became an Associate on 27 May 1784.

Although Johnson did not attend the monthly meetings, he had continued to be a subscriber from the time of his election to the society. Probably he felt that others were more capable of making the decisions. But there can be no doubt about his genuine interest in the two aims of the Associates. He had once said that "the qualifications of a minister are well known to be learning and piety."[4] How could one better encourage these essentials than by the establishment of parochial libraries? He must have favoured even more the society's program to educate and christianize the Negro. Always a stalwart Christian, he particularly condemned the failure of the plantation owners to

4. *Life*, II.245.

be concerned about the salvation of their slaves. His views on this subject were well expressed in a letter he wrote in 1766:[5]

> Christianity is the highest perfection of humanity; and as no man is good but as he wishes the good of others, no man can be good in the highest degree, who wishes not to others the largest measures of the greatest good. To omit for a year, or for a day, the most efficacious method of advancing Christianity, in compliance with any purposes that terminate on this side of the grave, is a crime of which I know not that the world has yet had an example, except in the practice of the planters of America, a race of mortals whom, I suppose, no other man wishes to resemble.

Johnson's interest in the Associates of Dr. Bray was further revealed by his contributions. The Minutes for 27 May 1784 note that he had recently made the organization a gift of ten guineas. Shortly before his death, at the end of that year, he again demonstrated his esteem for the society. Although he did not mention it in his final will, he provided that it should receive the royalties from the first edition of his posthumously published prayers. The execution of this bequest was left to George Strahan, to whom he entrusted the manuscript. Strahan mentions the provision briefly in his preface to *Prayers and Meditations*: "Dr. Bray's Associates are to receive the profits of the first edition by the Author's appointment, and any further advantages that accrue will be distributed among his relatives."[6] The proceeds of the first edition amounted to £47 7s. 2d.[7] This sum made Johnson one of the chief benefactors of the Associates of Dr. Bray.

It is interesting to observe that at one time Johnson had

5. *Ibid.*, 27.
6. *Prayers and Meditations Composed by Samuel Johnson* (1785), vi.
7. Minutes, 26 Mar 1787.

apparently intended to leave the society a still larger amount. His final will, which George Strahan and John Hawkins helped him to execute, was drawn up on 8 December 1784, with a codicil attached the following day. This final document provided that Johnson's Negro servant, Francis Barber, should receive the bulk of his estate and become his residual heir.[8] But Johnson had made an earlier will, on 27 November 1784. Here the only provision for Barber had been an annuity of seventy pounds. The earlier will differed from the final one in another rather remarkable way. According to John Hawkins, "The residue of his estate and effects, which took in, though he intended it not, the house at Lichfield, he bequeathed to his executors in trust for a religious association, which it is needless to describe."[9]

The organization which Hawkins chose not to name was probably the Associates of Dr. Bray. As we have seen, Johnson had long been a member of this society, and it is the only one for which he provided in disposing of his estate. Strahan does not say just when Johnson stipulated that the Associates should have the profits from his book, but it was probably about the time he changed his will. Although the society received a smaller sum from the first edition of *Prayers and Meditations* than it might have received under the terms of the first will, the designation of the royalties shows that Johnson was determined that the Associates should have some part of his estate.

If he had lived a few years longer, Johnson's strong aversion to the institution of slavery might have led him to take part in the abolitionist movement that developed in England shortly after his death. Probably the plight of the Negro was in his mind when he left a large part of his estate to his colored servant and a smaller amount to a society for improving the lot of

8. *Life*, IV.402 ff. (n. 2).
9. *The Life of Samuel Johnson* (1787), 581.

the Negro. The aged Franklin, back in Philadelphia after serving as Ambassador to France, also had the welfare of the Negro close at heart. In 1787 this most distinguished American of his time became President of the Pennsylvania Society for Promoting the Abolition of Slavery, and in 1789, a month before his death, he wrote his final essay, *On The Slave Trade.*[1] One may regret that these two great men who had so much in common did not become better acquainted. Yet it is gratifying to know that they met at least once, on 1 May 1760, as fellow members of a society dedicated to a humanitarian purpose.

1. Carl Van Doren, *Benjamin Franklin* (1938), 774–75.

A Biographer Looks at Dr. Johnson

JAMES L. CLIFFORD

"It's easy to put together a biography," said one of my novelist friends enviously. "All you have to do is to dig up the facts and string them together in chronological order." According to this point of view there is nothing essentially creative about the writing of a life. The biographer is firmly caught in a web of fact, his imagination hopelessly entangled.

But can a biographer ever be truly objective? Frankly, I doubt it. From the very start he is involved with his subject in many subtle ways. When choosing evidence he is subjected to terrific pressures—from his emotional response to the person he is describing, from his own education and environment, and—perhaps most importantly—from the general sensibility of the age. That one man in the nineteenth and another in the mid-twentieth century, having available the same source material, would produce very different portraits is almost too obvious to mention. The shift from prudery to license, from a respect for human reticence to a desire to penetrate deeply into inner motives, has produced an entirely different context for biography.

Even if complete objectivity were possible in a biographer, I am not sure it would be wholly desirable. Of course, what I say does not apply to a scholarly edition or a basic reference work. But when attempting a re-creation of character the mere assembling of evidence is not enough. There must also be intuitive insight, deep understanding, sympathy, and interpretation, all of them requiring creative imagination.

The question is, how much latitude does the biographer

have? How far may he use his imagination and still claim to be writing a life and not a novel? What kinds of devices are valid, and what too dangerous?

There is the matter of getting inside the subject's mind. Is it ever legitimate to assume that we know what some other person was thinking at any given time? Some biographers think that it is. Glibly we are given a long train of musings or a violent inner debate. More defensible, of course, is the transference of material from known letters or diary entries to thought processes. Because the subject wrote in a particular way to one of his friends, we assume that this was his general mood at the time. Yet there is always the possibility that he was merely playing a part.

An inconspicuously placed "perhaps" or a "possibly" may get the biographer out of this difficulty. Lytton Strachey set the pattern in the remarkable closing scene of his *Queen Victoria*. "Perhaps" Victoria, as she lay dying, remembered the spring woods at Osborne, Lord Palmerston's queer clothes, Albert in his uniform, or Lord M. dreaming at Windsor. No one can prove him wrong. Possibly she did. But the reader tends to forget the protective qualification and remember as vivid fact what is purely hypothetical.

That the device is dangerous no one will deny. And yet surely there are times when the risk is worth taking. When there is some historical evidence to back up the assumption, and when the reader will not be seriously misled on a vital point if the guess is wrong, a creative biographer should be able to take some liberties with his material. To illustrate the point, let me use one small incident in the early life of Samuel Johnson.

For about two years, from 1726 to 1728, before he was able to go to Oxford, the youthful Johnson was forced to remain at Lichfield in his father's bookshop. He was through with his grammar school education, and apparently there was no prospect that he would be able to continue further. Suppose that one were to describe him as unhappily watching his old schoolmates, many of whom he knew to be foolish and stupid, going up to the universities, as listening hungrily to their accounts of college pranks and of the vagaries of their tutors, and as imagining himself, with ill-repressed longing, in such surroundings. How far would such a description be justified?

There is little contemporary evidence. We cannot be absolutely certain that Johnson talked to any of his former schoolmates about their college experiences or their tutors. So far as we know he never unburdened himself about his unhappiness in his surroundings. And yet I think that the chances are almost ninety-nine to one that the re-creation is true.

From the researches of scholars, we know that many of Johnson's Lichfield playmates did go to the universities during this period. We know their names and something about them. We know from Johnson's own fragment of an autobiography, and from his later remarks, that he considered himself their superior mentally. Moreover, there is the story told Boswell by Edmund Hector, one of Johnson's earliest friends, that Andrew Corbet, a well-to-do boarder at the Lichfield Grammar School, had generously offered financial aid because he knew so well Johnson's eagerness to go to the university. Add to all this the known character of Johnson as a young man— moody, distraught, dispirited—and practically all the elements of the description are accounted for.

I have cited this example because it seems to me to illustrate legitimate imaginative creation. When there is sufficient authentic evidence from the records to suggest the amplification, and when it accords with normal human experience as well as with the total picture of the subject of the biography, then one may depart temporarily from strict historical relation.

Of course, any biographer, however slipshod and careless of

the truth, will claim to have followed my prescribed formula. Therein lies its danger; there is no denying that it does open the doors to the most flagrant kind of fictionalizing. Yet without some experimenting of this kind, a biography tends to be merely a dry compilation of facts. Without some license to the imagination biography becomes lifeless and dull; with too much it becomes fiction. Surely somewhere in between there is a sort of golden mean, which the successful biographer must find—a kind of justifiable calculated risk taken with eyes open and with all possible precautions.

When a writer dramatizes a scene to such an extent that he gives visual descriptions of events for which he has no genuine evidence, it seems to me he violates his contract as a biographer. It would be easy to point out specific examples in recent books where this is done. Events are described with dramatic effect—doors slam, chairs are pushed away from tables, speakers smile or frown, talk is easy and fluent—all of it with no supporting historical authority. This we at once recognize as popular fictionalized biography.

The sober scholar has no difficulty in pointing out deficiencies in this kind of writing, and is properly scornful. But must we, then, throw out all use of physical description unless quoted from some specific documentary source? Not at all. Again it seems to me that there is a permissible middle ground, which a sensible biographer will strive to attain. Using the vast body of available peripheral material, he can place his subject in a vivid setting, and still not indulge in fanciful fiction. He has every right to sketch in the background with as much color as possible, again assuming the authenticity of the diverse material used.

Another problem, even more puzzling, is the handling of differing accounts of the same episode. The historian and the scholarly biographer merely list the variant versions and make the reader judge for himself what actually happened. The creative biographer, on the other hand, may produce an imaginative fusion of the several versions, presenting the reader with a single hypothetical account. Using all the information available, not only concerning this particular episode, but also in relation to the people involved, and evaluating the credibility of each authority, the author may synthesize the evidence into what appears to him to be the most credible story. Again, there is risk. The reader is given no opportunity, without serious research on his own part, to check the reliability of the final account. He is completely dependent on the honesty and good judgement of the author. Yet who is better prepared to make such a synthesis?

For my part I am convinced that there can be no hard and fast rule about making composite versions. Sometimes justified, they are at other times to be avoided. Take, for example, two separate incidents from Johnson's early years.

Probably shortly after his marriage to the widow twenty years his senior, whom he called "Tetty," and while he was conducting the ill-fated school at Edial, Johnson is supposed to have attended the performance of some strolling players in the Guildhall in Lichfield. When he happened to quit his chair for a moment, and it was taken by another man who rudely refused to give it up, Johnson is reputed to have picked up chair and man and hurled them both into the pit. Three of the best known of Johnson's contemporary biographers— Sir John Hawkins, Mrs. Thrale-Piozzi, and Boswell—tell the story, but with varying details. The fullest account comes from Hawkins. Yet all three admit that the great actor, David Garrick, who presumably watched the affair, was their sole authority.

What, then, should the biographer do? Must he quote all

versions? Or should he quote only the very full but stylistically involved account by Hawkins? Or may he put together a smooth composite anecdote using what seems most credible from each source? To me the latter appears much the best choice. When there is only one primary source, who may himself have varied his account depending on his audience, it is the duty of the modern biographer to reproduce as closely as he can what he thinks actually occurred.

Another kind of decision comes with one of the most celebrated incidents in Johnson's early life, his reputed knocking down of the insolent publisher Osborne with a huge folio volume. For this colorful anecdote there are scores of variants, none carrying the stamp of authority. Both Mrs. Thrale and Boswell tried to draw the whole story out of Johnson. The lady recorded in her diary:

> I asked him the other day about his Combat with that Osborne, how much of the Story was true: It was true said he that I beat the fellow, & that was all; but the World so hated poor Osborne; that they have never done multiplying the blows, and increasing the weight of them for twenty Years together; The Blockhead told the story himself too originally, for I am sure I should not,—but says Osborne Johnson beat me this Morning in my own house—For what says his Friend—why for telling him that he *lied* forsooth.

In her published *Anecdotes*, printed years later, she added a further remark by Johnson: "I have beat many a fellow, but the rest had the wit to hold their tongues."

Boswell also tried to draw Johnson out about the affair.

> It has been confidently related, with many embellishments, that Johnson one day knocked Osborne down in

his shop, with a folio, and put his foot upon his neck. The simple truth I had from Johnson himself. "Sir, he was impertinent to me, and I beat him. But it was not in his shop: it was in my own chamber."

After Johnson's death all sorts of variants appeared in print. William Cooke, in 1785, added: "Osborne alarmed the family with his cries; but Mr. Johnson, clapping his foot on his breast, told him 'he need not be in a hurry to rise; for if he did, he would have the further trouble of kicking him downstairs.' " Another stated that Johnson, with his feet on his victim, sonorously declaimed, "Lie there, thou son of dullness, ignorance, and obscurity." One account had Johnson's foot on Osborne's neck, another on his breast. With each retelling, new variations were created. The actual volume supposed to have been used as the weapon—a huge Greek folio Bible—was later offered for sale by an enterprising bookseller.

To produce a satisfactory composite anecdote from these diverse versions would be next to impossible. First there is the basic problem of where the fracas took place, and why. The most popular account had it in Osborne's own house, and Mrs. Thrale quotes Johnson as confirming the location. Yet Boswell insists that Johnson categorically told him that it occurred in his own chamber. Moreover, the variations which involve Johnson's further threat to kick his opponent downstairs suggest that the fray was not located in Osborne's shop, which would likely have been on the ground floor.

Since it is impossible to reconcile the differing versions, the biographer cannot honestly put together a satisfactory composite story. He must either accept Boswell's stripped-down anecdote and ignore all the rest; or he must, as I have done here, summarize all the accounts. Perhaps, where the embroidery is so amusing, the latter choice is best.

A twentieth-century biographer is constantly faced with the problem of how much to use modern psychological techniques. Should he, or should he not, use Freudian analysis on his subject? Should he isolate certain patterns and symbols which crop up in the evidence and use them as the basis of his characterization? If he does, how certain can he be that his hypothesis is correct? Is it ever safe to analyse someone who is dead, when it is so difficult to find the truth about the living? One thing is obvious: the new techniques provide opportunities for greater variation in interpretation than ever before. By using modern analytical methods excellent scholars may come to diametrically opposed answers, after studying exactly the same evidence. Let me cite only one example.

One of our best eighteenth-century scholars, using various cryptic references to "fetters" and "manacles," to "padlocks" and "using the rod," in letters and diary entries, finds an erotic, masochistic relationship between Johnson and Mrs. Thrale. And this hypothetical condition is used to help explain Johnson's deep melancholy and fear of insanity. On the other hand, another admirable scholar insists that "chains" and references to being shackled are common figurative expressions in Johnson's writing, and normally refer only to his fear of being enslaved by indolence. Here we see that the interpretation of a single word or phrase may involve a modern biographer in major decisions of a kind never dreamed of in another age.

Again and again in writing a life there are crucial decisions where even the most rigorous logical analysis is unavailing. The existing evidence turns out to be conflicting or insufficient, many motivations uncertain. In such cases, the biographer's total concept of his subject must be the deciding factor.

A prime example is the relationship of Johnson to his wife, "Tetty." Was the husband always completely devoted? Or was there ever any serious friction? Did they once separate, as Sir

John Hawkins suggests? And did Johnson on occasions complain to his intimate friends about the wretchedness of his domestic situation? Was his later sentimental attitude towards his departed wife "a lesson that he had learned by rote"?

Boswell, who met Johnson eleven years after the death of Tetty, was horrified by this suggestion. Angrily he lashed out at Hawkins for having made it, and a century and a half of Boswellians have piously echoed the horror. Hawkins' uncharitable interpretation, it has been assumed, was merely an example of his unsympathetic attitude towards his old friend, and should be scornfully disregarded.

As a result, the picture of the devoted though ill-matched couple has become an essential part of the Johnsonian legend. Nothing, perhaps, can ever shake it. Moreover, it is based on genuine documentary evidence in Johnson's prayers and meditations. As the years stretched on, he did look back on his married life with nostalgia and lachrymose sentiment. "Dear Tetty," though many years dead, was constantly in his mind.

But a modern student might well wonder whether this was merely a later rationalization. The emotional entries could have been a psychological release for old complexes, compensation for guilt feelings, rather than proof of Johnson's actual attitude towards Tetty while she was alive. How, then, can we decide which is true?

In this instance there is very little contemporary evidence. One surviving letter from Johnson to his wife, not quite five years after their marriage, is affectionate but in places equivocal, and does certainly suggest the possibility of a temporary estrangement. Yet except for this there is nothing specific to rely on for these years, no pertinent diary entries or revealing notes.

The testimony of those who knew the pair during the 1740's —from David Garrick; Dr. Taylor of Ashbourne, one of Johnson's old schoolmates; Mrs. Desmoulins, the daughter of his godfather; and Dr. Levet, the strange, crude physician who lived for so long in his house—all this comes down to us only through much later recollections, some rather dubious. No early documents survive to support the colorful stories of Tetty's excessive drinking and taking of opium. To be sure, all the authorities agree about the drinking and hypochondria. But it is possible that these unflattering portraits were casual exaggerations, brought out merely to offset Johnson's excessive praise. Hawkins, who had probably met Johnson early in the 1740's, admitted that he never met Tetty and was merely passing on hearsay. Much of what he wrote may be only inference.

Each biographer of Johnson thus is faced with a crucial decision, whether to accept the view of Boswell, who never knew Tetty, or the unfavourable recollections of the others. Does the truth lie completely on one side, or somewhere in between? Somehow the conflicting points of view must be fitted into the comprehensive picture of Johnson the man. Inevitably one biographer will cling to the conventional version, and put his faith in Boswell and in Johnson's own later memories. Another will rely on the reports of those others, and will discount Johnson's subsequent emotional outpourings. The choice depends entirely on the pattern which has been set up in the biographer's own mind. As a creator of character, he interprets the evidence to fit his idea of what Johnson was really like.

For years I myself wrestled with this problem. Gradually— it is hard to tell just why—I came to accept Hawkins and to reject Boswell. As I studied the documents I was irresistibly drawn in that direction. Though Hawkins' remarks in this instance may have sounded uncharitable, they impressed me as representing a more probable condition.

According to my reading of Johnson's character, he would inevitably have romanticized his departed wife, no matter how difficult she had been during her last days. Indeed, the more troubled he had been, the more convinced he would later have become of his own responsibility for her break-up. And with this increased feeling of guilt the tearful remembrances would have been unavoidable. If at times he had been unhappy in his marriage and had complained to others, his over-developed conscience would have forced personal recriminations after his wife was gone. Thus his later sentimental entries in his diary cannot be taken as evidence of earlier relationship, but merely of his subsequent mental condition.

This is my interpretation; it cannot be proved. While it is based on a long study of the facts, it is nevertheless subjective, and has no standing as history. For me this interpretation fits into the pattern of Johnson's life as it has been built up in my mind. Moreover, it is intimately connected with my other theories concerning Johnson's relationship with his mother and his only brother. All the complex forces which produced his well-known eccentric temperament were involved. The explanation represents a fusion of the evidence in the light of my own total concept of Johnson's character.

Naturally I hope that my re-creation is neither wilful nor opinionated. Yet I know that others may disagree violently. And the probability is that fifty years from now my conclusions may all be discarded. Even if there are no more Malahide Castle discoveries, no more croquet boxes or ebony cabinets, another biographer, writing in the next age, with a new sensibility and new interests, will fashion from the same material a very different portrait.

Of one thing I am certain: to be successful any biographer must be creative. Within the limits of ascertainable facts—and these, of course, must never be violated—he has almost limitless opportunity for choice. Like a classical poet or composer, who gladly works within certain self-imposed structural confines, he always has the opportunity to shape his material into a work of art.

✝ March 28 1753

I kept this day as the anniversary of my
Tetty's death with prayer & tears in the morning.
In the evening I prayed for her conditionally if
it were lawful.

Apr. 3 1753 I began the 2d vol of my
Dictionary room being left in the first for
Preface Grammar & History none of them yet
begun.

O God who hast hitherto supported me
enable me to proceed in this labour & in the
Whole task of my present state that when I
shall render up at ye last day an account
of the talent committed to me I may receive
pardon for the sake of Jesus Christ Amen.

April 22 1753
As I purpose to try on Monday to seek a new
wife without any derogation from dear Tetty's
memory I purpose at sacrament in the morning
to take my leave of Tetty in a solemn commen-
:dation of her soul to God.

Apr 23 Easter Monday.
Yesterday, as I purposed I went to Bromley
where dear Tetty lies buried & received the sacrament
first praying before I went to the altar accor-
:ding to the prayers fore composed for Tetty

Extracts from Johnson's Diary, 22 and 23 April 1753

Dr. Johnson's Second Wife

DONALD AND MARY HYDE

The period of Samuel Johnson's marriage to Tetty has always
been provocative and perplexing to his biographers and critics.
Their conclusions have been conflicting and they have experienced difficulty in picturing Johnson as a lover, a bridegroom,
and a married man, because these roles are inconsistent with
their conception of him as a man of philosophy and piety, of
tenderness rather than passion. With one marriage they have
been forced to cope, but none of them has ever considered or
even hinted at the possibility of a second marriage. A manuscript now in the Hyde Collection reveals that Johnson at forty-
four, then a widower of some thirteen months, planned to take
a second wife. This manuscript is in Boswell's hand, a transcript of entries from a Johnson journal made at Johnson's
house in Bolt Court, Fleet Street, on 5 May 1776. This journal
was probably the most extensive diary that Johnson kept and,
since he burned it before his death, any surviving portion has
significance. More than this, the fact that Boswell with limited
time and an eye to the future chose these particular items gives
them the utmost importance.

The transcript shows that on Easter Sunday, 22 April 1753,
Johnson recorded, "As I purpose to try on Monday to seek a
new wife without any derogation from dear Tettys memory
I purpose at sacrament in the morning to take my leave of
Tetty in a solemn commendation of her soul to God." On
Monday, he recalled the preceding day, "During the whole
service I was never once distracted by any thoughts of any other
woman or with my design of a new wife which freedom of mind
I remembered with gladness in the Garden. God guide me."

Boswell's failure to include these two entries in his *Life of Johnson* lacks the candor usually shown by him. Surely, he must have been tempted, since his material was meagre for 1753; also he must have been sympathetic, for he was contemplating the same decision himself. It was not a matter Boswell forgot for he wrote of Johnson's "design" to his friend William Temple, who urged him to enrich his next edition with this curious and humanizing circumstance. Boswell refrained from doing so, probably in part from "respect" and "delicacy," also in part because he wished to defend Johnson's first marriage against Hawkins' "dark uncharitable" charges, and he realized that the consideration of a second marriage would rouse curiosity, perhaps excite misunderstanding, and certainly add fuel to the fire he labored to extinguish.

In his zeal to combat Hawkins' accusations, Boswell used certain material from his transcript, but manipulated the "two memorials" in such a way that they showed Johnson's "love for his wife was of the most ardent kind, and during the long period of fifty years, was unimpaired by the lapse of time." In the events of 1752, as related in the *Life*, he gave from his transcript the entry for 28 March 1753 and another which he dated "April 23, 1753." The latter is in reality Johnson's entry for 29 April. If Boswell had used the proper entry for 23 April it would have included the second mention of Johnson's design for a new wife. The entry of 28 March was the only true demonstration of Johnson's preoccupation with grief for Tetty, that he kept the anniversary of her death "with prayer and tears." As will be shown later, the entry for 29 April, if read in context with the other diary entries, does not necessarily convey the meaning which Boswell intended.

Boswell's obsession to paint the marriage of Johnson and Tetty as idyllic is unrealistic. He stirs incredulity by lack of knowledge and bias. He met Johnson eleven years after Tetty's death, when sentimental memory had blurred fact. Further-more, Hawkins' interpretation of Tetty in his *Life of Johnson* so angered Boswell that he was determined to defend Johnson's marriage, even though it required romanticizing what he did not know and omitting known facts contrary to his interpreta-tion. This is a logical reason for his failure to include the un-usual notes for 1753 which he possessed.

Hawkins' treatment of Johnson and Tetty had its short-comings. Like Boswell, he lacked knowledge, for he was never asked to meet Tetty and there is no indication that he ever dis-cussed the marriage with Johnson. His assertions when based upon personal opinion are unconvincing. He could not pos-sibly support his statement that Johnson never loved Tetty and that if he showed affection for her it was learned by rote. Such "uncharitable" and dogmatic conclusions betray his own inability to understand the varieties of human relationship. However, Hawkins has a clearer claim to accuracy than Bos-well because he knew Johnson well in London as early as the late forties. Johnson's failure to introduce him to Tetty, to-gether with the reports he heard from her friends, were ample cause to rouse his suspicions and to inspire his "dark" interpre-tation.

In support of Boswell's point of view it would be difficult to believe that Johnson married Tetty except for genuine affec-tion, because of his determination to proceed in spite of un-conventional circumstances. He was not yet twenty-six, while Tetty at forty-six was more than old enough to be his mother. She was a widow with three children, two of whom considered the marriage a disgrace to the family and violently opposed it, never seeing their mother again. Johnson's mother also op-posed the match and gave her consent reluctantly. In addition, it was improbable that their union would be blessed with chil-dren. On the other hand, Tetty had definite qualities to inspire

Johnson's love; though a fading beauty, she was attractive to him, her intellectual judgment pleased him, and her wit, which was something like his, amused him. She also had a little means, which made marriage possible.

Boswell has additional support. From the time of their wedding until Tetty's death, there is evidence that when they were together Johnson treated her with sentimental attentions and gallantries, sometimes exaggerated and comical to onlookers. Mrs. Thrale said she knew he adored her. Even Hawkins contradicted his statement of lack of affection by saying that Johnson's "attachment to her appears . . . to have been equal to what it ought to be." It is generally acknowledged that Johnson showed unflagging and tender concern during her long illness. He granted every request that might aid her health, though his financial position made each expenditure a great personal sacrifice. His desolation at her death is sincere and affecting and he often, in conversations and letters inspired by friends in bereavement, confessed great loneliness for her.

In support of Hawkins' point of view there are convincing indications that there was something wrong in Johnson's marriage. Dr. Taylor, who knew Johnson and Tetty intimately, is quoted as saying that poor dear Tetty "was the plague of Johnson's life, was abominably drunken and despicable every way, and Johnson had frequently complained to him of the wretchedness of his situation with such a wife." Garrick reported that "the woman was a little painted poppet; full of affectation and rural airs of elegance." Dr. Levet related that "she was always drunk and reading romances in her bed, where she killed herself by taking opium." There are added assertions of Tetty's drunkenness and the taking of drugs by Shaw, an early biographer. His authority was Mrs. Desmoulins, a person in a position to know.

During their entire residence in London few friends were

asked to their house, though Johnson loved company. During this time also there is no evidence that Tetty ever appeared with him in public. This is significant, for later Johnson carried blind and peevish Anna Williams to friends' houses with the best nature, showing her the gentlest consideration and care. Then there is Johnson's only known surviving letter to Tetty, now in the Hyde Collection, which, though superficially affectionate and generous, is in truth a demonstration of unhappiness and an attempt by Johnson to make amends. They had been separated for some months prior to the letter, during which time he had enjoyed the gay company of Richard Savage and rambles of his own in the Midlands. There are also two curious though probably inconsequential instances of forgetfulness on Johnson's part. He placed wrong dates on Tetty's wedding ring and on her gravestone; marriage and death are two dates which most devoted husbands remember.

There is no doubt that there was a void in the marriage. In view of the age differential, as time passed, Tetty found it hard to respond to the physical side of marriage. This is shown by her attitude and by Johnson's in the passage on conjugal infidelity which Boswell cancelled from the *Life*. There is suggestion that Johnson sometimes forced her against her will, which afterwards caused him regret and mortification. This would explain his self-reproach in passages of his "precomposed" prayer for Tetty, offered on that Easter Sunday when he resolved to marry again. In this prayer he asked to be forgiven "all the sins committed" in his union and he begged that the loss of his wife might "mortify all inordinate affections." He made the prayer before the sacrament; more than this, during the sermon which he could not perfectly hear, he composed a prayer against unchastity.

These two prayers are closely related to the thoughts expressed in Johnson's journal entry for 29 April. Boswell's use of this to illustrate Johnson's grief for Tetty as the only possible interpretation is misleading. Hawkins' record should not be forgotten—that Johnson at this period, when meetings of the Club in Ivy Lane were over at eleven at night, often wandered the streets and joined in the conversation of "those miserable females who were there to be met with." Johnson's "vain longings of affection" were not necessarily for his departed wife, but could very well have been concerned with his present distraction and his physical needs. He prayed that his longings would incite him to piety, and that he would "not deviate too much from common and received methods of devotion."

In weighing the two points of view, it is not without significance that all the people who had actually known Tetty in her later years, or who had known Johnson at that time, agreed with the "dark uncharitable" portrait that Hawkins painted. The only people who agreed with Boswell's interpretation were those who obtained their information in the same manner, from sentimental memories related by Johnson long after Tetty's death.

The source material now available indicates that the true story of Johnson's unusual marriage lies somewhere between Boswell and Hawkins. Johnson married Tetty with sincere love and an appreciation of her merits. As the marriage progressed, his original ardor turned into tenderness. There was always a strong bond, despite periods of strain and even separation. Her death brought profound melancholy.

The omitted journal entries, showing Johnson's determination to remarry, illustrate once again his human qualities. Like many other men before and after him who have taken second wives, Johnson was motivated by having enjoyed at least a reasonably happy first marriage, a fear of solitude in the future, and a physical longing that needed fulfilment. Boswell, with his interest in and his ability to understand and describe human qualities, must have appreciated this. With his special knowledge and journalistic acumen, it is hard to believe that he never questioned Johnson about the person or persons he might have considered; perhaps it was a personal question he did not dare ask. But Boswell's interest in the general subject is shown clearly in his biography by several lively conversations with Johnson on second marriages, and these warrant rereading with this in mind.

Irresistible speculations remain: did Johnson simply resolve to marry again, or did he have a particular person in mind? There is no direct knowledge; so to answer the question one must first consider Johnson's requirements. He would have sought a wife of proper, though not necessarily distinguished background, someone of good reputation who shared in some measure his religious beliefs and to a minor degree his political sympathies. She would have been required to have at least natural intelligence and some wit, and be good company. There would have been one other essential according to current mores and Johnson's principles—the lady must not be already married.

With these qualifications in mind, who among Johnson's known acquaintances might have been candidates? The first young lady reported to have enchanted him can hardly have been a possibility, for when Johnson met Olivia Lloyd, the daughter of Sampson Lloyd of Birmingham, he was a boy of sixteen in school at Stourbridge. She was two years his senior, an attractive young woman interested in the classics. According to Johnson's early friend, Edmund Hector, the romance was not serious but typically youthful and transient. There is no later mention of Olivia, and if Johnson had thought of her in 1753 it could only have been in pleasant recollection, for she married Thomas Kirton, the same year Johnson married Tetty.

A more plausible candidate would have been Molly Aston

whom Johnson had known while a young man in Lichfield. Molly was one of the many daughters of Sir Thomas Aston, and her social position, so far above his, doubtless curbed him at the time from seeking anything more than friendship. His admiration for Molly was intense and endured throughout his life. "Molly was a beauty, and a scholar and a wit and a Whig ... she was the loveliest creature I ever saw." Years later he told Mr. Thrale that the happiest period of his past life was the year in which he had spent one whole evening with Molly Aston, "That indeed was not happiness, it was rapture; but the thoughts of it sweetened the whole year." And he once told Mrs. Thrale that Molly Aston's letters would be the last papers he would destroy, then quoted in a faltering voice a verse of great tenderness for Molly. Even during his married life Johnson's admiration for Molly did not pass unnoticed by Tetty. The episode of his fortune being told by a gypsy, at Mrs. Johnson's urging, had an unfortunate result, for the gypsy said, "Your heart is divided, Sir, between a Betty and a Molly: Betty loves you best, but you take most delight in Molly's company." At this Tetty cried. "Pretty charmer!" he commented, "she had no reason!" By 1753 Johnson had attained considerable literary reputation and perhaps the knowledge of his growing importance in the world might have given him sufficient courage to approach the lovely Molly Aston, but unfortunately by that time she was the wife of a Naval officer, Captain Brodie.

To be sure, Elizabeth Aston, an unmarried sister of Molly, was in Lichfield in 1753; about that time she was building the lovely house on Stowe Hill. Johnson always had the warmest admiration for Elizabeth, but she never exerted the electric attraction of Molly; she was solitary, stubborn, and uncommunicative. In later years, when Johnson came to Lichfield and panted up Stowe Hill once a day to call, it was more in general remembrance of the past, its delights, its plans and hopes, than any immediate and particular prospect of pleasure. "I took a walk in quest of juvenile images," he wrote on a visit to Lichfield in 1771, "but caught a cloud instead of Juno." However, comfort and kindness were always to be found in the company of substantial Elizabeth Aston, closely attended in her last years by her widowed sister, brisk and lively Jane Gastrell. Johnson's letters to Elizabeth after her stroke in 1777, urging that she take care of herself, strive for improvement, and keep busy and cheerful, were always answered by Jane, and in the end he addressed and considered them both in the same breath, "Dear Ladies" of Stowe Hill—friends who shared cherished memories.

A likelier candidate in 1753 would have been Ann Hector, his friend Hector's sister, if she had not been married by then to the Reverend Mr. Carless. Johnson once said of Ann that she was "the first woman with whom I was in love. It dropt out of my head imperceptibly; but she and I shall always have a kindness for each other." When he met her again many years later, he told Boswell, "If I had married her it might have been as happy for me." But though Johnson continued to remember Mrs. Brodie and Mrs. Carless with the lasting sentiment which is characteristic of him, he considered neither in 1753. They were married and lived far from London. He did not even see them during this period.

The situation was different with Charlotte Lennox, who was thirty-three at the time in question, gay, vivacious, and talented. Johnson saw her often and found great pleasure in her company. It is said that when Johnson first met her a few years before, he had taken her on his knee as if she were a child, carried her in his arms to show her his library, and sent for cakes for her. On this occasion Charlotte was considerably embarrassed, but her respect for Johnson stifled any idea of resentment. Hawkins described a party which Johnson gave for her in 1751 to celebrate the publication of her first book. At this party, during the course of revelry, Johnson "invoked the muses by some ceremonies of his own invention" and encircled her brows with a crown of laurel. Nearly twenty guests attended the party, which went on all night, but ailing Mrs. Johnson was not one of the number.

Johnson showed Charlotte Lennox many favors and gave her generous assistance and criticism. In 1753 he wrote a dedication for her *Shakespear Illustrated* and assisted in preparing proposals for a collection of her works. He was laboring on the second volume of his *Dictionary* at this time, and in it he paid her the gracious compliment of citing her words on "Talent" among his quotations. He also paid her a more flattering, veiled compliment by commenting in this connection that he used living authors most sparingly, only when "some performance of uncommon excellence excited my veneration . . . or when my heart, in tenderness of friendship, solicited admission for a favourite name." Between Johnson and the attractive Charlotte Lennox, however, there could be tender friendship only, for she too, albeit unhappily, was in the group of the married. Her husband was Alexander Lennox, an employee of William Strahan, the London printer. It was her husband who probably introduced her to Johnson, which "seems to be the only entirely helpful and auspicious act that Mr. Lennox ever performed for his wife."

Mrs. Gardiner and Mrs. Masters, noted as visiting Johnson after his wife's death, cannot be considered as serious candidates. Their interest was polite but their affections were otherwise engaged. Mrs. Gardiner was the wife of a tallow chandler on Snow-hill and Mrs. Masters, the poetess, was dedicated to Cave, Johnson's first London publisher.

Johnson told Boswell in 1776 that he had once been in love with a Mrs. Emmet, an actress in a travelling troupe which came to Lichfield. This was during the time of his early marriage to Tetty if his "forty years ago" is to be taken literally and not as a simple approximation. It is probable that Johnson's infatuation was bounded by the footlights.

A more eligible candidate would have been Hester Mulso, a young woman of twenty-six, of excellent family and formidable mind, who did not become the wife of the attorney Chapone until 1760. Though Johnson accepted four billets of hers for *The Rambler* and concurred in the general opinion that her attainments were admirable, there is no evidence that he took a personal interest in her in any way equivalent to the attentions he gave Charlotte Lennox. On her part, Miss Mulso was critical of Johnson and indifferent to him. He was not the outstanding figure he was later to become, and her close literary association was with the most eminent and popular man of letters at the time, Samuel Richardson, twenty years older than Johnson; with him she enjoyed a playful friendship, calling herself his affectionate child, and being called by Richardson in return his "little spitfire."

Elizabeth Carter was a greater friend of Johnson's than Miss Mulso. Miss Carter was thirty-six in 1753, and had known Johnson since the thirties. He must have been charmed on first acquaintance, for he wrote an epigram to her both in Greek and Latin, commenting to Cave, who had introduced them, that Eliza should be celebrated "in as many different Languages as Lewis le Grand." She was an extraordinary woman, with talent, great intellectual capacity, and drive. She was stubborn and at the same time painfully timid. She preferred the company of her own sex and confessed that as a child she had "looked upon having a sweetheart with as much horror as if it had been one of the seven deadly sins." At twenty-six, however, she expressed herself less violently upon the subject, merely saying that her greatest fears were "may-bugs and men." As time passed, further metamorphosis took place. Though she continued to live a sheltered existence in her father's house, she began to assume some of the usual, solid, and understanding attributes of a housewife. She cooked her famous plum dumplings, embroidered, knitted, sewed, and supervised the education of the young children in the family. She became less averse to society and more relaxed in it; she even experienced without displeasure the advances of a few of the opposite sex.

It was during this approachable period of her life that Johnson accepted two of her contributions to *The Rambler*, a publication she admired and defended. It is interesting that Miss Carter came from her home in Deal and spent a few months in lodgings near St. Paul's at the time of Johnson's deliberations upon a second wife. If Johnson had attempted to seek her out, details of his actions would have been given to her admired friend, Miss Talbot, whom she wrote regularly and fully on such personal subjects. There is no indication that such attention was paid her.

Catherine Talbot, Miss Carter's friend, was an acquaintance of Johnson and had contributed a number to *The Rambler*. Upon certain occasions she spoke in criticism of the paper, but more frequently defended it as well as the editor, whom she regarded highly. At the time in question Miss Talbot was thirty-two, charming, spirited, and generally admired for her intellectual prowess. Like Miss Carter, she still lived with her family, but she moved in a more fashionable sphere, changing residence from city to country according to the custom of society. Despite her protests of hating London smoke and bustle and racket, she was always to be found there during the season. She thus had a better opportunity to see Johnson than did Miss Carter, whose journeys to London were rare, but there is no record of Miss Talbot's enjoying a close friendship with him. Perhaps she did not desire it, for her literary enthusiasm, like

Miss Mulso's, was for the eminent Mr. Richardson. Besides this, there was little room in her life for a man's affections; in her own words she was a "confirmed spinster."

Another young woman with whom Johnson was acquainted in 1753 was Catharine Sawbridge, then twenty-two; she did not marry Dr. Macaulay until 1760. Yet it is doubtful, though she was eligible in certain ways, that Johnson could have been drawn to her. Her chief object of ardor at the time was the cause of militant Republicanism, and this in itself must have been extremely distasteful to Johnson. Molly Aston's Whig sympathies had been a different matter, for a man in his youth, if he is troubled at all by a difference of political conviction, hopes to mold the lady's opinion to his own. Molly had been able to bewitch as well as to disturb, but there is nothing to indicate that Miss Sawbridge had other power than the latter.

Johnson's consideration of another maiden lady is suggested by Anna Seward, who told Boswell that Johnson was attached to Lucy Porter before he met her mother. This story has been substantially refuted by Hector, and it is inconceivable that Johnson could have contemplated matrimony later with his stepdaughter, on the ground of mores, if not on the ground of her temperament, by which Johnson had already been miserably plagued.

Hill Boothby, in contrast to this suggestion, is a tantalizing possibility. Johnson first met her in the late thirties when on the rambles referred to in the letter to his wife. The purpose of his trip was to seek the mastership of the Appleby School; he failed in his purpose, but during his endeavour he enjoyed several pleasant visits to Dr. Taylor at Ashbourne, through whom he met Mr. Littleton Meynell at Bradley, three miles away. While being entertained at Mr. Meynell's house Johnson was introduced to the host's remarkable older daughter, Mary, and to her dearest friend, Hill Boothby, who was a year

Johnson's senior. As his acquaintance with Hill Boothby grew, he formed the highest opinion of her attractions, purity of mind, intellect, wit, and grace of manner. According to one account his jealousy of her attentions to Lord Lyttelton, another guest, was never forgotten and caused his disparaging appraisal years later of Lyttelton as a poet.

There is no doubt that Johnson thought of Hill Boothby in affectionate terms after his wife's death, and it is known that she had a high regard for him. There are letters from Hill Boothby to Johnson in 1753 referring to letters from him, though the latter are not known to survive. She was the only woman, Johnson told Dr. Taylor in 1756, with whom he had ever exchanged letters regularly. There are phrases in Johnson's letters to her which reflect deep emotion: "I am alive therefore I love Miss Boothby," "Dear Angel, do not forget me. My heart is full of tenderness," "I love you and honour you, and am very unwilling to lose you," "none but you on whom my heart reposes." It is true that the quoted letters to Hill Boothby were written two and three years after the time of his resolution, and he knew then she was dying. Yet his words give the sense of a renewed declaration of affection. He was in despair at the prospect of her death, and when it occurred his friend Baretti said that Johnson "was almost distracted with his grief; and that the friends about him had much ado to calm the violence of his emotion."

The year 1753 may well have been crucial in Johnson's relationship to Hill Boothby, and when he made his resolution in April to seek a new wife it is unlikely that he realized the full significance of the tragic event which had taken place a month before. Hill Boothby's dearest friend, Mary Meynell, who had for some years been married to William Fitzherbert, had died. Miss Boothby was named her sole executor and residuary legatee. She dutifully assumed the management of Mr.

Fitzherbert's household and care of the six strenuous children. Her life became, in hard reality, the role she had imagined very prettily in fancy ten years before. Then, she had directed a portrait painter to portray her "in snowy white, a vestal maid," standing by a rustic altar, holding a "flaming heart" in her hand:

> Emblems that best may paint my warm desire
> To watch and cherish friendship's sacred fire.

If Tetty had died earlier or if Mrs. Fitzherbert had died later, Johnson might well have sought Hill Boothby, but as events fell out, her dedication to friendship, and soon her failing health, placed her "flaming heart" beyond reach.

Time passed, and Johnson's resolve was not furthered. For a while he took a lively interest in Charlotte Cotterell, daughter of the Admiral. In answer to a letter from her in 1755, he responded, "A letter indeed can but imperfectly supply the place of its writer, at least such a writer as Miss Cotterel, and a letter which makes me still more desire your presence is but a weak consolation under the necessity of living longer without you, with this however I must be for a time content." Baretti, according to the letter, was also on close terms with Charlotte, and Johnson lamented this rival's attentions, "for which if I could blame him, I should punish him, but my own heart tells me that he only does to me, what, if I could, I should do to him." Charlotte Cotterell must have been a captivating young woman, for also in pursuit was the Dean of Ossory, Mr. Lewis, despite the fact that his wife was still living. Mrs. Lewis died the next year, 1756, and the Dean married Charlotte.

It was Charlotte who interested Johnson, not Frances, her sister, who was apparently known by the name of "Calamity." In his letters of later years his casual references to Frances, who never married, are in sharp contrast to his mentions of Charlotte, for whose welfare he maintained a lasting concern. Several months before he died, Johnson heard that she, by then a widow, was in London, and he wrote asking her to dine with him. "I hope you do not think," he said, "that I have forgotten or can forget Miss Charlotte Cotterel."

There was always Mrs. Desmoulins, seven years Johnson's junior, whom he had known since he was a young man. She was the daughter of Johnson's godfather, Dr. Swinfen, a gentleman of very ancient family, an excellent physician, but a poor manager who died leaving a large family in indigence. While very young, Elizabeth Swinfen married Mr. Desmoulins, a Huguenot refugee and writing master in Birmingham. Her married life was of short duration, for within a few years she was in London, a widow, maintaining herself and her children, working first at a machine for stamping crape and subsequently keeping a boarding school. She had left the latter employment by 1748, for she then came to be with Tetty at the Hampstead lodgings which Johnson had taken in the hope that the country air would be beneficial. Mrs. Desmoulins lived for some while with Tetty, and Johnson came out from London to Hampstead from time to time. During this period Johnson treated Mrs. Desmoulins with marked affection. How long their playfulness continued is not certain, but when Tetty died in 1752 Mrs. Desmoulins is not mentioned as being one of the household. Yet a bond must have remained, for Johnson took her into his house some years later and she lived there for many years. In 1753 Mrs. Desmoulins was still a widow, but Johnson knew that her ill temper and her lack of intellectual interest, incapable of development, made her an unsatisfactory candidate. Perhaps, also, he had known her too well during Tetty's lifetime.

For almost as many years as Johnson had known Mrs. Desmoulins, he had also known Anna Williams. This literary lady, the daughter of an ingenious Welsh physician, had come to London in the hopes of having an operation for cataracts on both eyes. She was a constant visitor to the house in Gough Square while Tetty was still living, and after her death came there to have the operation performed more comfortably than in lodgings. Her operation, which Johnson urged, resulted in total blindness. With pity and kindness after the tragic outcome, Johnson continued to offer Miss Williams a home with him, while ever he had a house, till the end of her life, which came only shortly before his own.

Anna Williams was forty-seven in 1753. She was blind, unprepossessing in appearance and cold in temperament, yet her companionship must have alleviated the solitude he dreaded. She must also have contributed in some measure to his comfort, for she regulated the domestic matters of the house. In this she was handicapped, but she managed as well as she could. Johnson never complained, though his friends sometimes did. Baretti resented her carving the victuals by pawing them and Boswell lamented her sticking her finger in his teacup to test its fullness. Boswell was also depressed to discover that Miss Williams was exacting and peevish and exerted a power over his friend which turned Johnson's dominating spirit into meek and abject submission.

In 1753, the year in question, Mrs. Chapone described Johnson's bringing Miss Williams to a reception, where he watched over her and guided her about as a fond father would his daughter. Johnson took her various places and made considerable effort to contribute to her pleasure, even when it caused annoyance to his friends. Unfortunately, her feeling for him seems to have manifested itself as time passed by increasing ill nature, raillery, and jealousy. When Johnson's household attained the size familiar to most Johnsonians, dissension and chaos reigned. No member of it liked any other, and despite

Miss Williams' protestations of envy that Johnson sought all his pleasures abroad, she combined with the others to deprive him of all pleasure at home. She hated everybody, particularly Mrs. Desmoulins. Johnson seemed at this time to have little affection for either of these women. "Without any great dearness in the comparison," he wrote Mrs. Thrale in 1777, "Williams I think is the dearer of the two." Later, when Miss Williams threatened to go away, he "bid her not turn tail, and she came back, and rather got the upper hand." It was Mrs. Desmoulins who was ultimately vanquished in this interminable battle of acrimony. She was finally driven away by Miss Williams in 1783, and Johnson wrote Mrs. Thrale that now "I have only one sick woman to fight or play with instead of two, and there is more peace in the house." A few months later, however, Miss Williams died and this event stirred his affection and impelled him to strong expressions of grief. "My Loss is very great," he wrote Reynolds, "She had been my domestick companion for more than thirty years." He wrote to Lucy Porter that Miss Williams had been "for thirty years in the place of a sister" and that he now lived "in cheerless solitude." It is probably true that the highest regard in which Johnson ever held Miss Williams was that of a sister. He held her in affection, and seeing beyond the disagreeable side of her personality deeply appreciated her attributes of mind, her conversation, her principles, and piety.

One wonders what evidences of affection and grief the death of Mrs. Desmoulins might have evoked. She did not have Miss Williams' qualities of mind, and though she had once pleased him, his expressions of esteem for her in later years were few. Yet her affection for him was remembered. She cheered him after Miss Williams was gone, and was at his bedside when he died.

The course of these two long friendships was foreknowledge

which Johnson could not have glimpsed in 1753. At that time he knew only that neither Mrs. Desmoulins nor Miss Williams was a satisfactory choice for a second wife. It is apparent that from among his other friends and acquaintances such a person was not easily found. He never fulfilled his resolution but his later interest in Charlotte Cotterell is indicative that he did not abandon the idea. The passage of time, however, and the complications and responsibilities of his life weakened his purpose. Johnson was not a man who was easily stirred to action.

As the years went by, Johnson grew to accept his celibacy. Though it produced emptiness and misery, he had never been a stranger to emptiness, even in his marriage to Tetty. His loneliness he tried to lessen in various ways. He took into his household many types of unfortunate humanity and accepted philosophically its unhappy wrangling in exchange for company. He warmed his heart with many friendships outside his household. And the greatest ease to his wretchedness came thirteen years after his unrealized resolution, when he became absorbed in the life of the Thrale family, with its welcome comfort, entertainment, and affection. This consolation soothed him for twenty years, almost his remaining life span.

The Dark Hints of
Sir John Hawkins and Boswell

FREDERICK A. POTTLE

As Boswell foresaw, no portion of his *Life of Johnson* has been so unpopular with the commentators as that in which he attributes Johnson's agonies of remorse in his last days to sexual irregularities into which he had been led by Savage years before.[1] Croker feels obliged to declare his opinion that "Boswell's introduction of this topic, his pretended candour, and hollow defence, were unwarranted by any evidence, and are the most, indeed almost the only, discreditable points of his whole work." In another note he is even more condemnatory, speaking of "sinister authority," "low and filthy guilt," "calumniated friend," "hearsay or . . . guess"; and he concludes that "Boswell's good sense, good taste, and good feeling, must have . . . given way under some powerful *self-delusion*."[2] Fitzgerald expands this into the explicit charge that Boswell gratuitously inserted the passage in order to pay Johnson off for not remembering him in his will, and to sanction his own shortcomings.[3] Dr. Hill is silent, but Dr. Powell says the whole thing comes

1. *Life*, IV.395–98.

2. *Life of Samuel Johnson*, ed. J. W. Croker (1831), v.306, n. 1; 309, n. 1. In the (later) one-vol. edition the notes are somewhat different but no less violent.

3. Percy Fitzgerald, *Boswell's Autobiography* (1912), 265–71. No one who knows Fitzgerald will be surprised to find that this reverses his earlier opinion in his edition of the *Life* (1874, III.157, n. 1). There his opinion was one that might well serve as summary of the present article: "The evidence of Hawkins and Boswell, who had seen [Johnson's] private diaries, is more to be relied on than such speculations as Mr. Croker's."

down to "vague insinuations."[4] Professor Clifford reverts to Fitzgerald's view, suggesting that Boswell "was perhaps judging from his own thorough knowledge of the temptations of the London stews."[5]

Professor W. B. C. Watkins performed a real service to scholarship some years ago by pointing out that Boswell's statements on this subject are linked to those of Sir John Hawkins, and that Boswell merely made explicit (though in guarded and general language) a charge that Hawkins had already hinted. Watkins' conclusion is that "while it is possible that Boswell refers to some secret confidence, it seems fairly clear that Hawkins is merely making the rash assumption on the basis that Johnson knew intimately a man of dissolute morals. . . . His sense of sin is explicable on other grounds."[6]

The topic is an ungracious one, but since it will always have to be discussed by every serious biographer of Johnson, it is well to have somewhere a full statement of everything in Boswell's private papers that seems to bear on it. Watkins did not take Boswell's journal into account, and Powell and Clifford fail to explore the implications of one entry of the journal that seems to me highly significant.

There is nothing in the papers to indicate that Boswell may have been the recipient of a secret confidence. So far as is known, he never heard from Johnson himself any confession of sexual irregularity, and there is no known record that he ever questioned him directly on the subject. He told Sir John Pringle in 1776 that he did not dare to.[7] The known comments on the subject which he collected from others contain nothing that he himself considered even faintly incriminatory. He dis-

4. *Life*, IV.552.
5. J. L. Clifford, *Young Sam Johnson* (1955), 211.
6. W. B. C. Watkins, *Perilous Balance* (1939), 51, 53.
7. *Private Papers*, XI.233 (10 Apr 1776).

missed as absurd the apparently frequent rumors that Johnson was guilty of improper relations with Anna Williams and Mrs. Thrale.[8] When Peter Garrick told him that Johnson was suspected of having seduced "a Lady, a very fine woman," he thought the charge "not very probable."[9] He concluded that Johnson's relations with Mrs. Desmoulins had been, by Johnson's own standards, curious but not criminal: hungry for the fulfillment which his wife denied him, he had deliberately put himself in the way of temptation with Mrs. Desmoulins, but (to quote the lady herself) had never gone beyond the limits of decency.[1] The manuscript of *The Life of Johnson* shows Boswell's usual anxious stylistic revision in the passages in question, but reveals no authority for his unqualified statement that Johnson, "after he came to London, and had associated with Savage and others, was not so strictly virtuous, in one respect, as when he was a younger man."[2]

Yet we should not be too quick to conclude that he had no positive evidence. He was not given either to making unfounded assertions or to presenting conjectures as statements of fact. His sense of propriety often seems capricious, but he could be very close-mouthed in matters where he felt secrecy was called for. I have no doubt that he had authority which he considered adequate. There is evidence that this authority was certain private records of Johnson which Johnson destroyed in the last week of his life.

On 7 May 1785, Boswell met Hawkins at dinner at Bennet Langton's. His journal for the day contains the following: "Sir J. Hawkins and I did very well. Stood in a corner, and talked

8. Journal, 20 Apr 1783 (unpublished); *Private Papers*, VI.92 (7 Apr 1773).

9. *Private Papers*, X.142 (24 Mar 1775).

1. Journal, 20 Apr 1783 (unpublished). Boswell has written at the top of the first page of this interview, "Extraordinary Johnsoniana—Tacenda."

2. *Life*, IV.395; see also I.164.

grave and earnest. He accounted for Johnson's fear of death: 'I have read his diary. I wish I had not read so much. He had strong amorous passions.' BOS. 'But he did not indulge them?' HAWK. 'I have said enough.' "[3]

We shall probably never know the extent of the autobiographical records that perished in Johnson's hasty bonfire. There is, however, no reason to question Boswell's belief that they included a record in two quarto volumes which on one occasion he calls "a pretty full and curious Diary of his Life" and on another "a full, fair, and most particular account of his own life, from his earliest recollection."[4] Boswell had seen one of these volumes in a drawer in his own house in Edinburgh when he and Johnson were starting off on the tour to the Hebrides; and in the *Life* he admitted that at some time which he does not specify he had read surreptitiously "a great deal in them," and had even copied out some passages.[5] Two quarto leaves answering to this description turned up at Malahide in 1940 and may well constitute his entire transcript. (They are now in the collection of Donald and Mary Hyde.) Boswell's heading shows that the copying was done in Johnson's house in Bolt Court, London, on 5 May 1776, which we may safely assume to have been the occasion of his extended perusal.[6] According to his own account, he afterwards told Johnson of his reading. Johnson was surprisingly placid, but admitted that if Boswell had carried the books off, he might have gone mad.[7] When I first collected my thoughts on this matter eighteen years ago, I assumed that Boswell himself could have seen nothing in the diary to substantiate the charge of incontinency because in no

3. *Private Papers*, XVI.84.
4. *Life*, V.53; IV.405.
5. *Ibid.*, IV.405; I.251.
6. *Diaries*, xviii, 49–54; Donald and Mary Hyde, *Dr. Johnson's Second Wife* (privately printed, 1953), [10] (facsimile).
7. *Life*, IV.405–6.

known record does he say that he did. Now I am by no means sure. His papers provide more instances of reticence and complete silence on delicate points than I was then aware of.

Boswell also asserts in the *Life* that Hawkins pocketed one of these volumes shortly before Johnson's death, and surmises that it was the agitation into which Johnson was thrown by this incident that caused him to burn the diary and other personal papers.[8] Hawkins' own account, which appeared in the second edition of his book but not the first, was that he went on Sunday, 5 December 1784, eight days before Johnson's death, to partake the Holy Sacrament with him. Several other people had been invited: John Hoole, his wife and son, Langton, Mrs. Gardiner, young Desmoulins, Frank the Negro, and the Reverend George Strahan, who officiated. While Johnson was dressing and preparing himself, he missed a paper containing instructions to his executors, and several of the company went into his bedroom to search for it. Hawkins came upon a parchment-covered book and opened it, thinking the paper might be inside. Finding it to be "meditations and reflections" in Johnson's hand, he slipped it into his pocket, together with a lesser manuscript book of Johnson's, his excuse being that he wished to secure it from George Steevens, who would have got it if he could, and would have "made an ill use of it." He however told Langton and Strahan what he had done; Langton warned Johnson. As soon as the celebration was over (that is, at the first possible moment) Johnson, in great agitation, demanded the book back.[9]

8. *Ibid.*, iv.406, n. 1.

9. Sir John Hawkins, *Life of Samuel Johnson* (2d ed., 1787), 586. Hawkins does not name Steevens, but, as Boswell says, describes him "so as to make it sufficiently clear who is meant." His daughter, Lætitia Matilda Hawkins, supplies the name (*Memoirs*, I.265). The material from Hawkins, with Boswell's commentary, is conveniently collected in *Johnsonian Miscellanies*, II.128–30. The list of persons who were present at the

There are difficulties in the way of supposing that Hawkins could have done much reading of Johnson's baffling hand in the few moments allowed him in Johnson's crowded rooms on that morning of 5 December 1784. So far as his own description goes, the one book he admits looking into on that occasion might well have been the surviving diary of 1765–84, which certainly contains nothing to justify the head-shaking he indulged in in his conversation with Boswell at Langton's. I do not know how to resolve these difficulties. Perhaps he simply happened to open the book at the right place. Perhaps he managed to get another look at the diary before it was burned. Perhaps the whole alarm about the pocketed volume is a mare's nest so far as our inquiry is concerned, and he had done his reading on a previous day. Perhaps what he saw was a diary not otherwise recorded. Granting all the difficulties, they seem to me less impressive than Boswell's statement that Hawkins said that he had read Johnson's diary and was shocked by what he found there. I am also ready to believe that Hawkins put the correct interpretation on what he read. He was something of a prig, but he was not a fool. On the contrary, he was a hard-headed lawyer and magistrate with extensive practice in the weighing of evidence. There is no reason to suppose that he was not as well equipped to read and understand the literal sense of a Johnsonian document as any twentieth-century editor or biographer.

As historical scholars, we must be cautious about allowing our own sense of the fitness of things to lead us into easy dismissal of the testimony of a good contemporary witness, even when that testimony is no more than an *ipse dixit*. It must be insisted over and over that it is inconsistent and irresponsible

---

celebration is partly from Hawkins and partly from John Hoole's narrative (*ibid.*, II.155).

to accept Boswell's unsupported assertions when they fit one's own picture of what is right and to reject them when they don't. If Boswell is generally a good witness, then he is *generally* a good witness. Our speculative reconstructions of episodes in which he had testified to a matter of fact without citing evidence should at least *start* with a presumption that he is right.

I am acutely aware of the inconclusiveness of all speculation in biography. Many years ago I started writing the life of a man, for whom, even at that time, the documentation was of perhaps unparalleled richness. I had no dearth of materials to base my conjectures on, and I made many of them. After I had finished my draft, my materials were trebled, and I had the opportunity to confront many of my conjectures with the facts. My conclusion is that in the field of bibliography, given a reasonable amount of fact to go on, one can make conjectures which later acquired evidence will confirm to a gratifying degree. In the field of biography proper, one's most plausible conjectures are likely to be wrong more often than right. Unless one is blinded by prejudice, one comes to see that it is possible to make an unlimited number of plausible conjectures as to what happened in any given human situation. Weight of evidence counts for simply nothing, one's sense of the fitness of things for very little. What does count is the *right* piece of evidence, the piece that tells you what really *did* happen.

This is not an injunction against biographers' engaging in speculation; it is merely prelude to an ambitious biographical speculation of my own. But before I begin that speculation I need to quote a bit more from Boswell.

Boswell began the composition of the *Life* in London on 9 July 1786. In the entry of his journal for the preceding day occurs a sentence which seems to me of equal significance with those I have quoted from the entry for 7 May 1785: "Drank tea at Langton's and had a conference with him and Sir John

Hawkins upon a delicate question, which Langton assured me I weighed and decided upon as well as he could suppose it to be done."[1] Since this occurs in a fully written portion of the journal (the entire entry for the day runs to nearly three hundred words), its cryptic quality cannot be due to haste. Boswell is deliberately concealing something.

I suggest that he felt that he could not start on the *Life* until he had found out more about what Hawkins had read, and had settled with him the whole problem of the destroyed diary. Both of them had read in it and had learned important things from it. But they had read without Johnson's permission, and by burning the book Johnson had indicated that there was matter in it he wished suppressed. Boswell wanted to know what course Hawkins proposed to take. He presumably also wanted to influence Hawkins' own policy, and since Hawkins' book did not appear till more than eight months later, he would seem to have been in time.[2] I suggest that they agreed that the destroyed diary could not be referred to as a source for "delicate" matter (Johnson must not be quoted against himself), but that Johnson's sexual irregularities ought to be guardedly mentioned without authority, not because either of them thought these moral lapses particularly important in themselves, but because they furnished the necessary key to his remorse of conscience. As Watkins has said, they seriously considered it more creditable to Johnson to be shown as suffering from a sin of magnitude than to be weakly scrupulous.[3]

1. *Private Papers*, XVI.203 (8 July 1786).

2. The first "this day was published" advertisement in *The London Chronicle* appears in the number for Tuesday 20 Mar–Thursday 22 Mar (LXI.279), which also prints extracts from the book. The publication date was probably Monday 19 Mar 1787. The advertisement asserts that Hawkins "collected" it "from a Diary kept by [Johnson], and other documents."

3. *Perilous Balance*, 50.

They presented this matter at exactly the same spots in their respective narratives, and in terms that strongly suggest some kind of agreement. Hawkins, speaking of Savage's "vagrant course of life" which "had made him acquainted with the town and its vices," goes on, "and though I am not warranted to say, that Johnson was infected by them . . ."[4]—somebody long before this should have remarked that this is a lawyer's ploy for getting in excluded testimony. It does not mean, "I have no evidence for the reflection I am about to make," but rather, "I have evidence for the reflection I am about to make, but I am forbidden to cite it." Similarly, Boswell, leading into his final statement, says, "On that account, therefore, as well as from the regard to truth which he inculcated, I am to mention, (with all possible respect and delicacy however) . . ."[5] That *I am to mention* has no parallel anywhere else in his book.

There is one piece of evidence not yet cited that seems to me to fit with this interpretation. As Donald and Mary Hyde have pointed out in their essay in this volume, the extracts which Boswell made on 5 May 1776 from the destroyed diary contained two entries (22 and 23 April 1753) in which Johnson made unequivocal reference to an intention "to seek a new wife." Boswell never printed these entries, and never hinted at the matter in any way in the *Life*. It is suggested that he suppressed them because they would have disturbed the picture of Johnson's relations with his wife which he was offering as a corrective to Hawkins' "dark, uncharitable" interpretation.[6] This is an attractive suggestion, but there are difficulties with it, as the Hydes themselves realize. Apart from the reflection on Boswell's candor, which (as I have argued above) counts *against* any speculation of this sort, it is hard to see why those

4. *Life of Samuel Johnson* (1st and 2d eds.), 54.
5. *Life*, IV.395.
6. See above, p. 134.

161

two poignantly tender entries would have disturbed Boswell's picture at all. I should like to suggest that he suppressed all mention of Johnson's proposed second marriage *because he could not cite the source of his information.* He could print matter from his extracts that was not "delicate" (matter resembling the *Prayers and Meditations* which Johnson himself had given George Strahan with an understanding that they might be published), but he felt the proposed second marriage was "delicate," and as he had no evidence whatever for it except his entries from the destroyed journal, his lips were sealed.

Sealed, that is, so far as the public was concerned. In early spring 1792, reporting to his most intimate friend, the Reverend William Johnson Temple, that a scheme of his own for a second marriage had fallen through, he confided to him at least one of the secrets of Johnson's diary. The letter is lost, having presumably been used by Mme. Noel to wrap a parcel in. If we had it, it is probable that no part of the present article would have been written. But Temple's reply, I think, makes sufficiently clear what reason Boswell had given for not divulging Johnson's thoughts of a second marriage:

> If you can be truly attached again at our time of life, the other obstacle that presses at present would easily give way. The similar circumstance you mention of Johnson is curious, and as it serves still further to paint the man, and to shew the tender sensibility of his mind, ought to enrich your next edition. If conscious of what passes here, it will sooth his venerable shade and he will not look upon it as a breach of trust.[7]

7. W. J. Temple to James Boswell, 11 Mar 1792 (unpublished), among the Boswell Papers in the Yale University Library.

Dr. Johnson as Bibliographer
and Book Collector

E. L. McADAM, JR.

We all know that Johnson knew a great many books and that he had a considerable library. My purpose is to enquire into the extent of his technical knowledge of the history of printing, of books which were milestones in that history, and the existence of such books in his own library.

Though Johnson began his acquaintance with books in his father's store, there is little evidence that Michael Johnson was greatly interested in books other than as saleable commodities, and no unusual or particularly early editions are mentioned among the titles which we know he sold. Perhaps Johnson saw some such books as an undergraduate at Oxford, but the earliest date we can be sure of when he became interested in printing as such is 1740. In that year, this paragraph appeared in the *Gentleman's Magazine*:

> *Strasbourg, Feb. 19.* N.S. Here was lately celebrated the third hundred Year's Feast of the noble Art and Mystery of PRINTING, discover'd in 1440, the Honour of which is claim'd by this City, which disputes it with *Mentz* and *Harlem*. It is remarkable that two other Arts were discover'd in the same Century, *viz.* the Use of the Loadstone and Compass, and that of Gunpowder, which three made a total Change in the Affairs of the World, *viz.* Printing in Politicks and Divinity, the Compass in Trade and Navigation, and Gunpowder in the Art of War.

Johnson as sub-editor may have inserted this account, perhaps wrote part of it. At any rate his reference to it twenty-eight years later shows his interest, and he was correct as to the date of its appearance, a matter about which he is often careless.

But what in 1740 may have been an amateur interest, became in 1743 a professional one, when Johnson began work on the *Harleian Catalogue* for the bookseller Tom Osborne. Michael Maittaire, perhaps the best known bibliographer in England at the time, was employed to write the Dedication and sketch out the plan of the Catalogue, but, at seventy-five, he probably had no other concern with the work. His three-volume *Annales Typographici*, however, which had been published in Holland between 1719 and 1726, was almost certainly Johnson's guide in preparing the catalogue and its Preface. It is not known whether Johnson knew Maittaire, but he told Boswell that Maittaire "seems to have been a puzzle-headed man, with a large share of scholarship, but with little geometry or logick in his head, without method, and possessed of little genius."[1]

Johnson's Preface shows that he profited from Maittaire's difficult volumes, and that he probably ranged elsewhere as well. He hopes that this catalogue "will not be of less use to men of letters than those of the Thuanian, Heinsian, or Barberinian libraries"; he comments that "the boasted Bodleian library is far from a perfect model," and adds that a collector will find that "even the learned Fabricius cannot completely instruct him in the early editions of the classic writers." Naturally, in this display of names, Johnson does not neglect moral aspects of book-collecting, paying his respects to the Harleys' "ardour for literature, to that generous and exalted curiosity which they gratified with incessant searches and immense expence, and to which they dedicated their time, and that su-

1. *Life*, IV.2.

perfluity of fortune, which many others of their rank employ in the pursuit of contemptible amusements, or the gratification of guilty passions."

Johnson continues his Preface with a brief account of the Bibles in the collection, beginning with Fust's edition of 1462, which at this time he thought was the first one printed, though he was later to learn better, and he mentions in connection with the English Bibles four criteria which have since interested collectors: "the pomp and beauty of the impression . . . the notes with which the text is accompanied . . . any controversy or persecution that it produced, or . . . the peculiarity of any single passage." It is notable that he does not mention rarity as such. Later in the Preface he points out the importance to scholars of a library which contains rare editions of the classics available for collation in producing good modern editions, and adds that the Harleian library contains not only "the most ancient editions of Faustus [Fust], Jenson, Spira, Sweynheim, and Pannartz, but the most accurate likewise and beautiful of Colinaeus, the Juntae, Plantin, Aldus, the Stephens, and Elzevir."

No one has yet examined the Latin accounts of the books which, according to Boswell, Johnson wrote during the next two years for the *Catalogue*, or the notes in the third and fourth volumes which Hawkins thought Johnson wrote, but there can be little doubt that this is the period when Johnson learned most of what he knew of bibliography. At no time in his life was he likely to stop with the title page of a book: he looked into it, and Tom Tyers says that it was this deplorable habit which caused Osborne to object to Johnson's slowness in cataloguing, whereupon Johnson knocked him down with the folio he was working on.[2]

2. *Miscellanies*, II.347.

In 1759 Johnson made a casual reference to the history of printing which shows his continuing interest in the subject. In his essay on translation (*Idler* 69), he says, "Caxton taught us typography about the year 1474. The first book printed in English was a translation . . . the Destruccion of Troye. . . ." In 1778 he reverted to Caxton in a discussion of the place of France in the Revival of Learning: "Paris was the second city for the revival of letters: Italy had it first, to be sure. What have we done for literature, equal to what was done by the Stephani and others in France? Our literature came to us through France. Caxton printed only two books, Chaucer and Gower, that were not translations from the French; and Chaucer, we know, took much from the Italians."[3]

The respectful reference to the great scholar family of the Estiennes, whom he had mentioned in the Preface to the *Harleian Catalogue*, is worth noting.

The next direct evidence of Johnson's knowledge of bibliography is found in his letter of 28 May 1768 to Frederick Augusta Barnard, the King's Librarian, on the occasion of Barnard's setting off on a book-buying trip to the Continent. We do not know when Johnson met Barnard, but Boswell says that through this acquaintance Johnson had frequently visited George III's library in Buckingham House, and it is hardly a guess to say that Johnson enlarged his knowledge of scarce or splendid books by reading in that collection. It is not easy to tell which of the books mentioned in his letter Johnson has seen. The first edition of Cicero's *De Officiis*, 1465, he would have known about from reading, but a few years later, in Paris, he is intimately familiar with its typography; his discussing the book suggests that it was not in the King's Library in 1768. Where he saw Roberts' Welsh grammar, 1567, is also unknown (he had not yet been in Wales), but perhaps it was at a bookseller's.

3. *Life*, III.254.

He has his information about the first book with a complete printed date, the *Psalmorum Codex*, 14 August 1457, so much at his finger-tips that he does not bother to check his date, and is off by a year. He has, by more extended reading and perhaps conversation found out that there are three Bibles earlier than that of 1462, which he had once thought the earliest. And he has seen enough books produced by Fust and Schoeffer to be confident that all those from 1457 onwards have their usual printer's device of shields hanging from a bough. And from an obscure poem of Gabriel Naudé, one of the great seventeenth-century librarians, he has picked up the notion that earlier books of Fust and Schoeffer (the Gutenberg Bible, for example) are marked with horns. That Naudé was talking about water-marks, Johnson did not guess. I doubt whether he ever became expert on that subject. One would be hard put to recommend to him a contemporary book or article about watermarks: the *OED* gives only one occurrence of the word before the date of Johnson's letter. And finally he gives Barnard the names of two authorities useful to consult for information on Aldine and other early books, Fabricius, whose fourteen-volume work he had mentioned in the Preface to the *Harleian Catalogue*, and Baillet's *Jugemens des savans*, 9 volumes, 1685–86.

The whole of Johnson's letter to Barnard might be charac-terized as "advice to a librarian to be shown to the patron." Johnson advises the purchase of early books containing en-gravings, probably thinking of Holbein and Dürer among others, since "the designs were often made by great Masters, and the prints are such as cannot be made by any artist now living." He advises against the purchase of general libraries because of inevitable duplicates, but suggests that libraries specializing in particular fields be bought: the collection of an eminent civil or feudal lawyer or mathematician "will per-haps have very few Superfluities." And his interest in law adds a further recommendation: the "feudal and civil Law I cannot but wish to see complete. The feudal Constitution is the original of the law of property over all the civilized part of Europe, and the civil Law, as it is generally understood to include the law of Nations, may be called with great propriety a regal study."

He urges the purchase of local maps rather than those of a whole country since "it must not be expected that the exactness of actual mensuration will be preserved when Maps are reduced by a contracted scale, and incorporated into a general system." One piece of advice is not out of date for librarians who have to think of donors, scholars, and exhibitions: "a royal library should have at least the most curious Edition, the most splendid, and the most useful." And he specifies the first and the latest scholarly editions, adding, "The most splendid the eye will discover." A last bit of advice on buying has not lost any of its force: "In the purchase of old books let me recommend to you to examine with great caution whether they are perfect. In the first editions the loss of a leaf is not easily observed. You remember how near we both were to purchasing a mutilated Missal at a high price." That Johnson and Barnard were considering buying an old missal apparently means that they were considering it for the King's library. But a "Missale romanorum," three volumes, was Lot 134 in the sale of Johnson's library, no date given. Johnson perhaps continued to advise Barnard and the King: in 1774 he saw and admired the first printed book in Greek, Lascaris' Greek Grammar, 1476, and in the next year a copy was purchased for the King's library at the Agnew Sale for £21 10s.

It is tempting to suppose that Johnson gained some of his knowledge of early books from the most learned printer in London, William Bowyer, but I have no evidence that they were acquainted. Nevertheless, when Bowyer's little book *The*

Origin of Printing appeared in 1774, Johnson read it within two months of publication and made a note on Lascaris' Greek Grammar of 1476—an item buried in an appendix to Bowyer's book. And this may prove that Johnson not only read books through but read appendixes, in spite of his laughter about dull people who did such things. In the *Welsh Diary* where he records this he also notes seeing this edition of Lascaris in the library at Blenheim Palace, and comments that it is "well printed, but much less [so] than latter[!] editions." He knew what he was talking about: he owned an Aldine edition of Lascaris; it was in Lot 296 in the sale of his library.

In the same diary Johnson shows some familiarity with early Welsh books other than the first grammar of that language, which has been mentioned. He recommended that Davydd Rhys' grammar, 1592, be reprinted; he had some conversation about Edmund Prys' Welsh metrical version of the Psalms, 1621; and he mentioned the first translation of the Old Testament into Welsh, 1588, which, by the way, was in the Harleian Library.

Returning from Wales he saw the *Nuremberg Chronicle* in the library of Worcester Cathedral, most famous picture book among incunabula, and as he is writing "thinks" it is the first edition, 1493. Since he does not carry reference books about with him, he can't be sure. It was the first edition, and it is still at Worcester. In Shrewsbury he saw the large library which John Taylor, a classical scholar, had bequeathed to the grammar school, but since he was with the volatile Mrs. Thrale it is unlikely that he had a chance to handle many books before resuming their hurried tour of the town. At Hagley, William Lyttelton rudely interrupted Johnson's bibliographical progress by taking away his candle, but at Blenheim he was more fortunate, when the Duke's Secretary, the courtly Jacob Bryant, showed him not only the Lascaris grammar but the beautiful first edition of Durand's *Rationale*, 1459, and the *Battle of the Frogs and Mice*, the first part of the Homeric poems to be printed, Venice, 1486. Other books Johnson surely saw, but he mentions only these.

Next year in Paris Johnson continued to visit libraries. At D'Argenson's, he made so merry over the trifling books in the lady's cabinet that their party was not admitted to the upper rooms of the house. But in the Royal library he had better luck. There he saw an edition of the *Speculum Humanae Salvationis* (Holland? 1470?), of great typographical importance. He says it is "rudely printed, with ink, sometimes pale, sometimes black; part supposed to be with wooden types, and part with pages cut on boards." For a purblind old man, this is a pretty close description. It is a block book containing twenty leaves of xylographic plates and forty-four leaves printed in movable type, but probably not wooden. Note that Johnson says "supposed to be with wooden types."

Next he saw the copy of the Gutenberg Bible which he had written Barnard about. Here he says it is "supposed to be older than that of Mentz, in 62: it has no date; it is supposed to have been printed with wooden types. —I am in doubt; the print is large and fair, in two folios." His doubt that it was printed with wooden types—it was not—shows both how much information Johnson had absorbed about early books and how well he is using his eyes. His next comment bears this out: "Another book was shown me, supposed to have been printed with wooden types; —I think, *Durandi Sanctuarium* in 58. This is inferred from the difference of form sometimes seen in the same letter, which might be struck with different puncheons. The regular similitude of most letters proves better that they are metal." His inference is correct. The book was probably Durand's *Rationale*, 1459, which he had seen at Blenheim, here masquerading under a binder's title; no early edition has a title-page.

His last remark about the library is astonishing: "I saw nothing but the *Speculum* which I had not seen, I think, before." He had seen the Durand at Blenheim, but no one knows where or when he could have seen a Gutenberg Bible before, and since he must have been shown many more than the three books he names, one is impressed both with his acquaintance with early books and his memory of them.

It is just possible that he had handled a Gutenberg Bible without knowing it in cataloguing the Harleian Library, where he lists one, square letter, two volumes folio, without date, but clearly before 1500.

At the Sorbonne he saw, or at least mentioned, only some large historical collections, principally of the eighteenth century. At St. Cloud he apparently had time to read Beroald's *Orationes, Praelectiones, Praefationes et quaedam Mythicae Historiae*, 1508 or a later edition, as well as two seventeenth-century English pieces. At the Chartreux, Johnson evidently had no more than a glance at a friar's library, for he says, perhaps contemptuously, "His books seemed to be French." One would expect a friar to have at least *some* Latin books. But the friar gave Johnson some grapes, and probably softened Johnson's opinion of the man's intellectual poverty.

Toward the end of his stay in Paris Johnson saw the great library of St. Germain des Prés, which he rightly thought "a very noble collection." The first book he saw was Durand's *Rationale*, which he had seen at least twice before, here masquerading under the binder's title of *Codex Divinorum Officiorum*. He notes that it is printed in "a letter square like that of the Offices, perhaps the same." He is referring to Cicero's *De Officiis*, Fust and Schoeffer, 1465, which he had mentioned in his letter to Barnard, and his guess that the Durand, by the same printers, is in the same type, is borne out by the *Gesamtkatalog*. Since Johnson does not mention that he has the *Offices* at hand to compare the types, we may perhaps assume that he was depending on his remarkable memory and his excellent use of his poor eyes. Not many experts would be willing to venture such an opinion with so limited material. The very copy of Durand which Johnson saw here is probably that now in the Bibliothèque Nationale, as Dr. Powell has established.

The next volume was the *Psalmorum Codex* of the same printers, referred to in Johnson's letter to Barnard as the beginning of the annals of typography. Then Johnson looked at the twelve-volume set of the Dutch classical scholar Meursius and the first edition in French of three books of *Amadis de Gaula*, 1540–42, a romance Johnson liked well enough to borrow twice from Percy.[4]

The next book was Balbus' *Catholicon*, 1460, sometimes attributed to Gutenberg, which Johnson describes as without a colophon. No such copy is known, but Dr. Powell points out that "As the colophon occurs, not at the very end of the book, but before the 'tabula rubricarum,' it is possible that Johnson overlooked it."[5] He then looked at two other early editions of the same book, that printed in 1494 by Lathomi, Johannis, and de Villa, and that by Badius Ascensius, 1510.

Johnson next saw an edition of Augustine's *De Civitate Dei* which he describes as "without name, date, or place, but of Fust's square letter, as it seems." No such incunable edition is known. The only one without name, date, or place is that printed by Mentelin of Strasbourg, about 1468, in different type from the Durand. It is at least possible, however, that Johnson saw an imperfect copy, one lacking the colophon, of the edition of 1473 by Schoeffer, which does use the same type.

He spent part of the next day in the library of the English Benedictines, but he mentions only one book, Maffei's *History*

4. *Letters* 1145.
5. *Life*, II.526.

of India, 1589, in which he noted a Latin expression which he apparently thought new.

Although anyone reading all of the existing part of Johnson's *French Diary* knows that he did many things other than looking at early books, when his comments on these books are brought together, it becomes clear that he is not merely wandering through libraries and politely glancing at their treasures. One can readily believe that at each one he asked what early or remarkable books the library owned and then, with great interest, examined those which were handed him, comparing products of the same printers, remembering other books among the early incunabula, using his sound common sense about claims for the use of wooden types—in other words, acting like any other well-trained, skeptical bibliographer.

I have no evidence that Johnson owned any incunabula, though the miserably incomplete sale catalogue of his library may conceal one or more. The catalogue does show that he owned many Aldine editions (including Aeschines, 1513, Apollonius Argonauticus, 1521, and the Lascaris Greek Grammar already mentioned), the Plantin Aeschylus, 1580, and many works issued by Foulis in Glasgow. Products of almost every press of importance after Aldus can be easily found in that catalogue. Johnson can hardly have bought these because they were the most easily available texts, or the best, because usually they were neither one nor the other. He loved old books—he particularly mentions books in black letter.

Dr. Chapman says that Johnson "had all the qualities of a book-collector except greed and habits of tidiness."[6] But these seem to me to be relatively small concerns compared with one which Dr. Chapman does not raise: Did Johnson read his books?

6. *Letters* 206 n.

We are still assured by some of our best scholars that Johnson did not read books through. This is a dreadful canard, though it is often applied to book collectors who have not known R. B. Adam, Newton, Tinker, or some of the younger Johnsonians. A good collector knows his books, and not merely their bindings, title-pages, and cancels.

What is the origin of this myth about Johnson? In 1773, Boswell reports, "Mr. Elphinston talked of a new book that was much admired, and asked Dr. Johnson if he had read it. JOHNSON. 'I have looked into it.' 'What (said Elphinston,) have you not read it through?' Johnson, offended at being thus pressed, and so obliged to own his cursory mode of reading, answered tartly, 'No, Sir; do *you* read books *through*?' "[7] Note that this report concerns a new book much admired (too much, perhaps Johnson thought), and that Johnson was pressed, when, as usual, he reacted with characteristic violence. But he does not say "*I* do not read books through," and he may, as he often did, have taken off the edge of his remark with laughter.

Against this we may put Adam Smith's remark, and Adam Smith was not a disciple, that "Johnson knew more books than any man alive."[8] It is a very dangerous assumption that Johnson had not read any book he mentions or which is listed in the Sale Catalogue of his library. He does indeed say that he had not finished Mrs. Montagu's *Essay on Shakespear*, but he had read enough of it to judge its quality. He also told Langton— this is a *third*-hand report, through Boswell, and not dated— that the only book in Greek which he had finished was Xenophon's *Cyropaedia*, which he was reading to improve his Greek. But we know that he read the Greek dramatists in college, and there is impressive evidence that he read them later. We know that he read Virgil through and the Bible—the New

7. *Life*, II.226.
8. *Life*, I.71.

Testament, at least, in Greek as well as in English. I have mentioned a book in which Johnson read the appendix, and there is another in which he read the footnotes, in very small type, double columns. Johnson refers, in his diaries, to page 256, or the like, of huge, forgotten, double-column folios. He refers to works of the early Church Fathers, Chrysostom, for one, which are not now considered in the canon.

I suggest, in conclusion, that Johnson as a bibliographer and book collector was about as professional as any eighteenth-century Englishman, and deserves study as well as admiration.

Dr. Johnson's Spectacles

M. H. ABRAMS

"Of all skill," Dr. Johnson said, "part is infused by precept, and part is obtained by habit."[1] This remark applies to our skill in reading poetry. Guided, usually, by precept, we apply ourselves to specific poems and inaugurate a process of tentative adaptations, marked by success or failure in comprehension, which result, ultimately, in a pattern of established responses to the printed word. Whatever a reader's innate sensibility, and however definite his critical principles, these attributes must finally engage with a poem through an intricate set of expectations and habitual reactions, of which the reader himself may be largely unaware. For skills are simply advantageous habits. The difficulty is that habits which are advantageous for one kind of poetry may be ill adapted to poetry of a different order. Our interpretative habits compose a kind of spectacles, without which we could not read a poem. But the same lenses which bring the poetry of Pope or Dryden into sharp focus may blur the poetry of Milton, or distort it beyond possibility of appreciation.

Dr. Johnson's own criticism illustrates how the very skills of an experienced reader may restrict the range of his appreciation. Johnson is apt to our purpose because, though he applied to poetry an almost unexampled minuteness of scrutiny, our own perspective has shifted so sharply that we are able to recognize the limitations, as well as the powers, of the lenses through which he gazed. There is not space to consider how

1. Preface to Shakespeare, in *The Works of Samuel Johnson*, ed. Arthur Murphy (1824), II.129.

many of Johnson's prepossessions about poetry may derive
from his manner of reading, as well as from his critical principles—his condemnation of mythology, for example; or his
preference for poems which are perfectly unambiguous, to all
people, at first sight; or his proscription of words which "become low by the occasions to which they are applied, or the
general character of them who use them."[2] Two aspects of
Johnson's approach to poetry must stand in the place of many:
his treatment of metaphor, and his treatment of meter.

A number of critics in the generation of Johnson thought it
necessary to go to considerable pains to justify and delimit the
use of poetic figures. These were held to be an indispensable
means of adorning the matter of a poem; but it was considered
that they might be deceptive, and that they certainly ran the
danger of becoming extravagant, or obscure. We find that
metaphors and similes were admitted to poetry only under
strict conditions. The two foremost rhetoricians of the day,
Lord Kames and Hugh Blair, systematically laid down a long
list of such restrictions: a metaphor must be briefly presented
and quickly dropped; there ought not to be more than one
metaphor to a sentence; a metaphor must never be mixed, or
broken; and so on.[3] An instance or two in which Johnson discussed metaphors will reveal how tight were the limits that a
similar manner of reading imposed on the free play of poetic
language.

John Dryden, in his fable, "Of the Pythagorean Philosophy," had used the phrase

And bees [bring] their honey redolent of spring.

2. *Rambler* 168.

3. See Henry Home, Lord Kames, *Elements of Criticism* (1762), chap.
20; and Hugh Blair, *Lectures on Rhetoric and Belles Lettres* (1793), lecture 15.

The figure pleased Thomas Gray, who introduced a variation upon it into his ode "On a Distant Prospect of Eton College." Of the "gales" that blew to him from the Eton of his boyhood, Gray said:

> My weary soul they seem to soothe,
> And, redolent of joy and youth,
> To breathe a second spring.

And lest the allusion be overlooked, Gray, like some poets of our own day, took care to identify its origin in a note.

This is Johnson's comment on the passage, in his *Life of Gray*:

> Gray thought his language more poetical as it was more remote from common use: finding in Dryden "honey redolent of spring," an expression that reaches the utmost limits of our language, Gray drove it a little more beyond common apprehension, by making "gales" to be "redolent of joy and youth."

Now whether we like these figures or not, certainly both of them, far from being "beyond common apprehension," are readily intelligible to a modern reader. Gray's expression seems not even complex, unless in an effort to explain its workings we analyze "gales . . . redolent of joy and youth" as elliptical, perhaps, for "gales bearing odors reminding me of odors I experienced in the days of my happy childhood." Only upon analysis does it seem queer that "gales" should smell of the abstractions "joy" and "youth"; but upon analysis, almost any metaphor begins to seem queer. Apparently, what Johnson did was to analyze the passage in the very process of reading it: he interposed the demand that he understand how a figure works, and the qualification that its foundation be neither far-fetched nor difficult to discover, before allowing it to become poetically effective. The result was inevitably to restrict the freedom and complexity of the metaphors he was able to enjoy.[4]

As another example, take Johnson's treatment of a metaphor of Shakespeare's. In his edition of the plays Johnson was usually too scrupulous to emend a text merely because it offended his sensibility. Occasionally, however, Johnson nodded, and then he imposed changes on the language of Shakespeare which in fact betrayed his own implicit habits of reading. Thus, Macbeth's despairing cry,

> I have liv'd long enough. My way of life
> Is fall'n into the sere, the yellow leaf;[5]

apparently transgressed too far "the utmost limits of our language" for Johnson to attribute it even to the notorious licentiousness of the Elizabethans. He emended "My way of life" to "My *May* of life Is fall'n into the sere, the yellow leaf"; with the explanation that Shakespeare probably had not written "way," because "there is no relation between the *way of life,* and *fallen into the sere.*"[6]

4. Cf. Blair, *Lectures*, lecture 15: "particular care should be taken that the resemblance, which is the foundation of the Metaphor be clear and perspicuous, not far-fetched, nor difficult to discover. The transgression of this rule makes, what are called harsh or forced Metaphors, which are always displeasing, because they puzzle the reader, and instead of illustrating the thought, render it perplexed and intricate." Also, Kames, *Elements*, chap. 20, sec. 6: a metaphor, like a simile, "cannot be agreeable where the resemblance is . . . too faint."

5. *Macbeth*, v.iii.22–23.

6. For contemporary limitations on the reading of Shakespeare's metaphors, see, e.g., Blair, *Lectures*, lecture 15:

> "As glorious
> As is the winged messenger from heaven
> Unto the white upturn'd wondering eyes
> Of mortals, that fall back to gaze on him,
> When he bestrides the lazy pacing clouds,
> And sails upon the bosom of the air.

Now, what were the expectations and established responses which Johnson applied to the reading of poetic meters? This question is of particular interest, because Johnson's attacks on the versification of the sweetest singers in the language have become one of the scandals of English criticism. Blank verse, Johnson believed, is no better than cut-up prose; of Milton's sonnets, only two are "not bad"; the songs from *Comus* are "harsh in their diction, and not very musical in their numbers"; in *Lycidas*, "the diction is harsh, the rhymes uncertain, and the numbers unpleasing."[7] In the face of such judgements, even Johnson's staunchest defenders have thrown up their hands and acknowledged that he was a critic who had no "ear" for verse. As Sir Leslie Stephen says of his "odd remarks upon Milton's versification": "The result is what one might expect from the attempt of a writer without an ear to sit in judgment upon the greatest master of harmony in the language."[8]

Such an explanation, based on a false analogy between melody and meter, explains nothing. There is abundant evidence

---

"Here, the angel is represented, as, at one moment, *bestriding* the clouds, and *sailing* upon the air; and upon the *bosom* of the air too; which forms such a confused picture, that it is impossible for any imagination to comprehend it."

Or see Kames, *Elements*, chap. 20, sec. 6:

"*Malcolm.*—But there's no bottom, none,
In my voluptuousness: your wives, your daughters,
Your matrons, and your maids, could not fill up
The cistern of my lust.

"The best way to judge of this metaphor, is to convert it into a simile; which would be bad, because there is scarce any resemblance between lust and a cistern, or betwixt enormous lust and a large cistern."

7. *Life of Milton*, in *Lives*, 1.169, 163.

8. *Samuel Johnson*, English Men of Letters Series (1878), 176. Also J. E. Brown, *The Critical Opinions of Samuel Johnson* (1926), xxx: "The truth is that Johnson, who had no ear for music, provided a poor standard by which to judge any but the simpler and more regular forms of versification. Here was one critical blind spot."

in Johnson's criticism that he was, in fact, strongly responsive to metrical and verbal music, which with unaccustomed warmth he called "that harmony that adds force to reason, and gives grace to sublimity; that shackles attention, and governs passions."[9] Far from lacking metrical discrimination, Johnson was an uncommonly sensitive connoisseur of certain kinds of verse. The scope of his enjoyment, however, was limited because he had become closely habituated to one kind of versification; and, I think, one reason that Johnson found unpleasing much of the poetry of Milton, or Collins, or Gray, was that their numbers clashed sharply with the reading skills, the anticipations and accustomed reactions, which had been formed mainly on the numbers of Dryden and of Pope.

Pope's couplets in particular were for Johnson the nonpareil of measures and the ultimate reach of poetic development. Pope, he said, "discovered the most perfect fabrick of English verse." "To attempt any further improvement of versification will be dangerous. Art and diligence have now done their best, and what shall be added will be the effort of tedious toil and needless curiosity."[1] And from time to time, we can catch Johnson in the act of reading other measures through the patterns of habit formed by the couplet of the Augustans.

In Pope's couplets each line is usually an entity separated even from its rhymed companion-line by a pause in the reading, and often by a break in the syntax. It is plain that Johnson attempted to read not only the heroic couplet but other stanza forms, and blank verse as well, single line by single line, seeking to make each a metrical unit. As he once said, with reference to the deficiencies of blank verse:

> The musick of the English heroick line strikes the ear
> so faintly that it is easily lost, unless all the syllables of

9. *Rambler* 88.
1. *Pope*, 248, 251.

every line co-operate together; this co-operation can be only obtained by *the preservation of every verse unmingled with another as a distinct system of sounds,* and this distinctness is obtained and preserved by the artifice of rhyme.[2]

And Johnson gave away the fashion in which he tried to read *Paradise Lost* when he added: "there are only a few skilful and happy readers of Milton who enable their audience to perceive where the lines end or begin. 'Blank-verse,' said an ingenious critic, 'seems to be verse only to the eye.' " Which is, of course, to imply that to Johnson's perception, unless each line remains the unmistakable unit of the measure, unless there is a decisive auditory clue as to where one line leaves off and the next begins, verse ceases to be verse at all.

Johnson also chided Milton for frequently placing his pauses and sentence stops at less than three syllables from the end of a verse-line. His reasoning was based on the same assumption that each line must be an independent unit, with a pause functioning as the caesura does in the closed couplet; a stop nearer than three syllables to either end of a line thus isolates a fragment which is, in itself, metrically indeterminate. As a result, Johnson found such passages from *Paradise Lost* as this one to be lacking in harmony:

> First in the east his glorious lamp was seen
> Regent of day; and all the horizon round
> Invested with bright rays, jocund to run
> His longitude through heaven's high road; the gray
> Dawn, and the Pleiades, before him danced,
> Shedding sweet influence.

The two syllables "the gray," cut off from the earlier part of the line by a syntactic pause, are faulty, because "no part of a

2. *Life of Milton,* 192. My italics.

verse ought to be so separated from the rest as not to remain still more harmonious than prose, or to show, by the disposition of the tones, that it is part of a verse."[3]

This reading of meter suited Pope's couplets but was entirely inappropriate to Milton's blank verse, which relied equally on the verse-line and on the full sentence or paragraph, and which generated its characteristic metric energy by playing the pull towards closure of the single line against the drive for continuation of the larger syntactic unit. In his *Life of Milton* Johnson complained that "the variety of pauses, so much boasted by the lovers of blank verse changes the measures of an English poet to the periods of a declaimer."[4] To Johnson's way of reading, it is clear, the terminal disposition of Milton's pauses and stops either chops off unmetric fragments, or else enforces, not a tension between metric and syntactic units, but the total replacement of the verse-line by the sentence (the "period") as the structural element, and so relaxes a metric rhythm into a prose declamation. And that these prepossessions determined Johnson's writing, no less than his reading of verse, is made obvious by his blank-verse tragedy, *Irene*. Not only are the pauses mainly medial and the great majority of the lines studiously end-stopped; often each pair of lines are so isolated that they fall neatly into a closed-couplet structure:

> Then let me once, in honour of our sex,
> Assume the boastful arrogance of man.
> Th' attractive softness, and th' endearing smile,
> And pow'rful glance, 'tis granted are our own;
> Nor has impartial Nature's frugal hand
> Exhausted all her nobler gifts on you.
> Do not we share the comprehensive thought,

3. *Rambler* 90.
4. *Lives*, I.192.

> Th' enlivening wit, the penetrating reason?
> Beats not the female breast with gen'rous passions,
> The thirst of empire, and the life of glory?[5]

As we reconstruct Johnson's habits of reading, then, we begin to understand how he could be so sensitive and discerning before the poetry of Dryden and Pope, yet so seemingly obtuse before poetry built on different principles of figure and meter. The poems of most pre-Augustan writers, looked at through Johnson's spectacles, must have worn an aspect remote from that which is apparent to the trained reader of our own day. And the question suggests itself just what Shakespeare, for example, was like, when read through Johnson's explicit and tacit expectations regarding decorum, diction, metaphor, and versification.

Of course, Johnson praised Shakespeare more lavishly than he did any other writer, and we are tempted to say that Shakespeare's greatness overwhelmed Johnson's usual tastes and standards. Such an opinion, however, rests on a fallacy; it assumes that all who admire the same author admire him for the same reasons. The significant point is not that Johnson admired Shakespeare, but what he admired Shakespeare for. Johnson admired Shakespeare as the "poet that holds up to his readers a faithful mirror of manners and of life"; as an inventor of characters who "are the genuine progeny of common humanity"; as a writer of dialogue who "excels in accommo-

---

5. *Irene*, ii.vii, in *The Works of Samuel Johnson*, 1.65. The couplet-cadence emerges more clearly if we supply the rhymes:

> Then let me once, in honour of our sex,
> Presume your boastful arrogance to vex.
> Th' attractive softness, and th' endearing frown,
> And pow'rful glance, 'tis granted are our own;
> Nor has impartial Nature's frugal plan
> Exhausted all her nobler gifts on man.

dating his sentiments to real life"; as a thinker whose plays are filled "with practical axioms and domestick wisdom."[6] This is Shakespeare "the poet of nature," the creator of convincing character, the moralist; these elements of Shakespeare's dramas accorded both with Johnson's manner of reading and his critical principles, and they sufficed to win his highest commendation. But when Johnson spoke of the language and style of the dramatic poet, his judgements were much more qualified. He praised the "familiar dialogue" of Shakespeare's comedies as reflecting the durable style of "conversation above grossness, and below refinement," although he hastened to add that even this dialogue is "not wholly without ruggedness or difficulty." In tragedy, however, "whenever he solicits his invention, or strains his faculties, the offspring of his throes is tumour, meanness, tediousness, and obscurity." "In narration he affects a disproportionate pomp of diction, and a wearisome train of circumlocution," his set speeches "are commonly cold and weak," and he is not long "soft and pathetick" without succumbing to his fatal Cleopatra, "some idle conceit, or contemptible equivocation." "The style of Shakespeare was in itself ungrammatical, perplexed, and obscure."

> We fix our eyes upon his graces, and turn them from his deformities, and endure in him what we should in another loath or despise. . . . I have seen, in the book of some modern critick, a collection of anomalies, which show that he has corrupted language by every mode of depravation, but which his admirer has accumulated as a monument of honour.[7]

This is strong language. It is likely that we must interpret more literally than we have supposed Johnson's repeated affirmation

6. Preface to Shakespeare, *The Works of Samuel Johnson*, II.80–81.
7. *The Works of Samuel Johnson*, II.89–90, 92–94, 113–15.

that "Shakespeare never has six lines together without a fault."[8] The same skills which made Johnson's appreciation of Pope more discriminating than a modern reader may hope to match, contributed towards making Shakespeare out to be, stylistically, perhaps the most fallible genius ever to hold a pen.

Johnson, nevertheless, was one of our greatest critics, and many later critics have proved no less limited in the range of their perception, without matching Johnson's virtues of particularity and acuteness of vision and candor in judgement. If Johnson read Milton and Donne through the spectacles of Pope, Wordsworth and Coleridge read Pope through the spectacles of Milton, while more recent critics have read Wordsworth and Coleridge and Milton through the spectacles of Donne. The supposed relativism of poetic taste is in considerable part a relativity of reading skills to particular kinds of poetry; while it is the recurrent need to adapt our reading skills to poetic innovation which validates Wordsworth's pronouncement that "every great and original writer . . . must himself create the taste by which he is to be relished"—for, as Wordsworth adds, "he must teach the art by which he is to be *seen*."[9]

What a critic sees in poetry is the result, in Johnson's terms, of both "precept" and "habit"—in other words, of both his conscious principles and his established responses. If Johnson himself was not equally apt for all kinds of poetry, no more is any other reader. For there is no perfect critic, only more or less adequate critics. And a critic is adequate for his total task in proportion to the scope of his theory, the range of his experience in reading, and the degree to which his responses remain adaptive to unforeseeable literary possibilities.

8. *Life*, II.110–11.

9. Letter to Lady Beaumont, 21 May 1807, in *Wordsworth's Literary Criticism*, ed. Nowell C. Smith (1905), 54. My italics. Wordsworth attributes the thought to Coleridge; see also Essay supplementary to Preface (1815), *ibid.*, 195.

Personification Reconsidered

BERTRAND H. BRONSON

Probably no page of criticism in the English language is better known than that in which Dr. Johnson dispatches *Lycidas* to the limbo of failures of which the little life is feebly sustained by the reputation of their authors. Let us briefly recall the grounds of that notorious verdict. They are as follows. The poem affects a personal grief in terms which belie the fact. Taken literally, lines like "We drove afield . . . batt'ning our flocks" are merely untrue, and therefore arouse, and ought to arouse, no answering sympathy. Taken allegorically, "the true meaning is so uncertain and remote that it is never sought, because it cannot be known when it is found." The poem is filled with second-hand invention in the exhausted pastoral tradition, loaded with classical allusions "such as a College easily supplies," and indecently—not to say impiously—mingled with the sacred truths of Christianity. "Where there is leisure for fiction there is little grief . . . He who thus grieves will excite no sympathy; he who thus praises will confer no honour." It is this last pair of assertions to which we should particularly attend.

Admittedly, Milton's professed grief over his personal loss in the death of Edward King fails to stir much pity. We cannot and do not meet Johnson's objection with a contradiction. Rather, we tax him with obtuseness for not perceiving, or not acknowledging, that Milton's sincerity is vindicated on other, and subtler, grounds. Yet, after we have pointed out how wrong, because irrelevant, Johnson was, his objection, on its own terms, still stands: personal grief for a friend has no foothold here; and Edward King's human merits are not in this place exalted.

It is worthy of remark that Johnson's objections to *Lycidas* are further produced and illustrated in reverse by his own elegy on the death of Dr. Levet. That poem is a positive restatement and demonstration of his negative criticism of the great monody. Moreover, the contrast between the two poems is in the highest degree illuminating. With no "leisure for fiction" —no time for telling "of rough satyrs and fauns with cloven heel"—Johnson here sets himself squarely to the task of "conferring honour" by his lines, and expects, if successful, to excite sympathy from our common humanity. To achieve these ends, he first utters a general truth about the transitory nature of human pleasures, and then goes on to show where in general, and why, Levet will be especially missed. Without exaggerating Levet's knowledge, Johnson illustrates his fidelity in welldoing, in terms that must command universal assent to the man's merit. The reader's response is simply: "How admirable a being! how natural to lament his loss!" The formal contrast between this poem and *Lycidas* is perfect: the one an expression of deep personal loss, but stated in language so general that we merely infer the private grief as a natural part of the common experience; the other a medley of general themes miraculously blended under the guise of private grief, a "melodious tear" bewailing "a learned Friend unfortunatly drown'd in ... 1637," a grief asserted literally and figuratively, but nonexistent, or present only as a gently pervasive melancholy. In the one poem, pretence; in the other, reserve: artful pretence of a personal loss; and actual private grief masked in general statement.

The latter formula, of particular emotion conveyed in generalities, was powerfully evocative and convincing to Johnson's age, whilst the other was, for him at least, a mockery. If, apart from the unimaginable beauty of the verse, we of to-day prefer the Miltonic and find the Johnsonian statement relatively cold, the fact has far-reaching causes and implications. The major difficulty—for our own time, at any rate—of eighteenth-century poetry is here epitomized.

To predict that the uninformed reader, confronted for the first time by Johnson's poem in an anthology, will be but mildly impressed requires no great hardihood to-day. And the reason is already evident: Johnson has been at pains to put his particulars in the most general form. His success is registered in stanzas like the following:

> No summons mock'd by chill delay,
>   No petty gain disdain'd by pride,
> The modest wants of every day
>   The toil of every day supplied

To the modern reader, this of all forms of statement is the least tolerable. Esoteric obscurity, utter unintelligibility, were far to be preferred: and under personal agony (another's), our heads are bloody, but unbowed. But this, this is too removed from breathing reality. Give us the quickening particular, and let us for ourselves perceive within it the class.

In the face of so alien a mode, the instructor resorts to biographical annotation. He reads from Boswell; he explains the mutual dependence, the mutual respect, which subsisted between Johnson and Levet for a third of a century; he points out Johnson's freedom from snobbery in praising so justly, so nobly, so uncondescendingly his pensioner, the uneducated, inarticulate fellow who had picked up all he knew of medicine from waiting in a tavern frequented by doctors. Thus enlightened, our average reader softens to the poem: gradually his prejudices disappear, and he even likes it very much. He may reach the point—many have—where, from emotion, only with difficulty can he read the poem aloud.

What is the meaning of this little parable? Not, we suspect, that the eighteenth-century style has reached its mark; but rather that that style has been circumvented, been counteracted by having the receiving mind supplied with the facts which reduce all those generals to particulars. The actual focus of the mind's attention has subtly shifted to the vital and undeniably moving relationship that gave rise to the poem, and the poem itself now but serves as the door to recollection. It is doubtful if many readers to-day get beyond this point to a genuine and unforced enjoyment of the generalized style for its own sake.

The situation is curious. It is a truism that the eighteenth century was fond of abstractions, but we do not stop to realize what this truly means. What it usually means is that since, on the whole, to-day abstractions fail to move us, the aesthetic response of the eighteenth century, nourished on such things, must therefore have been relatively thin. This attitude is all but universal in critical writing from Wordsworth's time to our own. See, for example, how it underlies the position of even so sympathetic a critic as Thomas Quayle, writing recently of poetic style in the eighteenth century:

> In its groping after the "grand style," as reflected in a deliberate avoidance of accidental and superficial "particularities," and in its insistence on generalized or abstract forms, eighteenth century poetry, or at least the "neo-classical" portion of it, reflected its inability to achieve that intensity of imaginative conception which is the supreme need of all art.[1]

Now, so interpreted, the truism, or at least its corollary, may not be true at all—in fact, is almost demonstrably false. No inference, surely, is more unforced than this: that if eighteenth-

1. Thomas Quayle, *Poetic Diction* (1924), 13.

century poets labored long and hard to raise their immediate personal experiences and emotions to the most general statement, they did so because their keenest aesthetic delight lay in that direction. They were neither humanly incurious of, nor emotionally insensitive to, particulars, as almost any page of Boswell will prove; but personal statement gained force, conviction, vaster horizons, when lifted to the plateau of the general consensus. Force, conviction, and vaster horizons do not weaken effects for those who experience them. We work to-day in an opposite direction: we are, roughly speaking, insensitive to the *emotional* appeal of a general statement. This insensitivity, I suspect, is our characteristic weakness—meaning by *us* all who have been vitally affected by the intellectual drift of the last hundred and fifty years toward Egocentricity. Impartially considered, however, *under*valuation of the general statement has no more valid claim to be taken as an absolute in aesthetic judgement than has *over*valuation.

It may be objected that such undervaluation on our part has not been proved. Now it is next to impossible to be aware of one's own under- or over-evaluations—or those of one's own time—because these are precisely level with the sensibilities of ourselves or our age, and therefore fully experienced as valid: just as young persons are more alive than their elders to certain ideas and images, which come to them with emotional over tones to which at their years they are naturally peculiarly susceptible. We can never be truly aware of our over- or under-valuations until we have outgrown them, whether as individuals or as an age.

At any rate, waiving for the present any final judgement in the matter, the fact of an enormous "shift of sensibility" (Frederick Pottle's useful phrase) in the area under discussion is beyond dispute. We have moved from a taste for the abstract—which (in other than aesthetic fields) is often supposed a mark of maturity—to a preference for the concrete. The fact permeates all our judgements and makes it very difficult for us to meet the eighteenth century on its own ground, to experience aesthetic satisfactions comparable to theirs. Our responses all tend to show, so to put it, a negative displacement. With regard to poetry like that of Johnson, we are in a position analogous to Johnson's with regard to *Lycidas,* in that the basic sensitivity to an alien mode of expression is lacking to us as to him. It may be guessed that one day the pendulum will swing back. Meanwhile, it is a capital duty of criticism to be aware of this parallax, and to try by imaginative sympathy and understanding to allow for and correct the ever-present displacement. Nowhere, perhaps, is the necessity more acute than in the field of eighteenth-century personification; and to a consideration of that problem we may now address our attention.

Personification, as it relates to poetry, is one portion of the total field of metaphor. It is impossible to discover any valid distinction in kind between personification and metaphor in general, and it follows that critical acceptance or approval of metaphor entails similar acceptance of personification, as a metaphorical species. Metaphor is everywhere acknowledged as the core of poetic statement. Contemporary critics, as it happens, are intensively engaged in examining the nature and functions of metaphor; and this fact should indicate, among other possibilities, that the present age is acutely sensitive to metaphor. So, with varying emphasis, was the age of the Romantic poets and critics, Coleridge, Wordsworth, Hazlitt.

Now, whilst Coleridge taught us more perhaps than anyone else, before or since, about the nature of poetic language and the working of poetic imagination, most of what the Romantics had to say about personification was unfavourable. They inveighed against it, and although their greatest spokesmen

194

made clear by qualifications that the warnings were directed primarily against its abuse, the negative injunction has generally been taken in the widest sense, and the critical rule been everywhere solemnly deferred to and reinforced.

It is therefore worth pausing to insist upon the radical inseparability of personification from other kinds of metaphor. All, of course, rest on submerged similes. The blood kinship becomes self-evident, however, if we set examples side by side. Here is Blake's description of the Charity-school children:

O what a multitude they seem'd, these flowers of London town!

Conversely, Herrick addresses violets in this manner:

> Welcome, Maids of Honour,
>   You doe bring
>   In the Spring;
> And wait upon her . . .
>
> Yet though thus respected,
>   By and by
>   Ye doe lie,
> Poore Girles, neglected.

Once again, Herrick writes:

> There's not a *budding* Boy, or Girle, this day,
> But is got up, and gone to bring in May.

It is obvious that the first two figures are basically identical, the same equation being implicit in each. In the one it is "Children equal Flowers"; in the other, "Flowers (violets) equal Children (girls)." In the third example, the propriety of the epithet, *budding*, is dependent upon the same proposition. We may call the first a case of metonymy, the third a metaphorical descriptive adjective, and reserve the name personification for

195

the second alone; but it is obvious that these distinctions are merely technical and superficial. Nor, fundamentally, does it matter whether the analogy be conveyed by means of noun, verb, adverb, or adjective. We may complete the present series by setting the budding boys and girls over against a *weeping* willow, where the name implies a forgotten but not obliterated personification.

If we turn to abstractions, the same process is evident: for examples, Marvell's "vegetable love"; Cleopatra's

> For his bounty,
> There was no winter in't; an autumn 'twas,
> That grew the more by reaping;

Rückert's

> Du bist die Ruh,
> Der Friede mild,
> Die Sehnsucht du,
> Und was sie stillt;

Vaughan's

> If thou canst get but thither,
> There growes the flowre of peace,
> The Rose that cannot wither;

Collins'

> Spring, with dewy Fingers cold,
> Returns to deck their hallow'd Mold.

And when we speak of a "coming-out party," we make use of an abstract concept which doubtless contains embedded in it the radical image of springtime budding—of a flower "newly springing," as Jeremy Taylor would say, "from the clefts of its hood."

In view of these vital interconnections, we need, when confronted by the Romantics' hostility to personification, to take some critical bearings. Are we to go on believing that metaphor is necessary and wholesome, but that personification, a portion of metaphor, is a slow poison, of which, they say, the eighteenth-century poets eventually died? It will be best to return to the laboratory and review our analyses in the hope of surer guidance. Some indulgence must be craved for so academic—not to say pedantic—an exercise. But without it, I fear, we cannot profitably proceed.

The threshold of personification is not by any means easy to fix. Initial distinguishing marks, in English, are indications of sex and active (as opposed to passive) qualifying, whether by noun-appositive, adjective, verb, or adverb. Apostrophe is one of the commonest and simplest ways of marking the intention. It will be generally agreed that personification ought to be perceptible through the ear as well as through the eye; and this raises the question of capitalization, which cannot be disposed of in an easy phrase.

Coleridge ran afoul of Gray's lines,

> In gallant trim the gilded vessel goes,
> Youth at the prow and pleasure at the helm,

on the ground that "it depended wholly on the compositor's putting, or not putting, a small capital . . . whether the words should be personifications, or mere abstractions."[2] It is certainly difficult to deduce from eighteenth-century practice any consistent principles of capitalization; but a few observations may be hazarded on this subject. In the first place, up to at least the middle of the century, in the more carefully and elegantly printed books, it was a widespread convention to capitalize *all*

2. *Biographia Literaria*, ch. I.

nouns.[3] Moreover, while this practice of capitalization remained a general habit, there was obviously no compulsion upon the reader to think personification whenever he saw a capital. Now, Gray's own MS of the first draft of his *Elegy* proves that he was in the habit of capitalizing *every* noun. In this respect there is an utter lack of correspondence between his MSS and the earliest and most authoritative printed texts. It follows that he was indifferent to the capitalization of his poems, and left the matter entirely to his printer. His own sense of personification, therefore, was quite independent of typographical distinction: so that the reader is at liberty to import just so much of a sense of personification as he feels appropriate to the particular case, and neither more nor less. When Gray wrote:

> Let not Ambition mock their useful toil,
> Their rustic joys and destiny obscure:
> Nor Grandeur hear with a disdainful smile
> The short and simple annals of the poor,

he capitalized Toil, Joys, Destiny, Smile, Annals, and Poor, as well as Ambition and Grandeur; but the edition of 1768, by reducing all but the last two to lower case, puts for us an entirely misleading and disproportionate emphasis on the per-

---

3. Where this custom was consistently observed, it made possible refinements in meaning which later were lost to view. Thus, for example, in the first edition of Parnell's *A Night-Piece on Death*, where almost without exception the nouns are capitalized, occur the lines:
> ... think, as softly-sad you tread
> Above the venerable Dead,
> Time was, like thee they Life possest,
> And Time shall be, that thou shalt Rest.

Here the capitalization of *Rest* proves that word a noun, and the whole couplet is knit together with a parallelism—"they formerly possessed life, thou shalt possess rest"—which gives an antithetical force to the thought, lost (I believe) in every later printing.

sonifications, one which there is no evidence to show that Gray intended. But even this later text, could we read it, as Gray did, with a capitalizing habit of mind, would not obtrude its personifications upon us as it does to-day.[4] The personifications are there, to be sure, in any typographical dress, but they were not intended to clamor for attention. Coleridge's objection, therefore, is doubly answered: first, Gray does not base his personifications on a typographical device; and, second, it matters not at all to Gray whether Coleridge or another decide to take the words as personifications, or as "mere abstractions." Why not Personifabstractions? Let the reader determine the proportions to suit his taste. Must we have always thwacking full-bodied personifications? In the Realms of Gold, has an edict gone forth to slay all but the most robust inhabitants? Surely, no. It is time, after a hundred and fifty years, to try anew to make a few simple distinctions between sorts of personification.

First, then, I shall distinguish between two main classes, object-personification and abstract-personification. The conferring of primary human attributes upon an object or objects inanimate, or animate but non-human, constitutes the first class. For example, Wordsworth's "Earth fills her lap with pleasures of her own." An older convention would also include here invocation of the dead or the absent, as Wordsworth's "Milton, thou shouldst be living at this hour!" The other main class, the abstract-personification, may be exemplified by Wordsworth's

> Truth fails not; but her outward forms that bear
> The longest date do melt like frosty rime, &c.

4. It is perhaps worth remark that our disregard of the capitals which commence every line of conventionally printed verse is a current analogy for the state of mind here desiderated. The German convention is of course another. By Coleridge's day, the older capitalizing habit had been all but universally abandoned in printing.

Now, each of these classes can be legitimately divided into two sorts which, it appears to me, are genuinely distinct in kind, apart from the degree to which they may be elaborated. Differences of degree[5] I forbear to categorize, as being impossible to sustain except in the most obvious instances. The difference in kind which I seek to establish holds equally for object- and abstract-personification. It is a difference which I shall discriminate by the terms *non-restrictive* and *restrictive*. I have in mind the distinction between a personification which imposes no particular image, apart from what may be felt by the reader as inherent in the personified concept, and a particularizing, or restrictive, characterization—the arbitrary bestowal of an image or pictorial figure upon the concept, which acts as a limitation controlling our imaginative freedom. A few examples will, I trust, clarify the distinction.

When Wordsworth writes, "The river glideth at his own sweet will," he is personifying in such a way as to allow us to continue to see the river as a river. This is a non-restrictive object-personification. Another is "Fair Star of evening . . . on the horizon's brink Thou hangest, stooping" etc. Another is the same poet's coy Primrose of the Rock:

> So blooms this lonely Plant, nor dreads
> Her annual funeral.

Or, once more,

> The moon doth with delight
> Look round her when the heavens are bare.

Similarly, a non-restrictive *abstract*-personification is Wordsworth's Nature, in "Three years she grew":

5. For example, Dr. Hugh Blair's "The first is, when some of the properties or qualities of living creatures are ascribed to inanimate objects; the second, when those inanimate objects are introduced as acting like such as have life; and the third, when they are represented, either as speaking to us, or as listening to what we say to them." *Lectures on Rhetoric*, lecture XVI (1813), I, 377.

> Then Nature said, "A lovelier flower" ...
> "This child I to myself will take.
> Myself will to my darling be
> Both law and impulse" ...
> Thus Nature spake—the work was done.

Or, again, his abstraction Immortality, in the *Ode*:

> Thou, over whom thy Immortality
> Broods like the day ...
> A presence which is not to be put by.

Now, when, on the contrary, Wordsworth particularizes his characterization of Earth in the following fashion:

> even with something of a mother's mind ...
> The homely nurse doth all she can
> To make her foster-child ...
> Forget the glories he hath known ...

he is making a restrictive object-personification. Similarly, when he addresses Duty as "Stern Daughter of the Voice of God," and continues:

> thou dost wear
> The Godhead's most benignant grace;
> Nor know we anything so fair
> As is the smile upon thy face,—

he asks us to picture the abstraction in a special form; and this is an example of restrictive abstract-personification.

Within these four types, I believe all instances of personification can be comprised—and it is a peculiar pleasure to be able to find illustrations of all the four in Wordsworth. Whilst it would, of course, be easy to continue subdividing and refining, these broad divisions are possibly sufficient. Since they are not determined according to degree of intensity or of elaboration, they allow for the utmost variety in these latter respects, and are comparatively objective.

I am anxious not to becloud these clear and, as I believe, unforced distinctions with qualifications and debatable border-
line cases. But it would be less than candid not to acknowledge
that the different kinds may be found in combination, and
sometimes shading into one another. If we bear in mind that
the non-restrictive figure characterizes *within* the normal field
of the concept, whilst the restrictive tends to characterize *outside* that field, we can usually agree on a particular case. Thus,
when Thomson conjures up a "bright patrol" of virtues,
among which are "Courage composed and keen" and "sound
Temperance, healthful in heart and look," we have little hesitation in calling them non-restrictive, for the epithets merely
reinforce the sense of the abstract, and may therefore be said
to lie within its proper sphere of definition. But when Milton
writes "speckl'd Vanity," he is characterizing beyond the normal or intrinsic range of definition, and is thus creating a restrictive personification. Again, when Thomson introduces
"Activity untired, with copious life informed, and all awake,"
we may confidently classify the figure as non-restrictive; but
there might be doubt about "rough Industry," or "white
Peace," or "undaunted Truth." One may venture the guess that
the personifications most likely to give offence will generally
be found, not among the bare personified abstractions like
Gray's "Youth at the prow, and Pleasure at the helm," which
every reader may take at his own pictorial level, but among the
non-restrictive abstracts which have been elaborated with the
semblance, but not the substance, of restrictive characterization.[6] These are usually flabby figures that have to be energized

6. It is, however, to be acknowledged that restrictive personifications,
carried to an extreme, have their own peculiar odor of over-ripeness. Léon
Morel noted an instance in Congreve's Ode *On Mrs Arabella Hunt, Sing-
ing*, of which one is tempted to remark, Ripeness is all:

And lo! Silence himself is here.
Methinks I see the Midnight God appear,

—if they can be—by the reader's own unaided effort; and they are probably responsible for much of the special insipidity of dilution which permeates too great a proportion of second- and third-rate eighteenth-century verse. For offensive example, the following pseudo-restrictive figure of Thomson may stand pre-eminent:

> While in the radiant front, superior shines
> That first paternal virtue, public Zeal;
> Who throws o'er all an equal wide survey,
> And, ever musing on the common weal,
> Still labours glorious with some great design.

Yet another sort of elaboration, blindly stumbling between restrictive and non restrictive object-personification, is exemplified by the passage immediately following the one just quoted. When Thomson proceeds, "Low walks the sun," the personification is evident, and the verb lends a restrictive force; but when he adds, "and broadens by degrees," the figure of a walker is withdrawn in favor of a more literal delineation; yet the verb is sufficiently neutral to allow of an animistic re-

---

> In all his downy pomp arrayed,
> Behold the rev'rend shade:
> An ancient sigh he sits upon,
> Whose memory of sound is long since gone,
> And purposely annihilated for his throne.
> Beneath, two soft transparent clouds do meet,
> In which he seems to sink his softer feet.
> A melancholy thought, condensed to air,
> Stol'n from a lover in despair,
> Like a thin mantle, serves to wrap
> In fluid folds his visionary shape.
> A wreath of darkness round his head he wears,
> Where curling mists supply the want of hairs,
> While the still vapours, which from poppies rise,
> Bedew his hoary face, and lull his eyes.

siduum. The next sentence re-establishes the latent human image with a new and positively restrictive force: the sun becomes a king assuming his state with ceremonial display, and a supplementary restrictive personification gives reinforcement:

> The shifting clouds
> Assembled gay, a richly gorgeous train,
> In all their pomp attend his setting throne.

This picture is completed by a three-fold non-restrictive object-personification:

> Air, earth, and ocean smile immense.

But hereupon we begin to perceive that idle decoration is the sum of Thomson's intention; for he continues:

> And now,
> As if his weary chariot sought the bowers
> Of Amphitrite and her tending nymphs,
> (So Grecian fable sung)—

the whole sequence thus far being from walking to fattening to sitting on a setting throne—no! say rather, playing Apollo on a weary chariot!—and, by this declension, to sea-bathing and, we surmise, drowning. For, momentarily regaining rotundity,

> he dips his orb;
> Now half-immersed; and now a golden curve
> Gives one bright glance, then total disappears.

A consummation unlamented. Observe the retreat from restrictive to non-restrictive in "he dips his *orb*," and the desperate snatch at a final non-restrictive compromise in the curious

> now a golden curve
> Gives one bright glance,

where the swimmer's head is depersonified to a geometrical shape, but a shape still human enough to cast a dazzling look of farewell. This exercise of decorative ingenuity will sufficiently illustrate the fluctuations that are possible between the restrictive and non-restrictive in object-personification. And now, with a clearer notion of the varieties of personification, we may revert to more general considerations.

The affiliations and ramifications of personification are so numerous and far-flung, even in literary expression alone, and apart from connections with other arts, that if we were to list them we should not soon have done. Personification is inseparably involved with myth, with fable, with allegory, satire, the morality play, the masque, the comedy of humours, the type "character." The personifying impulse is in fact a radical tendency of the human psyche in all stages of culture; it is embedded in the very roots of language itself; it is basic to every impulse towards dramatic representation. To condemn it is not merely to impugn the value of many of the most important literary forms, to which it is ancillary or essential, but to be guilty of the folly of King Canute. Yet depreciation of it, depreciation both general and particular, continues along various lines to this day.

It has, for example, been disparaged on moral or ethical grounds. In a famous passage which is probably the *locus classicus* of critical commentary in this field, Ruskin has written as follows:

> It is to be noted that personification is, in some sort, the reverse of symbolism, and is far less noble. Symbolism is the setting forth of a great truth by an imperfect and inferior sign (as, for instance, of the hope of the resurrection by the form of the phoenix); and it is almost always em-

ployed by men in their most serious moods of faith, rarely in recreation. Men who use symbolism forcibly are almost always true believers in what they symbolize. But Personification is the bestowing of a human or living form upon an abstract idea: it is, in most cases, a mere recreation of the fancy, and is apt to disturb the belief in the reality of the thing personified. Thus symbolism constituted the entire system of the Mosaic dispensation: it occurs in every word of Christ's teaching; it attaches perpetual mystery to the last and most solemn act of His life. But I do not recollect a single instance of personification in any of His words. And as we watch, thenceforward, the history of the Church, we shall find the declension of its faith exactly marked by the abandonment of symbolism, and the profuse employment of personification,—even to such extent that the virtues came, at last, to be confused with the saints...[7]

Thus Ruskin, although he admits that in the earlier phases of the Renaissance the fashion has been loftily used. This passage has more than once of late been cited with whole-hearted or modified approval; but nowhere have I seen it examined with any attention.

Now, certainly, in so far as the utterance contrasts personification with symbolism, it is an egregious piece of special pleading. Upon what principle could one prove personification "far less noble" than symbolism? How can it be determined, *a priori*, that the bestowing of a human or living form upon an abstract idea is "less noble" than the setting forth of a great truth by an imperfect and inferior sign? Is it not manifest that Ruskin's opposition lies solely between a *great* truth and an idea presumably minuscule? Which, of course, is logically ir-

7. *Stones of Venice*, Vol. II, ch. 8 (The Ducal Palace), section LV.

relevant. Unhappily, symbolism is potentially, and has ever been actually, as prompt to serve in the promulgation of any diabolical doctrine, for example Nazism, as of the highest truths. It is equally obsequious to the barber, the pander, and the pawnbroker. It readily provokes scorn of the good and every mischievous prejudice. It has no morals apart from those of its employer. And, on the other side, personification is equally neutral; nor is its sincerity, or the lack of that quality, inherent in its constitution, but in the use to which it is put. And that use may be of the loftiest kind. Ruskin might have bethought him that not merely in Renaissance art, but in the general conception of mankind, God Himself is a personification:—*Him*self, without impiety I say.

How, moreover, can this distinction in kind be ultimately sustained? When Fra Angelico shows us God the Father, he is personifying an idea; but is he not, at the same time, setting forth a great truth by an imperfect and inferior sign? Is not Botticelli's Truth, in the allegorical painting, "The Calumny of Apelles," a noble or exalted representation of the ideal, if yet inferior in the sense of more restricted; nevertheless, in fact both a symbol and a personification? (And for whom, we ask incidentally, would the representation disturb belief in the reality of the idea personified?) In truth, symbol and personification are not opposites. The two terms are not even commensurate, for the one includes and transcends the other. Symbol is a term which easily contains personification and much else: a personification is but one among many kinds of symbol.

Recently, however, Ruskin's distinction between symbol and personification has been taken up by C. S. Lewis, in his valuable book, *The Allegory of Love*, and subtly elaborated in a somewhat different direction, allegory taking the place of simple personification in his discussion. "On the one hand," he writes, you can start with an immaterial fact, such as the passions which you actually experience, and can then invent *visibilia* to express them. If you are hesitating between an angry retort and a soft answer, you can express your state of mind by inventing a person called *Ira* with a torch and letting her contend with another invented person called *Patientia*. This is allegory . . . But there is another way of using the equivalence [between the immaterial and the material], which is almost the opposite of allegory, and which I would call sacramentalism or symbolism. If our passions, being immaterial, can be copied by material inventions, then it is possible that our material world in its turn is the copy of an invisible world. As the god Amor and his figurative garden are to the actual passions of men, so perhaps we ourselves and our 'real' world are to something else. The attempt to read that something else through its sensible imitations, to see the archetype in the copy, is what I mean by symbolism or sacramentalism . . . The difference between the two can hardly be exaggerated. The allegorist leaves the given—his own passions—to talk of that which is confessedly less real, which is a fiction. The symbolist leaves the given to find that which is more real. To put the difference in another way, for the symbolist it is we who are the allegory . . . Symbolism is a mode of thought, but allegory is a mode of expression. It belongs to the form of poetry, more than to its content.[8]

Now it is impossible not to feel at once in this analysis the edge of a very keen intelligence, or to deny to the distinction here emphasized a large measure of plausibility. On general grounds, it is much to be desired that a distinction so clear-cut

8. *The Allegory of Love* (1936), 44–48.

should if possible be adopted. Yet I think that before we give ourselves to it wholly, we should try what weight it will bear.

For myself, I confess I am troubled at being asked to start by agreeing that the passions which I actually experience are immaterial facts in comparison to the allegorical figures I may invent to represent them. I find it hard not rather to regard the figures as idealizations of my states of mind, idealizations which may have a general pertinency and validity for all men who may be suffering the like emotions under whatever particular circumstances. I incline to regard these idealizations as in the nature of archetypes or archetypal images, of which my own and other men's experiences offer particular illustration. In the sense in which the Platonist can maintain that the ideal is more real than the world of phenomena, it is surely possible for the allegorist to claim that what he is seeking to portray is precisely that ideal world. And the firmer the hold which this visionary world takes upon his imagination, the more deeply rooted, pure, and satisfying will be the reflected images. In what sense, then, does he differ from Lewis' symbolist, who "leaves the given to find that which is more real"?

If, moreover, we consent to the proposition that "Symbolism is a mode of thought, but allegory is a mode of expression," it still has to be pointed out that a mode of thought is not operative in art until it has found utterance in a valid mode of artistic expression. If this be true, symbolism and allegory cannot thus be contrasted as opposites. The true opposite of allegory is naturalism, these two modes being at the extremes of the scale of expression. Symbolism, as a mode of thought, may therefore employ either extreme at will. The symbolist who is sufficiently convinced that we are the allegorical representatives, the "personifications" and "abstractions" of the world of reality, may give himself over to the task of depicting the natural world, secure in the conviction that the more faithfully he portrays this world, the closer he will come to the ultimate verities. Indeed, naturalism, consistently pushed towards meaningful ends, aspires to symbolism. And it is no accident, in turn, that the Symbolist Movement, so called, has been so deeply enmeshed in sense impression.

On the other hand, the symbolist may with equal propriety make use of allegory as a mode of expression. His choice of this mode or that will ultimately be determined, or at least profoundly affected, by the measure of his metaphysical assurance or religious faith. Granted sufficient confidence in the validity of his idealistic vision of reality, he may resort to allegory as the readiest means of conveying his positive affirmations, or, conversely, to satire as the negative expression of the same beliefs. Naturalism, on the contrary, is the mode of a symbolist who is uncertain about the ultimate significance of his symbols; sure only—or at worst merely hopeful—that they have a meaning, that they are veritable symbols. The truth, he feels, is latent in the phenomena, but inextricable.

Inherent in symbol is the idea of exchange, of one thing put for another. To employ it successfully, one must be familiar with its exchange value. This is at once the source of its weakness and of its strength. For the initiate, it can be shorthand for a whole congeries of conceptual meanings. Allusion to a Joseph, a Daniel, or a Babbitt may convey a wealth of significance. But to the uninitiated it means nothing. Of what effect is the Christian symbol mentioned with such approval by Ruskin, of the phoenix to figure the hope of resurrection, if we have no previous acquaintance with that intention? Or of a fish to suggest the Messiah? And it will be admitted that a symbol of which *no one* knows the meaning is of no more use than a hieroglyphic inscription without the Rosetta Stone.

The symbolist, therefore, who makes use of naturalism is faced with a serious dilemma. Although regarding all mankind as involuntary personifications or symbols of reality, he yet, of course, is limited to particular examples. The instances, taken together, constitute a sort of symbolic shorthand which neither he nor anyone else can translate into any other terms. By the very definition of his chosen method, all he can do is to describe what has been observed (*tranche de vie*). In so far as his figures are genuinely symbolic, they must be abstractly significant: that is, they are particulars standing for a general. They are types—but typical of what? In sober truth and strict logic, not typical at all. The total, infinite sum of such particulars would indeed together make an image, or type, of the phenomenal world. But the individual cases, by themselves, illustrate only the generalization—if indeed even this—that if in every contributory detail this particular configuration of phenomena could be duplicated, the result would be identical: an affirmation of little use or significance. A is all A's—but there is only one A.

How comes it then that we can be continually speaking with assurance of this or that figure in a naturalistic novel or play as a "typical" character? Is it not in every case because we ourselves, instinctively turning allegorists or personifiers, reduce these figures to embodiments of one or two predominant traits, or qualities; so that, as they pass current from mind to mind, they have no more three-dimensional actuality than what attaches to a personified abstraction—which is exactly what they have become: eponymous personified abstractions. But it is we who have created the symbol out of the original uniqueness and complexity; and, be it well observed, the symbol does not stand for that original figure, but for a class the members of which, in common with the original, all prominently exhibit some characteristic trait. When we call someone a Shylock, we think of the exacting of the pound of flesh, not of those qualities of racial and paternal pride and bitterness which make of

Shakespeare's creation a terrible and pathetic human individual; his use as symbol is restricted to the bare outline of an idea.

Almost automatically, therefore, and quite involuntarily, we find ourselves back in the world of idealized abstractions, where the mind is more at home, and where alone, perhaps, the multiplicity of experience can be brought to terms and made endurable. For we are so constituted that we have to make generals of our particulars or be drowned in the flood of phenomena.

If, then, we have to make eponymous personified abstractions out of naturalistic characters before they can become symbolic, the question arises: what advantage is served by leaving to such haphazard and roundabout means the achieving of a necessary end? For if the character is subtly and complexly portrayed, there is a likelihood that our secondary operations upon it will not coincide to produce an image identical or closely similar to that in the minds of others. Your Hamlet may not be mine; and if we are referring to him as a kind of character, as a "Hamlet," we must first sit down to definitions. As symbol, he is unsatisfactory: he will not easily circulate as ready currency because his value is too disputable. The simpler characters, flat, two-dimensional, are more serviceable, because already closer to personified abstractions. All that they lack is the label itself; which anyone may easily supply who knows their story; or which may even be suggested by a descriptive, Dickensian name.

Art has many legitimate uses for counters which are minted with a recognizable face value. The bestowing of a self-explanatory label is a device of great efficiency and economy. It obviates the inconvenient necessity of an initial reading to discover significance. It anticipates and prevents doubt of intention. It makes for a clarity of statement more precise than can be achieved by undenominated symbols. It advances upon and occupies the positions of an argumentative or expositional statement or series of propositions with a suddenness never approached by naturalistic methods, and clinches these with the force of logic—witness *Everyman*. Where the artist's meaning, in the sense of intellectual idea, is clear and unambiguous, and where also the focus of his attention is beyond the world of physical phenomena, he will instinctively employ the device of named abstractions in allegorical configuration. The religious and moral convictions of the Middle Ages made allegory, therefore, a natural mode of artistic utterance, and the ethical and intellectual convictions of the Age of Locke were to do the same for the simpler configurations of personified abstraction. An artist sure of what he wishes to say about the nature of the ordered, ideal world will not wait for chance and our own random inclinations to lead us to his meaning. Like Spenser, he will seek his goal by a more immediate and certain route. Rather than rely on our clumsy, hit-or-miss abstractions from phenomenal representation, he will invent his own personifications, give them appropriate and transparent names, and set them in motion to express his doctrine. For allegory is the most forthright method that we know, of conveying an ethical message in dramatic representational form.

Partly for that reason the method has latterly been unpopular—though there are signs of change in the air. Of the two extremes, explicit statement ("moral") and implication ("meaning"—our current fashionable name for "moral"), the Scylla and Charybdis between which the artist is always trying to steer, one seems a greater peril in one age, the other in another. Oppressed with the riddle of the world, yet afraid to be called naïve, the modern author shuns the first risk, of forthright statement, preferring intentional, and he hopes sophisticated, obscurity. His readers may even read more meaning into his work than he himself is able to see. If not, who can say that

that is not the reader's fault? Are we not already blessed with seven types of ambiguity? and who knows how many more remain to be disclosed?

Thus it is argued to-day that explicit statement is a relatively inferior and immature form of expression. Allen Tate has given positive and vigorous voice to this point of view in the following passage:

> The kind of poetry that is primarily allegorical . . . because its primary direction is towards that oversimplification of life which is the mark of the scientific will . . . is a one-sided poetry, ignoring the whole vision of experience . . . When the preponderance of meanings receives from the author himself the seal of his explicit approval, in face of the immense complication of our experience, then the work . . . is written in the interest of social, moral, and religious ideas apart from which it has neither existence nor significance. And it is aesthetic creation at a low level of intensity . . . the characters, images, symbols, ideas, are simple, and invite restatement in a paraphrase that exhausts their meaning; they stand, not in themselves, but merely for something else. The *Faerie Queene* belongs to this class of allegory . . . The narrative lacks inner necessity; it is pure illustration.[9]

Although the clarity of this statement excites admiration, its judgements raise a fundamental question. When it is said that a work of art has inner necessity, what in reality is the nature of the claim? Is it that the content of the work is literally the complex expression of antecedent and concomitant pressures of time and space, cause and effect and event, differing in no respect from actuality in the phenomenal world? If so, art

9. *Reactionary Essays* (1936), 89–91.

and life are indistinguishable, and *The Faerie Queene* has as much "inner necessity" as anything else, being like all else the involuntary resultant of universal forces. But clearly, this is not the critic's meaning: we have pushed his "inner necessity" too far when we equate it with physical actuality. It is, then, an imitation of such actuality. Such inner necessity as it can claim is the author's own contribution, the result of his shaping intention. It reflects a selection from various possibilities in accordance with his total purpose. It is therefore inevitably his reading of existence. Now, in what sense is all this not equally true of Spenser's allegory? It comes to this: that Tate is here expressing merely his personal inability to share in Spenser's kind of vision, preferring complications of a more naturalistic order. But why "a low level of intensity"? Has Tate read accurately the temperature of Spenser's imagination? Or shall we say that a documentary transcript from the diffuse phenomenal world, in Zola or Dreiser, is by its mere nature more "intense" than the simplicity of allegory? Is the play of haphazard circumstance necessarily more "intense" than the thrust or pull of two equal and opposite forces—say, duty and desire?

On the contrary, it is possible to hold that allegory is a more advanced form of intellectual and artistic expression than naturalism. Just as on the physical level it requires a concentration of will and effort to drive a road through the jungle, so in the world of the mind, it requires a greater intellectual and imaginative effort to divine or perceive order within the chaotic multiplicity of consciousness, and to represent that ideality with power and beauty, than to reproduce, even with high fidelity, our chaotic impressions and responses to the phenomenal world. Every such act is a reclamation, a little fiat in the divine image, and is entitled, if any aspect of our mental life has such a right, to be called mature. And this is Spenser's achievement. His subject, as Janet Spens very properly reminds us, is "the apprehension, description and organization of the inner world."[1] Being Elizabethan, he "tends to utter his more intense emotions through the imagery of human figures," having inherited the medieval view of reality as "a personal God fully reflected in miniature in man and faintly and partially in the different elements of the physical universe."[2] With man in a position of such pivotal importance, Spenser's primary concern is, as Miss Spens well says, "not so much with the sensuous fact as with the mental translation of the fact—with the use which the soul's faculty makes of the impact and stir of the physical sensation . . . He cared more for the artificial than for nature, because in the artifact the sensuous element is more visibly held in solution by the concept."[3]

An analogy may help to throw this question of relative sophistication between allegory and naturalism into clearer focus. Ruskin noted with disapproval the fact that as the hour of the Renaissance grew later, the tendency to personification increased, until the abstract virtues tended to become confused with the saints; so that, in the later litanies, we actually "find St. Faith, St. Hope, St. Charity, and St. Chastity, invoked immediately after St. Clara and St. Bridget."[4] Now, there are two ways of interpreting these data. We may take them, as Ruskin does, as an indication of the decline of faith. Or we may infer a gradually increasing awareness, a sharpening sense, purifying itself from association with particular persons and acts, of the loveliness and beauty of the abstract idea of these moral virtues—a sense which finally elevated them to a reality for the spiritual life no less vivid and vital than that of the human beings who in the historic or legendary past had

1. *Spenser's Faerie Queene* (1934), 52.
2. *Ibid.*, 55, 56.
3. *Ibid.*, 70.
4. *Loc. cit.*

aspired to exemplify similar virtues in their own lives. It may be thought a loftier, a more adult procedure, to sanctify the pure idea of a virtue than to sanctify a virtuous man or woman. This tendency may be taken as an index of increasing spirituality, if not in the Church, then in the minds of men.

Opportunely, C. S. Lewis' discussion of the beginnings of monotheism provides us with a second analogy. At first, he reminds us, we find a polytheistic universe, in which claims and counterclaims are made for various divinities, rivals in power and worship. The more popular divinities gradually assume the attributes of the lesser, and the hierarchy simplifies towards the point where relatively few gods stand as the presiding genii of particular areas of activity. The goal was never quite reached of a perfectly consistent and non-conflicting hierarchy, but the tendency in that direction was not arrested. Polytheism led inevitably to further simplification and to unification. Monotheism was the natural issue.

> The best minds [says Lewis] embrace monotheism. What is to be done with the gods of the popular religion? The answer—or at least that form of the answer which concerns us most—was given by the Stoics. 'Deus pertinens per naturam cuiusque rei, per terras Ceres, per maria Neptunus, alii per alia, poterunt intelligi.' [Cicero, *De natura deorum*]—where the very construction *Deus poterunt* hits off the corresponding state of mind to a nicety. The gods are to be aspects, manifestations, temporary or partial embodiments of the single power. They are, in fact, personifications of the abstracted attributes of the One.[5]

In this way, the older gods are, so to put it, spiritualized into the virtues and powers of God Himself. The advance in point

5. *Allegory of Love*, 57.

of intellectual and spiritual maturity is in no need of demonstration.

Now, between these instances of progress and the point at issue there is a manifest parallel. Just as, in the person of saint and pagan god, we find the imperfect and mixed embodiment of an abstract quality which we are enabled, by increasing intellectual and moral growth, to isolate and conceive in its pure essentiality, so likewise, in the naturalistic depiction of the finite individual, we find the potential symbol which, first by instinctive simplification and then by deliberate refinement, we may transform to a pure distillation, an abstract of the essential quality or idea. Such will be the personified abstraction, constituting the entity to be interwoven in narrative or dramatic context with other kindred entities, and forming with these the full-blown allegory. The intellectual and imaginative achievement of such a transformation is an affirmation of maturity, not immaturity. Hence a recent writer, in a highly provocative comparison of Elizabethan dramatic conventions with the hampering restraints of modern realistic drama, can roundly declare that the Elizabethan mind "had not been warped by the naïve incredulity of scientific naturalism."[6]

So lately as 1924, in a study sympathetic in the main to the eighteenth century, Thomas Quayle comes into collision with the abstractions of the neo-classical poets. He speaks of the prevalence of abstraction as a "contagion" and a "mania" in that school.[7] The personified abstractions, he says (p. 164), are "faint and faded relics" of medieval allegory. In this attitude, he is obviously at one with Wordsworth in the famous Preface

6. S. L. Bethell, *Shakespeare and the Popular Dramatic Tradition* (1944), 87.

7. *Poetic Diction* (1924), 139, 146.

of 1800. Wordsworth, we remember well, professes to reject these figures on the ground that they "do not make any natural or regular part of [the] language of men": he wishes "to keep the Reader in the company of flesh and blood."

The discussion in the foregoing pages will have served to remind us that we cannot so cavalierly dispose of the matter. We realize that there are losses as well as gains in the abandonment of this mode of expression—losses especially in clarity of aim, in precision and economy of statement. We have seen that any general attack is likely to involve itself in contradiction and inconsistency.

But, again, Quayle is not innocent of the assumption that the presence or absence of personification is determined by the depth and intensity of the poet's emotion—and this in inverse ratio. Thus, on the positive side, he finds that Johnson as a rule was saved from the danger of indulging in such figures "by the depth of feeling with which he unfolds the individual examples chosen to enforce his moral lessons."[8] In some of Young's evocations he finds "a tinge of personal emotion which invests these shadowy figures with something of a true lyrical effect."[9]

It was implied at the start that the bulk of historical evidence lies in the opposite direction. The proof of a lack of personal emotion cannot justly or safely be deduced from the hostile response of a later day; nor is such a lack in the least suggested by the presence of a liking so widespread that it can be called the "mania" of an age. On the contrary, when we listen to explicit statements on the subject by men of that time, we find, as we ought logically to expect, a very different sort of language. Goldsmith, for example—or whoever wrote his fifteenth essay—enumerates the devices of poetry that

8. *Ibid.*, 140.
9. *Ibid.*, 138.

"serve to animate the whole, and distinguish the glowing effusions of real inspiration from the cold efforts of mere science"; and of these resources he puts "above all, the enchanting use of the prosopopoeia, which is a kind of magic, by which the poet gives life and motion to every inanimate part of nature."[1]

The crucial question thus inescapably obtrudes itself, and we can no longer avoid it. Why did the eighteenth century derive such extreme satisfaction from a device which the nineteenth and twentieth centuries have joined to execrate as frigid and lifeless?

Fully to answer this query would require a better history of the last three hundred years in Western Europe than has yet been written. As may be inferred from Whitehead's masterly survey, the explanation has some of its roots in the development of mathematics. Mathematics, defined by Whitehead as "thought moving in the sphere of complete abstraction from any particular instance of what it is talking about,"[2] made breath-taking progress in the seventeenth and early eighteenth centuries; and its impulses were felt at many levels less rarefied than the purely abstract. On one level, it impelled towards classification. "Classification," as Whitehead writes without any thought of literary applications, "is a halfway house between the immediate concreteness of the individual thing and the complete abstraction of mathematical notions."[3] But halfway to complete mathematical abstraction is no mean distance in Everyman's Progress. Small wonder that he stopped long for rest and refreshment at this comfortable caravanserai, whose pavilions and gardens were thickly strewn with allegorical personifications, like the Groves of Blarney (of which Professor

1. Goldsmith, *Works*, Globe ed., 328.
2. Alfred N. Whitehead, *Science and The Modern World* (1925), 32.
3. *Ibid.*, 43.

Lowes lately reminded us) with their classical statues tastefully disposed about the pleasaunce—

> Bold Neptune, Plutarch, and Nicodemus,
> All standing naked in the open air.

Mathematics, as Whitehead makes clear, "supplied the background of imaginative thought with which the men of science approached the observation of nature."[4] So Kepler could apply the laws of periodicity to planetary motion, Newton to sound, Huyghens to light. How these in their turn affected and were reflected in the poets—Thomson, Akenside, and their school —has very recently been exhibited by Marjorie Nicolson.[5]

All these discoveries and revelations in the realm of physical laws of course encouraged and exemplified generalization on top of generalization, exciting the men of the eighteenth century with the heady vision of a supremely ordered universe, where

> All are but parts of one stupendous whole
> Whose body Nature is, and God the soul.

"Bliss was it in that dawn to be alive!" But, unfortunately for men's peace of mind, the growing increment of generalization was not ultimately a one-way traffic towards simpler and purer abstraction. There was a counter-effect. "Nothing," Whitehead memorably declares, "is more impressive than the fact that as mathematics withdrew increasingly into the upper regions of ever greater extremes of abstract thought, it returned back to earth with a corresponding growth of importance for the analysis of concrete fact."[6] New generalizations made possible new concrete discoveries, and these in turn exploded the

4. *Ibid.*, 46.
5. *Newton Demands the Muse* (1946).
6. *Ibid.*, 48.

old generalizations. The current of generalization was clogged with the mass of particulars, which continued to collect until they stopped the flow. Thus particulars came to be all that had immediacy and meaning. Preoccupation with individual experience became the rule and the egocentricity of the last century and a half bears witness to our all but universal inability to reach any compelling generalizations. The flower in the crannied wall became the symbol of our helplessness, a symbol repeated in an infinite variety of shapes and contexts to illustrate the same negative conclusion. With all man's intellectual and emotional life re-oriented towards this fundamental predicament, the abstractions of the eighteenth century had lost their meaning. The wheel had come round again to the primitive many; the one had receded into the intense inane. The primrose of the rock was faithful in a sense, Sir Galahad was pure; but fidelity and purity no longer had any purchase on the imagination. To speak at large, the Ice-man was a more endemic figure in this climate.

Looking back once more, we can see that the Romantic ideal was that poetry should in some way rectify this state of affairs. In poetry, the imaginative faculty was to reconcile the general with the concrete, to harmonize and even identify the idea with the image. Wordsworth's statement of the use and purpose of poetry was, in fact, perfectly in accord with Dr. Johnson's: to tell truth agreeably. "Poetry," said Johnson, "is the art of uniting pleasure with truth, by calling imagination to the help of reason."[7] "Its object," wrote Wordsworth, "is truth, not individual and local, but general, and operative." But it is a question whether the means employed by the Romantics and later poets were not better suited to convey truth individual and local than general; and whether, if they had been surer of the general truth they wished to convey, they would

7. *Lives*, 1.170.

have rested content with representations of it so idiosyncratic. When Wordsworth's idiot boy, Johnny, "burrs, and laughs aloud," the poet appears to most readers to be conveying truth individual and local. When Thomson, in the *Castle of Indolence*, writes

> The sleepless Gout here counts the crowing cock,

he equally appears to be expressing a general and operative truth. When Goldsmith writes, in *The Traveller*,

> Hence Ostentation here with tawdry art
> Pants for the vulgar praise which fools impart,

he is reducing to felicitous statement no very confined range of social experience. If we would judge truly the value of this device of personification, we must judge it by its successes, not by a dismal parade of its failures. No accumulation of languid and lamentable examples from the flaccid fancy of third-, fourth-, and fifth-rate versifiers should be allowed to discount the merit of a single triumph in the hands of a genuine poet, if we are to learn what is possible in this kind, and this kind alone. At its best, it can, in fact, provide a very special sort of delight. Is there any other resource at the disposal of the poet so perfectly calculated to unite the general with the particular, the abstract with the concrete? It opens views of the widest conceptual horizons, and at the same time brings them into close and familiar neighbourhood. It lends strangeness to the conventional; it brings the dead to life. As of everything else in the domain of human expression, Shakespeare is the greatest, most inexhaustible master of it, as every page of his work stands ready to testify: "Liberty plucks Justice by the nose," "Time hath . . . a wallet at his back Wherein he puts alms for oblivion."

There is nothing inherently unpoetic about abstraction in itself, as will always be demonstrated afresh whenever a great poet employs it. As a touchstone of this truth, need one mention the last twenty-five lines of *The Dunciad*, where concept follows concept into the night of sense,

> And universal Darkness buries All.

Now, the course of eighteenth-century poetry suggests that the maximum intensity of satisfaction in generalization was reached somewhere about the middle of the century. By that date the positive influence of scientific thought was strongly operative with the least amount of its undermining negative influence. It is important to understand how at this maximum point the device of personification played a vital—and vitalizing—role. Although the age might derive excitement and pleasure from the new revelations of science, men were temperamentally no more "scientific" then than at other times: they needed to humanize their abstractions and generalizations. And this they managed, as Goldsmith emphasized in the passage quoted, through the mechanism of personifying. Generalization was of the utmost importance to them: it was one of the chief ways in which man transcended his private experience and became adult. They would not have exchanged it for any merely private vision of happiness. To generalize was, in fact, to be civilized, and in poetry, no matter how intensely one might feel, it was not decent to autobiographize. Hence the crucial importance and intense satisfaction found in personified abstraction. The device enabled one to particularize in socially, intellectually, and aesthetically acceptable forms. The *mores* of the time demanded that they keep their private concerns in the background; their intellectual preoccupations demanded that they should raise these interests to the level of generalization; and personification allowed them to recapture the most valuable part of the immediacy of personal statement. It allowed them to make the best of both worlds, the public and the private, to be at the same time general and specific, abstract and concrete. Thus they first translated personal experience to decorous generalization; and then, without surrendering the general, re-individualized it by means of personification. By this combination of opposites they gained access to a kind of aesthetic tension hardly present where the particular alone finds explicit statement.

Returning now for a closer inspection of Johnson's elegy on the death of Levet, we can perceive more clearly the functions of this abstract-concrete mode of expression. Johnson's problem, as we saw at the commencement, is two-fold: to express a personal grief, and to celebrate the merit of the departed. There is nothing out of the common order in the death of an old man; and where the life has been useful and fulfilled, lamentation is unseemly. This thought does not lessen the vacuum of personal loss, however; and that sense is itself a testimony to the merit of a good man. It is right, therefore, that grief should find utterance. The conflict can only be resolved by reflecting that, if one cannot ask the public to pity and share one's private grief, that grief may with justice be regarded as part of the general condition: *Sunt lacrimae rerum, et mentem mortalia tangunt.* There is no impropriety in voicing such an idea; and, seen thus in wide perspective, our private woe gains in humility, and wisdom, and dignity. Nearly a third of a century earlier, Johnson had given memorable expression, in *The Vanity of Human Wishes*, to the "doom of man," and had written:

> Year chases Year, Decay pursues Decay,
> Still drops some Joy from with'ring Life away.

It is with the weight of half a lifetime's sombre meditation, therefore, and with a perceptible reverberation from that earlier statement, that he opens his elegy:

> Condemn'd to Hope's delusive mine,
>   As on we toil from day to day,
> By sudden blasts, or slow decline,
>   Our social comforts drop away.

The opening metaphor has been censured—unjustly, in my opinion. The idea is still that of the vanity of human wishes: "*delusive* mine" because the ore which we hopefully extract never yields the expected return; *condemn'd,* because while life endures we cannot escape from this futile labor. It is a pregnant image of the "doom of man" ... The last line of the stanza is one of the two glimpses Johnson allows us into his personal deprivation. Or suddenly or slowly, he says, "our social comforts drop away"; and within this decorum we may hear, if we care to listen, the footfalls of a lonely old man in an empty room. Half a century later, a poet similarly oppressed with the tears of things would cry, "I fall upon the thorns of life! I bleed!" At least Johnson escaped the distress of surviving into a world which admired that exclamation, though his comment upon it would have been worth hearing. "Dear Sir," he had expostulated to Boswell on a lesser occasion, "I hoped you had got rid of all this hypocrisy of misery."[8]

His own declaration, with its personal implications, provides the transition from the opening generalization to the second and principal subject: the just appreciation of a humble man's simple merit, before God and his fellowmen:

> Well tried through many a varying year,
>   See Levet to the grave descend.

8. *Letters* 715.

Johnson does not say, "My comfortable companion upon whom I have long depended, and my valued friend." He says:

> Officious, innocent, sincere,
>   Of every friendless name the friend—

and we can acknowledge the sense of proportion which rendered praise for the repeated Samaritan gifts of friendly aid in quarters destitute of friendliness, instead of commemorating personal ties where friendship was abundant. Yet Johnson loved Levet; and he tells us he is not forgetting him, in the personified abstraction that opens the next stanza:

> Yet still he fills Affection's eye,
>   Obscurely wise, and coarsely kind.

He continues with a series of abstract-personifications, some restrictive, some non-restrictive, which with the utmost economy—as anyone may see who tries to paraphrase—place in the broadest possible view the scope and nature of Levet's charitable life:

> Nor, letter'd Arrogance, deny
>   Thy praise to Merit unrefin'd.

> When fainting Nature call'd for aid,
>   And hovering Death prepar'd the blow,
> His vigorous remedy display'd
>   The power of Art without the show.

> In Misery's darkest caverns known,
>   His useful care was ever nigh,
> Where hopeless Anguish pour'd his groan,
>   And lonely Want retir'd to die.

> No summons mock'd by chill Delay,
>   No petty gain disdain'd by Pride,

The modest wants of every day
The toil of every day supplied.

His Virtues walk'd their narrow round,
Nor made a pause, nor left a void;
And sure the Eternal Master found
The single talent well employ'd.

The two final stanzas need not be quoted. It is regrettable that they fall steeply off in power; and noteworthy that they do so in the degree to which they descend from abstract statement to the biographical particulars of Levet's latter days, to his age, and to the manner of his unexpected death. These were matters of record which meant much to Johnson, personally troubled as he was by fears of his own impending final illness and death; but he was unable to give them wider significance. Thus the stanzas serve to point the moral of what we have been considering.

So far, indeed, as concerns the personal or autobiographical element in neo-classical poetry, there is a genuine relation to the music of that age. The poets had invented, and at their best and most characteristic moments used with great distinction, a form of statement in which the unstated private meaning and emotion permeates the general statement which constitutes the explicit content, in much the same manner as that, say, in which the quintessential poignancy of Mozart's private emotional meaning eventually makes itself felt through the impersonal statement and decorous surface emotion of his instrumental compositions. Both poets and musicians have made it their business to keep that element out of sight, as the poets and musicians of the next age were to make it their main affair to parade it; but it can be sensed after long familiarity with the idiom.

We of to-day are the heirs of conflicting ideals. We are ensnared in the egocentricity of the past century and a half. Yet we also feel an affinity with the eighteenth century and are coming to acknowledge more and more readily an admiration for its characteristic virtues. Naturalism is pretty clearly at present on the way out and Romantic egoism has at least fewer admirers. There is, on the other hand, a cry to-day among certain of our younger critics, of a need for a new "mythology." The lack of any such compelling imaginative system, or set of controlling images, is suggested as a root cause of our contemporary malaise. The contention is that great literature, in particular, is impossible without "a ruling mythology that makes intelligible and unitive the whole of that experience from which particular fables spring and from which they, in turn, take their meaning."[9] Not only epic but even great lyric poetry can be based solely upon "adequate and explicit" myth, in this view. Yet we find, reassuringly, that if myth, understood in this very broad sense, is indispensable, it is also inescapable. The misfortune of the eighteenth century is held to be that, under the impact of seventeenth-century thought, the *good* old Christian mythology broke down, and the *bad* new mythology of Newtonian science took its place. Comparative mythology is a fascinating field, but for abundant reasons we must not venture upon it now. We may, however, attend briefly to the causal sequence here asserted. Eighteenth-century poetry, as such critics view it, was at its best no more than elegant or severe or vituperative; on its characteristic level, was prosaic; was never genuinely serious, nor "grand." *Ex hypothesi*, its short-comings are accounted for by its underlying mythology. Hence the Newtonian mythology was thin and impoverished. Now we are still existing under that dispensation, as revised and brought up to date by a succession of brilliant editors, of whom the latest is Einstein. On this hypothesis, how are we to

9. Mark Schorer, *William Blake* (1946), 29.

account for the enormous fluctuations, in artistic tone and temper and achievement, which have occurred in the last two hundred and fifty years? That the impact of science upon literature has been profound has been already fully acknowledged. But it is to be remarked that in so far as neo-classicism, taken by these recent critics as the baleful reflection of the scientific myth, encouraged generalization and abstract-personification, it was at one with the medieval and Renaissance impulse toward allegorizing, which reached its zenith when the Christian "mythology" was most strongly dominant. It was not neo-classicism, in truth, which exemplified the break-up of the older unifying concepts. Rather, neo-classicism is the last historical effort to stave off the collapse of those sustaining postulates which for centuries had given dignity and importance to mankind. That much eighteenth-century poetry is thin is doubtless true. That "it means no more than it intends to mean," as Mr. Schorer has it, is potentially as great a compliment as it was intended to be disparaging. It invites the retort that poetry ever since has been intending to mean more than it means. The great virtue of neo-classical poetry at its best is that it intends to mean a great deal: it intends to mean that human life is significant according as it corresponds to ultimate ideas of order and value which are not beyond the power of man to apprehend in the largest sense. And it strives to give clear and appropriate expression to this meaning. To say this is to say that it often intends to mean more than it—not *means*, but *says*. Thus, when the poet writes

> Condemn'd to Hope's delusive mine,
>   As on we toil . . .
>   Our social comforts drop away,

he feels it unnecessary, in order to be understood as a man speaking to men, to cry,

I fall upon the thorns of life! I bleed!,

or even, But O,—

But O the difference to me!

Whether we shall ever regain a view of the world so comprehensive and assured as to enable us to state common experience in general terms, ridding us of our ego-rooted private dread of uttering a platitude, is yet to be learned. If such a time arrives, we shall unquestionably find that again we shall need, and freely employ, those ideational fictions, personifications, which spring from, and give visible form to, and implement the structure of abstract thought. Indeed, Janet Spens has suggested that we are already evolving a new mythology. "We think," she declares, "that we are dealing with scientific fact when we talk of mind, matter, silence, vacuum, but in truth we are creating entities, which are quite as much personifications as any of the figures in eighteenth-century poetry."[1] And as these abstracts impinge upon our imaginations, we shall discover as well that they carry emotional overtones along with their intellectual content; and we shall the better understand how it was that in the eighteenth century, as in earlier days, the personified abstraction wielded so potent, and so satisfying, an appeal.

1. Spens, 62.

"We Fell upon *Sir Eldred*"

HERMAN W. LIEBERT

Like all others in authority, Samuel Johnson was often asked to exercise his power for the benefit of those less capable or confident. "It is wonderful," Boswell says, "what a number and variety of writers, some of them even unknown to him, prevailed on his good-nature to look over their works, and suggest corrections and improvements."[1]

Johnson did not always grant these suitors their wishes. He sometimes satisfied them, with undeviating regard for the truth, by less than the actual exercise of his editorial pen. To the Reverend William Tasker's anxious, risible question as Johnson was reading one of his poems ("Is that poetry, Sir?— Is it Pindar?") he could reply with exquisite honesty, "Why, Sir, there is a great deal here of what is called poetry."

For a number of poets, however, he consented to use his critical powers in the task of revision. In 1745 he blotted a great many lines in Samuel Madden's *Boulter's Monument* and received ten guineas; the work of his friends Mary Masters and

1. It has not seemed necessary to burden with annotation a paper of this character. Quotations from the *Life* are available through Dr. Powell's excellent index. The letters of Hannah More and her sisters can be found in any edition of William Roberts, *Memoirs of the Life and Correspondence of Mrs. Hannah More,* under the date 1776. The two editions of the poem considered are *Sir Eldred of the Bower, and The Bleeding Rock: Two Legendary Tales. By Miss Hannah More* . . . (London, T. Cadell, 1776) and the same, 2d ed., corrected, 1778. Quotations from Johnson will be found, from the *Dictionary sub verbo,* and from other works in Joseph Epes Brown, *The Critical Opinions of Samuel Johnson* (Princeton, 1926) or William K. Wimsatt, *The Prose Style of Samuel Johnson* (New Haven, 1941).

Anna Williams he "illuminated here and there with a ray of his own genius"; he supplied passages for both of Goldsmith's greatest poems; and he encouraged young Henry Lucas and George Crabbe by mending their verses.

But unfortunately, except for whole lines newly added, the revisions he made have not been identified. We know much about Johnson's principles of poetry; if we could trace him at work altering words and phrases, recasting thoughts, and polishing commonplaces into elegance, we could learn more about his practice.

For one poem only that he revised is such a study possible. This is Hannah More's *Sir Eldred of the Bower*, the second edition of which displays changes made after the first, which are here attributed to Johnson. It is curious that this example of his work as a reviser has not sooner received attention.

In December 1775 Miss More published the poem, of 132 stanzas in ballad meter, together with another poem, *The Bleeding Rock*. *Sir Eldred* is the tale of Birtha, beautiful daughter of Sir Ardolph, who, on the day of her marriage to the peerless Sir Eldred, is discovered by him in the arms of her long-lost brother Edwy. Eldred slays Edwy, Ardolph expires at the sight, Birtha's spirit flees her body, a curtain is decently drawn over Eldred's end, and the author is left alone, moral in hand, on the corpse-strewn stage.

Immediately successful, the poem was praised by Johnson, Garrick, and Burke, and, like *Evelina* two years later, was soon on every lip.

Birtha, Miss Reynolds told one of Hannah's sisters, "has kindled a flame in the cold bosom of Johnson," and at the same time one of the sisters warned another at home that

> if a wedding should take place before our return, don't be surprised, —between the mother of Sir Eldred and the father of my much-loved Irene; nay, Mrs. Montagu says,

if tender words are the precursors of connubial engage-
ments, we may expect great things; for it is nothing but
"child," "little fool," "love," and "dearest."

Early in January 1776 Johnson and Miss More were among
nineteen at Mrs. Montagu's for dinner. Later the same day
Hannah wrote her sister

> I had the happiness to carry Dr. Johnson home from Hill-
> street, though Mrs. Montagu publicly declared she did
> not think it prudent to trust us together, with such a de-
> clared affection on both sides. She said she was afraid of a
> Scotch elopement. He has invited himself to drink tea
> with us tomorrow, that we may read Sir Eldred together.
> I shall not tell you what he said of it, but to me the best
> part of his flattery was, that he repeats all the best stanzas
> by heart, with the energy, though not with the grace, of a
> Garrick.

The next day Miss More hurried home from Garrick's in
time to receive Johnson at seven.

> Johnson, full of wisdom and piety, was very communica-
> tive. To enjoy Dr. Johnson perfectly, one must have him
> to one's self, as he seldom cares to speak in mixed parties.
> Our tea was not over till nine, we then fell upon Sir El
> dred: he read both poems through, suggested some little
> alterations in the first, and did me the honour to write
> one whole stanza; but in the Rock he has not altered a
> word. Though a tea-visit, he staid with us till twelve.

The changes in *Sir Eldred* were not printed until both
poems enjoyed a second edition in 1778. A comparison of
the two texts reveals a number of alterations, which it is the
purpose of this paper to examine.

That every one of the differences between the two texts is

certainly a change made by Johnson cannot be demonstrated by external evidence. Yet what is found accords with Miss More's account: changes and a stanza added in *Sir Eldred*, and no changes in *The Rock*. Knowing that Johnson did suggest changes, and finding changes where he is said to have made them, but none where he did not, seem adequate grounds for attributing them to him. Even more convincing is the nature of the changes. The reader, however, will make his own judgement as to the correctness of the attribution.

The "new" stanza which Johnson supplied is the forty-ninth of the poem, in which Sir Eldred, his smothered passion blaz ing forth, addresses Birtha. In the first edition it stands

> *Beauty* with coldness I've beheld,
> And 'scaped the shaft divine;
> But what my guardless heart can shield
> From *piety* like thine?[2]

This is replaced in the second edition by

> My scorn has oft the dart repell'd
> Which guileful beauty threw,
> But goodness heard, and grace beheld,
> Must every heart subdue.

This is accepted as Johnson's by the editors of his poems in the definitive edition of 1941, though an error ("heart" for "dart" in the first line) destroys the sense of their text.

The stanza is not strictly a new one, but rather a re-casting of Miss More's original. The nature of the re-casting is surely Johnsonian. Quite apart from the removal of such infelicities as awkward elision and inversion, the revision has replaced the particular (Eldred's heart) with the general (every heart),

2. In all quotations from the poem, the italics are those of the original.

and a rhetorical question by a universal affirmation. " 'The business of a poet,' said Imlac, 'is to examine, not the individual, but the species.' "

This stanza is the only change of Johnson's that has been previously recorded. But there are many other revisions to which attention is called here for the first time.

In the first edition, the second stanza opened

> Where gliding *Tay* her stream sends forth,
> To crown the neighbouring wood . . .

In the second edition, "crown" has been replaced by "feed." Johnson realized that the effect of rivers on trees is at their roots and not their summits.

The sixth stanza originally closed

> And every deed of lofty worth
> Is but a tax for more.

In the substitution of "claim" for "tax" may we not see an example of Johnson's dislike of mean diction, "sounds which we hear on small or on coarse occasions"? He did not like the vocabulary of the revenue office in *Sir Eldred* any more than that of the stable in *Macbeth*.

The eighth stanza read, in the first edition

> When *merit* raised the sufferer's name,
> He *doubly* serv'd him *then*;
> And those who cou'd not prove that claim,
> He thought they still were *men*.

This was revised to read

> When *merit* raised the sufferer's name,
> He show'r'd his bounty *then*;
> And those who cou'd not prove that claim,
> He succour'd still as *men*.

Hardly a memorable stanza in either version, though a little
clarity and strength have been added to the contrast.

The eleventh stanza first ran

> Yet if distrust his thoughts engage,
> Or jealousy inspires,
> His bosom wild and boundless rage
> Inflames with all its fires.

This is, of course, Sir Eldred, and the flaw of jealous rage in the
otherwise perfect gentle knight is introduced to prepare the
catastrophe. The effect was, in the revision, enforced by linking
distrust and jealousy, and by preserving the knight's virtues
save when overborne by rage. The clumsy third line was
abandoned.

> Yet if the passions storm'd his soul,
> By jealousy led on,
> The whirlwind rage disdain'd controul
> And bore his virtues down.

In the eighteenth stanza, Johnson was on familiar ground.

> The birds their amorous notes repeat,
> And glad the vernal grove,
> Their feather'd partners fondly greet
> With many a song of love.

These "mechanick echoes of the Mantuan song" must have
stirred his familiar impatience with myrtle bowers and purling
rivulets. We may guess that he was tempted to dispense with
the whole stanza. Instead, the birds are made amorous only in
the last rather than in both the first and the final line, and,
with faint novelty, the birdsong is made vernal and the grove
thickening, the last at least true to nature.

238

> The birds their vernal notes repeat,
> And glad the thick'ning grove,
> And feather'd partners fondly greet
> With many a song of love.

Johnson was no more friendly to the ballad than to pastorals, yet the substitution of "and" for "their" in the third line shows an ear sensitive to the flow of ballad meter.

A nice ear is also apparent in the thirty-third stanza, where "by" was substituted for "with" in the lines

> For wisdom, with a father's care,
> Was found in every field.

Thus a mouth-filling surfeit of "w" was avoided.

The most marked improvement in the poem is the thirty-seventh stanza. If this is Johnson's—and both the sound and the sense make it hard to reject—Miss More was not quite honest in describing his change as a "little alteration," for the stanza is substantially new. What formerly read

> While the sweet pink, and scented rose,
> In precious odours last;
> And when no more the colour glows,
> The sweetness is not past.

became in the second edition

> While the sweet-scented rose shall last,
> And boast its fragrant power,
> When life's imperfect day is past,
> And beauty's shorter hour.

Of the pink and the rose Johnson might have said what he said of the worthy and the good in Pope: that they "are distinguished only to lengthen the line." And are not the last two lines, totally new to the poem, darkened with the same shadows as *The Vanity of Human Wishes?* Certainly the insipid commonplace of the first version yields with benefit to the strength of the second.

In the fortieth stanza, Birtha is compared to the northern star

> When sailing thro' the liquid air,
>   It pours its lambent light.

This reads in the second edition

> When sailing thro' the cloudless air,
>   She sheds her silver light.

The change was not dictated by dislike of alliteration, for the thrice-repeated "l" is succeeded by "s" in equal number. One probably need not seek farther than that the new lines are more truly poetical. But it may be that Johnson the amateur chemist found liquid air and pouring light suggestive of the laboratory, and consequently "low." "Liquid" in the *Dictionary* is defined as "soft; clear" but the illustration refers to melody, and "lambent" in the sense of "gliding" is applied to flame.

The correction "Such Birtha shone" to "So Birtha shone" in the next stanza is a mere adjustment of grammar.

The forty-fifth stanza is considerably altered.

> The mountain breeze which paints her cheek
>   With Nature's purest dye,
> And all the dazzling fires which break
>   Illustrious from her eye:—

is replaced in the second edition with

> The virgin blush which spreads her cheek,
>   With Nature's purest dye,

> And all those dazzling beams which break,
>> Like Morning, from her eye.

The moment is Eldred's first sight of Birtha, surprised at prayer. The alteration in her complexion is patently better referred to maidenly modesty than to a hilltop draft. "Illustrious fires" is a curious phrase, wisely replaced. And when Morning was introduced, beams followed naturally enough. For all his bad eyesight, one feels, Johnson was a better observer of woman than Miss More.

In the next stanza, Eldred's "ravish'd eye" feasted on the sight of Birtha. Johnson admitted "ravish" in the sense of "delight" to the *Dictionary*, but he was probably offended by its constuprational ambiguity. In the second edition it became "raptur'd."

The next change is that of the "new" stanza already recognised as Johnson's and already quoted. Though not mentioned by Miss More, the stanza following has also been so much altered as to be substantially new. She had written

> She cast her mild eyes on the ground,
>> And rais'd their beams as fast;
> And close her Father dear she found,
>> Who haply that way past.

The substituted stanza was

> Quick on the ground her eyes were cast,
>> And now as quickly rais'd:—
> Her father haply that way past,
>> On whom she trembling gaz'd.

The parallelism in the first two lines is much sharpened, reminding one of Johnson's constant use of this effect in his own writing. The rather flat ending of the old stanza is brought up, if not to any eminence, at least to the level of the rest of the poem.

In Part II of the poem, only two changes were made, each of a single word. Though Miss More's account does not suggest it, perhaps Johnson's zeal for revision lagged.

Ignorance of medieval armory led Miss More, in the third stanza of Part II, to use an old word for "shield" as if it meant "helmet." "The targe and ample shield" of the first edition reads "The casque and ample shield" in the second.

The last change in the poem might be regarded as a typographical error if we did not know Johnson's own opinion of the words concerned. Coming upon the sanguinary catastrophe, Ardolph finds Birtha lying in the slaughtered Edwy's gore—"In brother's blood imbued." The second edition reads "imbrued." The *Dictionary* gives both words in the sense of "steeped" or "dyed," but of the admissibility of "imbue" Johnson expressed some doubt. "This word, which seems wanted in our language, has been proposed by several writers, but not yet adopted by the rest." He took the conservative course and substituted the older for the newer and less widely accepted word.

These, then, are the changes in *Sir Eldred*, made between the first and the second editions, and here attributed to Johnson. What does the sum of them tell us of Johnson as a reviser?

There are three ways, he pointed out to Boswell in 1784, of making a work better: "putting out, —adding, —or correcting." This may have been his practice in revising his own writing, but with Miss More's he seems to have confined himself to the last. Even in those places where stanzas might almost be called new, Johnson has taken the central meaning of the former text and clothed it in his own more forcible and nervous language. This is quite unlike what we know of his changes in the poems of other writers, which are true additions of wholly new and independent lines of his own composition. Perhaps the kind of correcting he did in *Sir Eldred* is all he felt he could do to a poem which he recited with pleasure, by a poetess he addressed as "darling."

Within the limits of correcting, Johnson has done to the poem what his theory would lead us to expect. He believed, for example, that art achieved grandeur through generality, and when he could he introduced generality into *Sir Eldred*. Goodness and grace do not merely subdue Eldred's heart; they must subdue every heart. The symbol of the transitory is not merely a rose, but life and beauty. It is no external mountain breeze that brings the blush to Birtha's cheek, but the inner turmoil of the virgin confronted with the emotions aroused by man. In short, when Johnson encountered what he felt were "descriptions descending to minuteness," he substituted general ones with elements of grandeur that he approved, such as "a nice display of passion in its progress."

To the same end, he purged the poem of a few expressions that he felt were tarnished by "the grossness of domestick use" or "the harshness of terms appropriated to particular arts." "Tax," "liquid," and "odour" were succeeded by "claim," "cloudless," and "fragrant power."

A few errors of fact were corrected by his changes. Rivers feed but do not crown trees; a targe is a shield and not a helmet.

When he undertook to rewrite freely, he introduced into his own lines that balance of elements characteristic of all his prose, poetry, and talk. "Goodness heard" is paired with "grace beheld," "life's imperfect day" with "beauty's shorter hour," and "succour'd" is set off against "show'r'd."

Several of his changes improve what he would have called the "cadence" of the poem. Lines of poetry that ended in unimportant words, he felt, disappointed the ear and lost their energy. He might have said to Miss More what he did say seven years later about the Earl of Carlisle's tragedy: "A rigid examiner of the diction might wish some lines more vigorously terminated." Thus, in *Sir Eldred*, "And close her Father dear she found / Who haply that way past" was altered to "Her father haply that way past, / On whom she trembling gaz'd." Johnson is here applying a principle that he both enunciated as a critic and practised as a writer.

But the most Johnsonian of all the elements we see exemplified by his revisions is the view of life apparent in what he added to the poem. The shortness and seriousness of human existence were never very far from Johnson's mind, and even the small bits of *Sir Eldred* that are his are suffused with a knowledge of the perilous balance of life and the little time we are given to adjust it. The brooding sense of unceasing conflict between virtue and vice, between imperfect man and the divine will, which cast its shadow over Johnson's own inner life, found expression even in these disconnected fragments. The scornful heart must be subdued by goodness and grace; rage gains control only after it wins the battle with virtue; the best of men live only imperfect lives compared with the ideal. It is no wonder that Johnson thought so highly of *Sir Eldred* as he did, for its concluding stanza, which he apparently could not contrive to improve, is an expression of his own view of life.

> Yet Heaven's decrees are just, and wise,
> And man is born to bear:
> Joy is the portion of the skies,
> Beneath them, all is care.

Unfortunately we do not know which were the "best stanzas" that he repeated by heart to Miss More's delight, but surely this must have been one of them. And it was just this reflection in Hannah More of Johnson's own deepest feelings that led him, with some suspension of his critical faculties, to praise her

244

poem, to revise it little, and to call her, as he did with great solemnity, "the most powerful versificatrix" in the English language. With this we can hardly agree today, but *Sir Eldred* still deserves our attention because it affords a unique opportunity to watch Johnson at work as a reviser.

Johnson and Intellectual History

WILLIAM R. KEAST

In defining Johnson's view of history—as of almost anything else—we make a choice between dissimilar images. It is well known that Johnson disliked much of the historical writing of his time, and that he disliked even more the use to which it was often put. We may be inclined, therefore, to picture his attitude through his report to Mrs. Thrale of a conversation with Charles James Fox. Fox was illustrating some point of contemporary politics by discoursing upon Catiline's conspiracy. Whereupon, says Johnson, "I withdrew my attention, and thought about Tom Thumb." This is a delightful image, but it is also a useful one, for it brings into focus several rays of Johnson's thought: his distaste for the great contemporary game of historical analogizing, his neglect of Gibbon and Hume, his preference for Goldsmith over Robertson as historian, his opinion that most histories, by omitting "motives and philosophy," were little better than almanacs or journals.

It is a useful image, but it is far from a perfect one. It will not assimilate Johnson's high praise of Raleigh, Clarendon, and Knolles in *Rambler* 122, against the view of Bolingbroke and others that England could boast no great historian. It will not square with the remarkable collection of historical works in Johnson's library, nor with his own projects for historical writing, including a history of the state of Venice and a history of the revival of learning. The man withdrawing his mind from a discussion of Roman history is hard to identify with the man who had said that "the study of *chronology* and *history* seems to be one of the most natural delights of the human mind," or with the man who was to condemn the syllabus of Milton's school because it substituted natural science for "those authors . . . that supply most axioms of prudence, most principles of moral truth, and most materials for conversation" —that is, "poets, orators, and historians."

Most important, this image—and the attitude towards history it seems to imply—scarcely prepares us for Johnson's opinion of biography. Professor Moore has reminded us of how strange it is that Johnson, who admired biography, should hold so low an opinion of history. Perhaps we should find it no less puzzling that a man whose opinion of history was so low should yet admire biography so much. Indeed, Johnson's remarks on biography are often as severe as his judgements on history. If there is "but a shallow stream of thought" in history, biographies, he says, "rarely afford any other account than might be collected from public papers"; and if history tends towards the almanac or the journal, biographers for their part often "imagine themselves writing a life when they exhibit a chronological series of action or preferment."

In Johnson's condemnation of history and historians we can discern a mingling of influences. Sometimes, as Boswell saw when Johnson said that Goldsmith's Roman history was better than Robertson's, he was talking for victory; sometimes he was indulging his notorious low opinion of the Scots, and at other times his abhorrence of atheists and deists. Frequently he was attacking the mindless repetition of a cliché, such as the use of the Punic War to decorate conversation. To these we must add his distaste for Whiggism, which found in Roman history a collection of what Johnson regarded as specious texts to bolster its position. And sometimes he used the defects of bad history to identify the virtues of good biography, without implying that he thought all biography good or all history bad.

248

For Johnson, whatever he may have thought of particular histories or particular historians, did not as a matter of fact have a low opinion of history at all. There is a kind of history in which the stream of thought is deepened, a kind of history whose power, like the power of biography, lies in its applicability to the general state of human life. History of this kind I will call, using Johnson's own term, intellectual history. Its nature and value are most fully set forth in *Rasselas*, chapter xxx. Rasselas and his sister, in Egypt, are discouraged because their search for happiness has so far been unsuccessful. When Imlac suggests that the monuments of Egypt may afford matter for contemplation, Rasselas and the princess make the conventional reply of the unhistorical:

> My curiosity, said Rasselas, does not very strongly lead me to survey piles of stone, or mounds of earth; my business is with man . . . The things that are now before us, said the princess, require attention and deserve it. What have I to do with the heroes or the monuments of ancient times? with times which never can return, and heroes, whose form of life was different from all that the present condition of mankind requires or allows?

Imlac is quick to show that this is nonsense: "to know anything," he argues, "we must know its effects"; "to see men we must see their works, that we may learn what reason has dictated, or passion has incited, and find what are the most powerful motives of action. To judge rightly of the present, we must oppose it to the past; for all judgement is comparative, and of the future nothing can be known." Since, Imlac goes on, "the present state of things is the consequence of the former, it is natural to inquire what were the sources of the good that we enjoy, or the evil that we suffer." The study of history, indeed, is not only natural; it is a moral obligation: "If we act only for ourselves, to neglect the study of history is not prudent; if we are entrusted with the care of others, it is not just. Ignorance, when it is voluntary, is criminal; and he may properly be charged with evil who refused to learn how he might prevent it."

Imlac is thinking of a special sort of history: "There is no part of history [he says] so generally useful as that which relates the progress of the human mind, the gradual improvement of reason, the successive advances of science, the vicissitudes of learning and ignorance which are the light and darkness of thinking beings, the extinction and resuscitation of arts, and the revolutions of the intellectual world." Intellectual history —the history of the progress of the human mind—bases itself on the products of art or industry and reasons to the powers which produced them. "When the eye or the imagination," Imlac continues,

> is struck with any uncommon work the next transition of an active mind is to the means by which it was performed. Here begins the true use of such contemplation; we enlarge our comprehension by new ideas, and perhaps recover some art lost to mankind, or learn what is less perfectly known in our own country. At least we compare our own with former times, and either rejoice at our improvements, or, what is the first motion towards good, discover our defects.

This concern for intellectual history may be seen in a hundred ways in Johnson's life and writings. We see it in the remarkably high and dignified place he gives to curiosity among the intellectual virtues. "A generous and elevated mind," he said in dedicating his translation of Father Lobo, "is distinguished by nothing more certainly than an eminent degree of curiosity." Curiosity is "one of the permanent and certain

250

characteristics of a vigorous intellect"; in great and generous minds it is "the first passion and the last; and perhaps always predominates in proportion to the strength of the contemplative faculties."

This praise of curiosity is no mere theoretical commitment; it is actively expressed in Johnson's own scholarship and in his zeal for the scholarly and antiquarian researches of others. "No active or comprehensive mind," Johnson said in his preface to Percy's *Reliques of Ancient English Poetry*, "can forbear some attention to the reliques of antiquity. It is prompted by natural curiosity to survey the progress of life and manners, and to inquire by what gradations barbarity was civilized, grossness refined, and ignorance instructed." Johnson's encouragement of Percy's work is well known; his promotion of other scholarly projects attests the seriousness of his interest in intellectual history. After busying himself among the Northern books in the library of Francis Wise, he presented Wise with a "Finnich" dictionary he had received from a learned Swede. He backed Warren Hastings' proposal for a professorship of Persian at Oxford, and encouraged a translation of the Bible into Gaelic. He asked Boswell to search for old charters in Scotland, suggested sources for Farmer's *History of Leicester*, encouraged Charles O'Connor's Irish researches, and gave his blessing to Evan Evans' work on Welsh bardic poetry. He hoped that Hastings, returning to India, would "enquire into many subjects of which the European world either thinks not at all, or thinks with deficient intelligence and uncertain conjecture," and that he would "examine nicely the Traditions and Histories of the East, that he [would] survey the remains of its ancient Edifices, and trace the vestiges of its ruined cities; and that at his return we shall know the arts and opinions of a Race of Men from whom very little has been hitherto derived."

It is true, of course, that in the *Rambler* and elsewhere

Johnson made fun of useless antiquarianism, of men "who are kept from sleep by the want of a shell particularly variegated; who are wasting their lives in stratagems to obtain a book in a language which they do not understand"—of men like Quis-quilius, whose collection boasts "a snail that has crawled upon the wall of China; a humming-bird which an American princess wore in her ear; the tooth of an elephant who carried the queen of Siam; [and] the skin of an ape that was kept in the palace of the great Mogul." But Johnson, unlike Pope and Swift, never allowed himself to be betrayed into unqualified attack on scholarship or antiquarian research. For even the mere collector has his uses: "To collect the productions of art, and examples of mechanical science or manual ability, is unquestionably useful, even when the things themselves are of small importance, because it is always advantageous to know how far the human powers have proceeded, and how much experience has found to be within the reach of diligence."

Intellectual history may take as its subject not the human mind in general, or the mind and manners of a particular country or time, but the mind of the individual. Johnson's biographies regularly include a section on the mental qualities of the subject; he is especially interested in preternatural exhibitions of intellectual power, as in Cowley, Pope, Congreve, and Milton; he is interested in men like Barretier and Boerhaave, whose intellectual distinction may provide a guide and measure for others. In this aspect of his biographical writing, it will be noticed, Johnson is not so much concerned with "those parallel circumstances and kindred images, to which we readily conform our minds" and to which he traces the general appeal of biography. He stresses rather the elements of distinction and rarity in the lives and works of his subjects. Thus Johnson expresses the hope that those who know Boerhaave's career will not permit any detail of his life to be lost.

Men are generally idle, and ready to satisfy themselves, and intimidate the industry of others, by calling that impossible which is only difficult. The skill to which Boerhaave attained, by a long and unwearied observation of nature, ought, therefore, to be transmitted, in all its particulars, to future ages, that his successors may be ashamed to fall below him, and that none may hereafter excuse his ignorance, by pleading the impossibility of clearer knowledge.

Again and again Johnson finds a place in the *Lives of the Poets* for histories of the genesis of literary works; the terms he uses to introduce them echo Imlac's discourse on the value of archaeology. Long passages from early versions of Pope's *Iliad* are given, for example, because "to those who have skill to estimate the excellence and difficulty of this great work, it must be very desirable to know how it was performed, and by what gradations it advanced to correctness." It seems likely, indeed, that this same principle may have helped persuade Johnson to sponsor Lauder's book on Milton's plagiarism, for he says in his preface to Lauder's work that

Among the inquiries to which [the] ardour of criticism has naturally given occasion, none is   more worthy of rational curiosity, than a retrospection of the progress of this mighty genius in the construction of his work, a view of the fabric gradually rising, perhaps from small beginnings, till its foundation rests in the centre, and its turrets sparkle in the skies; to trace back the structure through all its varieties to the simplicity of its first plan, to find what was first projected, whence the scheme was taken, how it was improved, by what assistance it was executed, and from what stores the materials were collected.

The enterprise described in such passages as these is something more than the use of history to illuminate literature, although this is an important part of its value. It is something more than exegetical scholarship in the usual sense. The reference goes beyond the work to the writer. The history of a work reveals the lineaments of genius in the same way that general intellectual history reveals the power of the human mind.

Intellectual history, whether of the man or of men, has several values for Johnson. Like any other sort of knowledge, it is valuable in itself. It may have practical importance, leading to the recovery of lost arts or to the improvement of present practice. But its great significance is in the structure of Johnson's thought, for it provides the measure or standard by which human works and human actions can be tested.

In criticism Johnson's ultimate interest is to identify and assess the genius of authors, and in morals, to appraise the extent to which men discharge their obligations to their Creator. The two tasks are alike—and morals and criticism are near allied—because both involve referring actions to their agents and measuring the powers or accomplishments of those agents against a general standard. The great problem is to fix the general standard, whether of poetic performance or moral action. The standard cannot be found where some of Johnson's predecessors had found it, in the great works or deeds of the past, for works are only ambiguously the signs of their authors, and genius or virtue may always manifest itself in new forms. Nor can it be derived, as still others had derived it, from a speculative analysis of the mind and the passions, for Johnson is sceptical of attempts to define the human faculties or to relate them to specific modes of action or expression. If the standard of judgement cannot be directly inferred from great works or deduced from speculative or rational psychology, where then is it to be found? It is to be found in what Johnson calls "the general and collective ability of man, as it is discovered in a long succession of endeavours"—in a conception, that is to say, of the limits of human capacity, as this may be inferred from what men have been able to do, given the circumstances under which they have worked and acted. The standard, while approaching the absolute, never attains it, because our knowledge of what men have done is never complete (and this is one ground of Johnson's interest in history, scholarship, and antiquarian study), and because a new genius may always exceed the limits previously established. The standard, moreover, can be determined only by historical inquiry: opportunity, materials, education, priority, and many other conditions affect the display of human ability, so that direct inferences from the work or the act itself must always be corrected by an examination of their circumstantial setting. "The palaces of Peru or Mexico," he says, "were certainly mean and incommodious habitations, if compared to the houses of European monarchs; yet who could forbear to view them with astonishment, who remembered that they were built without the use of iron?" History is therefore propaedeutic to judgement.

"There is always a silent reference," Johnson says in the *Preface to Shakespeare*, "of human works to human abilities, and as the inquiry, how far man may extend his designs, or how high he may rate his native force, is of far greater dignity than in what rank we shall place any particular performance, curiosity is always busy to discover the instruments, as well as to survey the workmanship, to know how much is to be ascribed to original powers, and how much to casual and adventitious help." The "far greater dignity" of the effort to see how far man may extend his designs measures the dignity, in Johnson's thought, of the history of manners and of intellect, for it is the method by which alone that discovery can be made. Far from being an object of disinterest or disdain, history in this sense is at the centre of Johnson's critical and moral theory; his repeated expressions of impatience with history as usually written reflect his deep conviction of its potential value.

Johnson, touring the Hebrides, came to Icolmkill, "that illustrious Island, which was once the luminary of the Caledonian regions, whence savage clans and roving barbarians derived the benefits of knowledge, and the blessings of religion." The train of thought aroused by the place, like Imlac's reflections on the pyramids, gives us an image of Johnson's sense of history which we should substitute for that of the man who withdrew his mind from Catiline to think about Tom Thumb.

> To abstract the mind from all local emotions [Johnson says] would be impossible, if it were endeavoured, and would be foolish, if it were possible. Whatever withdraws us from the power of our senses, whatever makes the past, the distant, or the future predominate over the present, advances us in the dignity of thinking beings. Far from me or from my friends, be such frigid philosophy as may conduct us indifferent or unmoved over any ground which has been dignified by wisdom, bravery, or virtue. That man is little to be envied, whose patriotism would not gain force upon the plain of Marathon, or whose piety would not grow warmer among the ruins of Iona!

The Making of *The Life of Pope*

FREDERICK W. HILLES

Of the various biographies that Johnson wrote, the *chef d'oeuvre*, according to Sir Joshua Reynolds, was his *Life of Pope*. It is the longest of them all, filling a complete volume of 373 pages in the original edition. It has been reprinted more often than any of the others. Professor Sherburn has termed it "easily the most satisfactory" of the many biographies of Pope that have appeared in the past two centuries,[1] and it has the added interest of being the last important work from Johnson's pen.

The life of the greatest poet of the century had been written by the most eminent man of letters of the day. Naturally anything pertaining to it was regarded as a valuable memorial. George Steevens, whose researches had been of great help to the biographer, secured the rough notes Johnson made when planning his work. Boswell acquired the original and only manuscript as well as a set of the proof-sheets. Another set of proof-sheets Johnson gave to Fanny Burney. Boswell's proof-sheets have disappeared, but the other documents have long since passed into great collections, where they have been available for study by scholars.[2] Strangely enough, no one seems to

1. George Sherburn, *Early Career of Alexander Pope* (1934), 13. Sir Joshua's characterization of the biography is in Horace Walpole's letter to Mason, 14 April 1781.

2. The memoranda, presented by Steevens to William Cole, are in the British Museum (Add. MS 5994.2); the MS, which in 1825 was in the sale of the younger James Boswell, is in the Pierpont Morgan Library; the proof-sheets are in the Hyde Collection. Boswell and Fanny Burney se-

have made the obvious use of them. When supplemented by letters and other records of the time, these materials enable us to sit at the author's elbow while he is shaping his last book. We can watch Dr. Johnson at work.

Something should be said at the outset about the date of composition, if only to clear up a number of conflicting statements. The first confusing chord was struck by Boswell, who under date of 10 October 1779 asserted that Johnson was "now employed" in writing Pope's life. Less pardonable is the error made by that great Johnsonian, Birkbeck Hill. In the *Life of Pope* Johnson quoted a still unidentified couplet:

> C'est que l'enfant toujours est homme,
> C'est que l'homme est toujours enfant.

Hill pointed out that Johnson also quoted these lines "in a letter to Mrs. Thrale written while he was writing the *Life of Pope*." That letter is dated 4 July 1780. Furthermore, in his edition of Johnson's letters Hill included an undated note to Nichols (No. 697) written after the *Life of Pope* had been set up in type. This Hill dated "Summer, 1780." Dr. Chapman knew better and deleted the conjectural dating but made no substitute. Hill's commentary doubtless led Professor Sherburn to write that the life was composed in the summer of 1780.

Against this is the word of the author himself. On his birthday, 18 September 1780, Johnson as was his custom reviewed his life and renewed his resolutions. "I have not at all studied; nor written diligently," he wrote. "I have Swift and Pope yet to

---

cured their documents with the author's knowledge and consent. From the hints of Hawkins one wonders whether Steevens quietly appropriated the memoranda. See above, p. 157, n. 9. Steevens' covering letter to Cole is in *Life*, IV.499.

write, Swift is just begun." A month later he was preparing to set out with the Thrales for Brighton. On Monday, 16 October, he wrote to Mrs. Thrale: "Pray let me know when it is that we *must* go. I will keep the day, but if it could be Saturday I should be glad, but the difference after all will be little more than that of burthening the luggage cart with more books or with fewer." What were the books to which he referred? Some time before 16 August he had asked Nichols to send him, among other books, Ruffhead's *Life of Pope*, Pope's *Works*, and Swift's *Works* with Dr. Hawkesworth's life. By mid-October he had probably completed his life of Swift. If so, the books he must have used at Brighton were Ruffhead and the nine volumes of Pope's *Works* edited by Warburton and published in 1751.[3] In Brighton he presumably devoted himself to reading and organizing his materials for Pope's life. From there he wrote to Nichols on 26 October begging that he be spared the bother of making trivial corrections in the proof-sheets of other lives. The next day George Steevens sent him information concerning the part played by Fenton and Broome in Pope's translation of Homer.[4] By mid-November the Thrales had settled once more in Streatham, where they were joined by Johnson, and it was there in all probability that the *Life of Pope* was actually written. Mrs. Thrale, who transcribed various documents for Johnson mentions in *Thraliana* the foul copy of Pope's Homer under date of 10 December.

Early in March 1781 Johnson announced that he had finished his work. Before the middle of April Reynolds and Horace Walpole had read an advance copy—or, more probably, a set of proof-sheets. The book was officially published on 18 May. The evidence here assembled suggests that Johnson

3. Johnson's references in the memoranda prove that this was the edition he used. For his request for books see *Letters* 696, 698.
4. The letter is in the Pierpont Morgan Library.

completed his manuscript early in 1781. Hill's conjectural date for Letter 697 is about six months too early.

Of course it could be argued that Johnson was "employed" in writing Pope's life well before the autumn of 1780. As soon as he had contracted to write little Lives for a little edition he knew that he was to be Pope's biographer, and while writing of Pope's contemporaries he was constantly dealing with matters that concerned Pope. Moreover his friends exerted themselves on his behalf and from time to time brought pertinent information to his attention.

Boswell's efforts to arrange a conference between Johnson and Lord Marchmont are well known. Marchmont had been an intimate friend of Pope, and Boswell was understandably proud to report to Johnson in May 1778 that his Lordship would be pleased to talk with him. To Boswell's astonishment and chagrin Johnson retorted: "I don't care to know about Pope." And when Mrs. Thrale came to Boswell's rescue she received the famous reply: "If it rained knowledge I'd hold out my hand; but I would not give myself the trouble to go in quest of it." Boswell persisted, and a year later had the pleasure of taking Johnson, who was "drest in his best suit and parisian Wig," to wait upon Marchmont. Johnson's first question was what sort of talker Pope was. Marchmont replied "that if the conversation did not take something of a lively or epigrammatic turn he fell asleep, or perhaps pretended to do so." Marchmont gave Johnson the unpleasant account of the last meeting between Pope and Martha Blount and assured him that a defamatory life of Swift was not among the papers which Pope left to his executors. He talked of an unpublished, unfinished satire, "One Thousand Seven Hundred and Forty," which he had often heard about from Pope. He "much lamented that he could not find it among Pope's papers." Other

remarks made by Marchmont were recorded by Boswell, who
sent them to Johnson early in 1780:

> He required sleep often. . . . Was excessively crooked. . . .
> Always in an iron case, like a man whom you hang in
> chains. . . . He was not *Un homme a bon mots*. His con-
> versation was something better, more manly. A flow of
> vivacity. But it was necessary he should lead the conversa-
> tion. If other people talked together he fell asleep. . . . He
> had a strange reserve and secrecy in little matters. Lady
> Bolingbroke said he was *Un politique aux choux et aux
> raves*. . . . He had no settled faith. . . . Kept connected with
> Catholicks. But Lord Marchmont believes had not for
> long period gone to Mass.

Doubtless other matters first recorded by Johnson derive from
this source, and Johnson was properly grateful. "Sir," he said
to Boswell, "I would rather have given twenty pounds than not
to have come."[5]

Meanwhile other sources of information were made available to him. Of these easily the most important was the New-
castle manuscript of Spence's Anecdotes. Cunningham credits
Mrs. Boscawen with having procured it for Johnson, but gives
no evidence. Better authorities, Boswell and Mrs. Thrale, say
that Dr. (later Sir Lucas) Pepys obtained it and brought it to
Streatham at the beginning of February 1780. In early April
Johnson speaks of Seward's reading Spence aloud to him.[6]
What was made available to Johnson was a handsome fair copy

5. *Life*, III.344, 392, 418. The information supplied by Marchmont is
put together from *Miscellanies*, II.4, from *Pope*, pars. 243, 288, and from
Boswell's journal for 1778. Extracts from this unpublished journal printed
by permission of Yale University and the McGraw-Hill Book Co.

6. *Lives of the Poets*, ed. Cunningham (1854), I.vii; *Life*, IV.63, 482;
Letters 654.

of the Anecdotes now in the collection of James M. Osborn, with pencilled references in the back apparently in Johnson's hand.

At the same time various scholars furnished him with help. In May 1780 Joseph Warton sent him some notes on Pope. George Steevens was working closely with him, gleaning for him many facts biographical and bibliographical. He it was, perhaps, who called to Johnson's attention the manuscript of Pope's Homer, and he may be suspected of having procured for Johnson "the testimony of Kennet," which at that time had not been published. Isaac Reed prepared a chronological list of Pope's writings and lent Johnson various rare pamphlets by or about Pope. Johnson examined Pope's copy of Tickell's Homer, and through the courtesy of his friend R. P. Jodrell secured a transcript of Pope's letter to Bridges.[7]

But most of the new material that Johnson included in his *Life of Pope* he obtained orally. Much of it he had heard long before he planned to become Pope's biographer. He made use of information that he had received from Savage before the death of Pope and from Dodsley, who had died in 1764. In France in 1775 he conversed with Pope's friend, Abbé Hooke, and with Mrs. Fermor, niece of Pope's Belinda.

Because of the familiarity of Boswell's story about "raining knowledge" it may be worth while to list some of the many others who contributed to this Life. Sir John Hawkins and Sir Joshua Reynolds had spoken to him about Pope's painting. Walter Harte as well as Steevens and Warton added information about Pope's relations with Fenton. Benjamin Victor threw light on the real character of the "Man of Ross." The younger Jonathan Richardson furnished the vivid anecdote

7. *Letters* 668; MS Malone 30, pp. 70 f., in the Bodleian Library; *Pope*, pars. 113, 383. The Reed MS in the Bodleian is described by J. M. Osborn in *PMLA*, L (1935), 928, n. 3.

illustrating Pope's sensitivity to personal criticism. Johnson asked Dobson how extensive Pope's learning was; he asked Warburton how many books of the Odyssey Pope had translated. Lord Orrery may be the source of some anecdotes. Langton and Dodsley, we know, contributed, as did "Lintot, the son of Bernard," and the bookseller Osborne.

When departing for Brighton in 1780, then, Johnson had already accumulated a considerable amount of material, but before he was ready to write he felt it necessary to re-examine Warburton's collected edition of Pope's *Works* and Ruffhead's *Life of Pope*. As he read these books he took notes, recording important dates in Pope's early life. He seems to have started by writing on one side of a sheet only, spacing his entries so that at a later time he could insert relevant information in its proper place. Ruffhead he found very useful up to the time when Pope's poetry is discussed. At that point, apparently, he picked up the last three volumes of Warburton's edition, volumes that contain all of Pope's authorized correspondence. From these letters Johnson selected enough information to round out a reasonably full biography. Warburton, following Pope, printed the letters as correspondences. Johnson, whose immediate task was to build up a chronology, therefore found himself moving back and forth in Pope's lifetime and occasionally recorded the same item twice because it had appeared in two different correspondences. After completing his reading of the letters he may have returned to Ruffhead. At least there are a few references to Ruffhead for Pope's later life. And some of the later entries derive from Spence's Anecdotes.

When rereading his notes Johnson often added his own comments, normally writing them on the blank page facing the notes. For example, from Ruffhead he had noted that Pope "lost ground" while attending the school near Hyde Park. Opposite this—that is, on the verso of the previous page—his comment is "He could not have lost much." The reading notes he supplemented with a few additional pages of memoranda, containing ideas he planned to develop or reminders of what he had heard about Pope from such people as Mrs. Fermor, Dobson, Marchmont.

He was now ready to write. He had collected his materials and knew how they were to be arranged. This was the last of the prefaces "biographical and critical" to be written. Between the biographical narrative and the critique Johnson had, for the more important poets, been inserting what he and his contemporaries called a "character" of his subject. *The Life of Pope*, then, was to be divided into three parts, the biography, the character sketch, and the commentary on Pope's poetry.

When writing the purely biographical section Johnson, with reading notes before him, seems to have opened once more his copy of Ruffhead. Verbal parallels here must be treated with caution, for all early commentators on the life of young Pope cheerfully take their phrases from the notes of Pope or Warburton or from one another. A comparison of all possible sources for a given statement, however, indicates that it was Ruffhead Johnson had before him as he began writing.

The way in which he has departed from Ruffhead's phraseology is often amusing. At times the alteration seems to have been made solely to avoid slavish copying. Ruffhead: "Our bard was naturally of a tender and delicate constitution. . . ." Johnson: "Pope was from his birth of a constitution tender and delicate." Ruffhead: "but of a temper nevertheless peculiarly sweet and engaging." Johnson: "but is said to have shown remarkable gentleness and sweetness of disposition." According to Ruffhead, Pope was "for a few months, placed under the tuition of *another priest, one Deane.*" According to Johnson "he had for a few months the assistance of *one Deane, another priest.*" Ruffhead, speaking of the comedy and tragedy written

by the youthful poet, wrote: "With regard to the subject of the
former, we are wholly in the dark; the latter however was
founded on a story taken from the legend of St. Genevieve."
Johnson transposed this: "The tragedy was founded on the
legend of St. Genevieve. Of the comedy there is no account."
Again, Ruffhead spoke of Mr. Secretary Caryll as "author of
the comedy of Sir Solomon Single," while Johnson, following
Ruffhead, called him "authour of *Sir Solomon Single, a comedy*."

Perhaps such transpositions were essential for the measured
sentences Johnson naturally wrote; perhaps they are the unconscious revelation of Johnson's independence, of his unwill-
ingness to adopt the sentence structure of those for whom he
had little respect. Certain it is that he did not wish to adver-
tise the assistance which he had received from his predecessor.
"No man," he said, "loves to be indebted to his contemporaries."[8]

How Johnson used his chief source deserves a more extended treatment, for from such a study a better understanding of his method of composition will result. Naturally there
are not many passages which are mere paraphrases. For clarity's sake the alterations which Johnson made may be classified
in three groups. Much that Ruffhead wrote, Johnson omitted;
much that Johnson included is not found in Ruffhead; and
much that is in Ruffhead Johnson corrected.

Ruffhead's book is more than three times longer than Johnson's, although it includes a good deal less biographical information. Ruffhead, as we have just seen, mentions "another
priest, one Deane," and adds: "from whose instructions, however, he received very little benefit, having made no farther

8. *Pope*, par. 86. At one place in the proof (par. 54) Johnson cancelled
Ruffhead's name. There are numerous references to his book in the memoranda (*R* followed by page number).

progress under him, than that of being able to construe a little of Tully's Offices." Here are twenty-eight words which are boiled down in Johnson's version to twelve: "of whom he learned only to construe a little of Tully's Offices." Johnson's diction is for the most part far simpler than Ruffhead's; his sentences are normally more terse and invariably more virile.

What has been added to Ruffhead's account is what makes Johnson the most readable of all of Pope's biographers. Remarks in passing which are drawn from his wide knowledge of literature and of life—pithy aphorisms, or those subacid comments of which Strachey must have been thinking when he spoke of the "foretaste of Stracheyan artistry" in Johnson's biographies[9]—such comments, absent in Ruffhead, add seasoning to what Johnson wrote. Occasionally the alteration from his source, though slight, is most significant. Ruffhead in his account of Pope's genealogy mentions the poet's uncles, "one of whom was killed, another died, in the service of King Charles I." Johnson, loyal to the Stuarts, refused to be as matter-of-fact on such a subject and wrote: "one of whom *had the honour of* being killed, and the other of dying, in the service of Charles the First."

When interpreting the same material the two biographers differ greatly. Take, for example, the case of the "unfortunate lady." All that Johnson knew of her derived from Ruffhead, whose account, wrote Johnson, is "given with evident intention to raise the lady's character." Ruffhead describes a distinguished lady who had too much truth and honour to lie to her uncle, and who, after languishing a considerable time in sickness and sorrow in a strait and severe confinement, was found a suicide "yet warm upon the ground." We are introduced to a "rigid guardian" who had upbraided her, employed spies to watch over her, forced her abroad, and intercepted her letters

9. In a letter dated 18 April 1921, in my collection.

to her lover. And now listen to Johnson: the lady "seems to have been impatient, violent, and ungovernable. . . . Nor is it discovered that the uncle, whoever he was, is with much justice delivered to posterity as a 'false Guardian'; he seems to have done only that for which a guardian is appointed; he endeavoured to direct his niece till she should be able to direct herself." Ruffhead's comment, after the facts have been presented, is characteristic: "Such a moving catastrophe might have inspired a savage with sensibility; but in Mr. Pope it awakened all the power of the Pathos." With this contrast Johnson: "Poetry has not often been worse employed than in dignifying the amorous fury of a raving girl."

The nature of Johnson's indebtedness to Ruffhead has been indicated. While he was writing the first part of the biographical section, covering roughly the first half of Pope's life, Johnson, having few materials to draw upon other than those used by Ruffhead, was content to take his facts and sometimes his very phrases from his predecessor. Thereafter Ruffhead was of little use to Johnson, who knew more about the last seventeen years of Pope's life than did his guide. For the *Dunciad*, the moral essays, and satirical epistles, and for the publication of the letters, Johnson relied upon what he had heard from others. For this part of the narrative the only important written sources are Pope's letters, Spence's unpublished anecdotes, and a few of Warburton's notes. The account of the conversations between Pope and Bolingbroke (pars. 191–93), as the memoranda indicate, as well as the concluding paragraphs (249–54)—a late addition written after the second section had been begun—derive from Ruffhead, but are exceptions.

Johnson gave relatively little thought to the writing of the biographical section. The structure adopted was a chronological one, and facts and comments fell easily into place. But the second section, the character sketch, required more literary craftsmanship and was written with more care. His chief sources here were oral tradition and Pope's published correspondence.

Before him as he wrote were his memoranda, which include many words and phrases that survive in the sketch as finally written. One line of notes reads: "Practised only one form of verse. Facility from use." This line is the germ of par. 300, in which Johnson writes: "By perpetual *practice* language had in his mind a systematical arrangement; having always the same *use* for words, he had words so selected and combined as to be ready at his call. This increase of *facility*," etc. The paragraph following this is based on the note immediately preceding this line: "Nothing occasional. No haste. No rivals. No compulsion."

The character begins with Pope's appearance, his health, and in general with what those who had seen him had observed of him. After describing the outer man Johnson attempted to get beneath the surface by examining Pope's personality as it is revealed in his letters. And finally he discussed Pope's mind and the way in which he composed his poetry. The section concludes with the brilliant comparison of Pope and Dryden. This part of the biography is well organized and is as effective a piece of writing as may be found in any of Johnson's works.

Johnson's task in the final section was to comment on Pope's poetry, and surely he was as well qualified to do this as any man living. But he was no longer young and seems to have adopted the easiest way to bring his labours to an end. It is almost certain that he did not bother to reread Pope's poetry. Instead he apparently leafed through a few of the more available commentaries and contented himself with remarks provoked by these commentaries. Professor Boyce has shown how dependent Johnson was on his predecessors for direction in his critical utterances. The readability of this section, Boyce remarks, "is due in part to the sense Johnson had of being in converse with worthy opponents; . . . in writing his criticism of Pope, Johnson listened to one speaker and then another, replying roughly to some remarks, ignoring others, borrowing the language of one man, handing a rare compliment to someone else in a moment of happy agreement, perpetually demanding the last word, even if he had to roar to get it."[1]

Professor Boyce's admirable study may give the unwary reader the impression that Johnson carefully reviewed all earlier comments on Pope's poetry. In fact, with minor exceptions such as allusions to the criticism of Lord Kames, Dennis, and Warburton, Johnson's critique is based on statements of only two of his predecessors. Joseph Warton's *Essay on the Writings and Genius of Pope* had been published in 1756. Thirteen years later Ruffhead brought out his biography "with a Critical Essay on his Writings and Genius," which is admittedly directed against Warton's commentary. Most of Johnson's dogmatic utterances have been called forth by the remarks of one or the other of these two writers. Ruffhead, said Johnson, "knew nothing of Pope and nothing of poetry." Warton's essay Johnson had reviewed without enthusiasm. He told Boswell it was "a very pleasing book," but he questioned Warton's critical judgement. "His taste," he once said, "is amazement." The two men are said to have quarrelled at Sir Joshua's because Warton had had the temerity to contradict Johnson.[2]

In any case they treat one another with great respect in their published criticisms of Pope's poetry. Warton speaks of the "excellent" dictionary which Mr. Johnson had given the world and more than once quotes "the excellent Rambler."

1. "Samuel Johnson's Criticism of Pope," *Review of English Studies*, new ser., v (1954), 46.
2. *Life*, ii.167, i.448, ii.41 n.

Johnson makes the retort courteous by mentioning "the learned author of the *Essay on the Life and Writings of Pope*; a book which teaches how the brow of criticism may be smoothed, and how she may be enabled, with all her severity, to attract and delight." When he has occasion to take exception to any of Warton's judgements, which is frequently the case, he carefully avoids any mention of Warton's name. Johnson may have been likened to a bear, but he cannot be accused of rudeness when referring in print to rival critics.

Warton dismissed Pope's pastorals with the remark that they do not contain "a single rural image that is new." Ruffhead, angered by any statement which depreciated Pope's genius, attempted to refute this by quoting among other samples the following couplet:

> The balmy *zephyrs*, silent since her death,
> Lament the ceasing of a sweeter breath.

Johnson, emphasizing the general structure and versification of the poems, praised them highly, but added: "I wish, however, that his fondness had not overlooked a line in which the 'Zephyrs' are made 'to lament in silence'." He then vigorously attacked Warton's position, in spite of the fact that in his review of Warton's book he had accepted it. It is characteristic that the one blemish to which he called attention was a couplet praised by Ruffhead, and that his general comment on these poems is a refutation of Warton's.

Warton's examination of *Windsor Forest* led him to say that "descriptive poetry was by no means the shining talent of Pope," but among the passages which receive his approbation is that in which "Old Father Thames is raised, and acts, and speaks with becoming dignity." Ruffhead was content to stress the passages which Warton praised. Johnson, after referring to

Denham and Waller, asserted that "Pope cannot be denied to excel his masters in . . . the art of interchanging description, narrative, and morality." But he commented adversely on two parts of the poem, one of which is "the appearance of Father Thames."

Warton gave high praise to Pope's *Messiah*, which "incontestably surpasses the Pollio of Virgil." "That the Messiah excels the Pollio," wrote Johnson, "is no great praise."

In general the three critics agreed in what they had to say of the *Ode for St. Cecilia's Day*. But it is worth noting that the second stanza, which was dismissed by Johnson as consisting of "hyperbolical common-places," was highly extolled by Ruffhead, who was not content with the faint praise Warton gave to the ending. Both Warton and Ruffhead condemned the end of the fifth and all of the sixth stanza, chiefly on metrical grounds. According to Johnson, in these stanzas "we have all that can be performed by elegance of diction or sweetness of versification."

In his discussion of the *Essay on Criticism* Warton singled out the simile of the Alps, which "is frequently mentioned, as an instance of the strength of fancy. The images however appear too general and indistinct, and the last line conveys no new idea to the mind." Ruffhead offered a lame defence, which he further weakened by admitting that the simile "seems to be spun out to a languid iteration of idea. 'The Alps rising on Alps', is but an echo of 'hills peeping o'er Hills'." To Johnson the simile is "perhaps the best that English poetry can shew." His retort to the strictures on the concluding lines was that the simile "has no useless parts." What he had in mind is made clear by reference to this sentence in his review of Warton's *Essay*: "That the last line conveys no new *idea*, is not true; it makes particular, what was before general."

The critics were united in making enthusiastic remarks

about the *Rape of the Lock*. But Warton at the end of his commentary declared that Pope "was not the FIRST former and creator of those beautiful machines, the sylphs; on which his claim to imagination is chiefly founded." This statement caused Johnson to refer to Warton directly, though not by name. "Pope is said by an objector not to have been the inventor of this petty nation." The rest of the paragraph is a vigorous attack on that opinion.

Johnson is not affected by Warton when criticizing the later poems. (Warton's second volume did not appear until 1782.) But his approach remained the same; his criticisms were in opposition to those which others had expressed. When discussing the Homer, for example, Johnson mentioned "a thousand cavils" directed at the un-Homerical qualities of Pope's translation—and defended his author. And what he says of *The Dunciad* or *The Essay on Man* is exactly the opposite of what Ruffhead had said.

After recording his opinions of individual poems, Johnson brought his biography to a close in ten paragraphs that treat of Pope's versification and his genius. Here again he was indirectly answering Warton, whose aim had been to encourage those contemporary poets who were breaking away from Pope's type of poetry and whose general thesis was that Pope, doubtless a man of wit and a man of sense, was not a true poet. Johnson's hostility to the new school of poetry was no secret. He began his peroration with this uncompromising statement: "Pope had, in proportions very nicely adjusted to each other, all the qualities that constitute genius." And the concluding paragraph contains the familiar question: "If Pope be not a poet, where is poetry to be found?" As he brought his biography to a close, Johnson trained his guns on his most dangerous opponent. His best criticism was called forth by the questions Warton had raised.

What he wrote for publication, said Johnson to Dr. Burney, he never wrote "twice over."[3] The manuscript of the *Life of Pope*, which Boswell described as "the original and indeed only manuscript," supports this statement. The fact that it was the printer's copy is obvious; written in at the proper places are the signatures C, E, G, K, L, M, N, O, P, U, X. That it was also the original copy is equally clear. Frequently Johnson begins a sentence with the main subject and verb, cancels what he has written, and begins again with an introductory phrase or clause. At times this first cast is surprisingly colloquial. "Aristotle," he wrote, "is praised for naming Courage the first of the cardinal virtues ... *but if he had got it after Prudence*"— he deleted the italicized words and supplied a more orthodox conclusion to the sentence.

At first glance the most striking thing about the manuscript is the number of words Johnson managed to crowd on a given page. He objected to Pope's "petty artifices of parsimony, such as the practice of writing his compositions on the back of letters," but he too deserves the epithet "paper-sparing." The *Life of Pope*, unlike most eighteenth-century manuscripts, is written on both sides of a sheet. One of the pages "in the fair hand of Mrs. Thrale" (the phrase is Boswell's) contains 97 words. A page of the same size written by Johnson contains 239 words. To be sure his hand was small, but this fact alone does not account for the difference. Margins are negligible, and when after starting a sentence he decided to alter it, the new form was squeezed in over the old, instead of after it. Perhaps this habit dates from the early days in London, when to him as to his friend Savage, paper was an expensive item, and care was taken to make each sheet go a long way.

3. Malone's note to the 5th ed. of *Life of Johnson* (1807), 1.47. Cf. Mme. d'Arblay, *Memoirs of Dr. Burney* (1832), 11.179. For Boswell's remark in the next sentence see *Life*, 1v.36.

While writing, Johnson worked as he said, "with vigour, and haste."[4] The chief signs of haste in the manuscript are the many slips of the pen, omission of words, and grammatical mistakes. Intending to say that Pope "was impressed with . . . veneration for his instructor," Johnson wrote that he "was impessed with . . . veneration for his instructed." *Necessary* is written for *necessarily*, *which* for *when*, *the* for *to*. With surprise we read that "Parnel wrote the Life of Parnel." And the phrase "it had been vain to ask Pope, who probably had never asked himself" appears as "it had it been vain to ask Pope, who probably had never asked him."

There are other indications that the biography was written under pressure. Frequently dates and figures were left blank in the copy, to be filled in after the page had been set up in type. The manuscript was sent to the press in installments. Twice on the proofs in the Hyde collection there is a respectful request: "Please to send more copy," "Pray send more Copy," and from the location of these requests we may judge that one of the delays was caused by the difficulty Johnson had in handling the Homer MS, the other by the task of arranging the materials in the character sketch. The result of the first request is known. The harassed author speeded his work by enlisting various amanuenses. The first pages of transcriptions from the Homer MS were written by Johnson, but some are in the hand of George Steevens, and a great many in that of Mrs. Thrale. She refers in her *Anecdotes* to these transcripts, and adds that when she had completed her task Johnson said with relief: "And now I fear not Mr. Nichols of a pin."[5] She also copied for him Savage's account of the quarrel with the dunces and the longer extracts from Spence's *Anecdotes* and Pope's letters.

That he seldom reread his manuscript before sending it to

4. *Diaries*, 304.
5. *Miscellanies*, I.178.

the printer is best indicated by the sentences that escaped correction until the reading of proof-sheets. The hastiness and carelessness with which he wrote led him into many faults. Of these the commonest was what Boswell called "a too near recurrence" of a given word.[6] In par. 273 Johnson had written: "Such *friendships* were friendships of the golden age, and are now the friendships only of children." The next paragraph began: "Friendship has no tendency to secure veracity, for by whom can a man so much wish to be thought better than he is, as by him whose *friendship* he desires to gain or keep?" The words italicized disappeared in proof. This is but one of some seventy examples of revision made necessary by what he seems to have considered needless repetition.

A second major fault in Johnson's original composition was the tendency to connect in one long and clumsy sentence a number of statements. Originally par. 194 read as follows: "From this time Pope and his commentator lived in the closest intimacy and the good offices of Warburton were amply rewarded, for he introduced [him] to Mr. Murray, by whose interest he became Preacher at Lincoln's Inn, and to Mr. Allen, who gave him his niece and his estate, and by consequence a Bishoprick and when he died left him the property of his Works, a Legacy which may be reasonably estimated at four thousand pounds."

Occasionally after he had written a sentence he revised it in manuscript, giving it the authentic Johnsonian ring. "In conversation," he wrote in par. 273, "the first emotions of the mind often burst out without consideration, in business interest and passion have their genuine effect." Evidently he decided that the beginning of each of the two parts of this sentence was outweighed by the end. The alteration would

6. *Life*, III.357.

indicate this. *"In the eagerness of conversation* the first emotions of the mind often burst out before they are considered; *in the storm of business* interest and passion have their genuine effect."* Presumably he felt that a monosyllable did not properly balance *eagerness*, for *storm* was then changed to *tumult*. This sort of emendation, common enough in the proof-sheets, is rare in the manuscript. The great majority of revisions before printing are caused by a last-minute decision to make an active verb passive or to interpolate a phrase or clause.

A notable exception to what has been said is the comparison of Pope and Dryden that concludes the second section. It was thoroughly worked over in manuscript, with the result that the changes in proof were slight, nor did the author see fit to revise it in a subsequent edition.

The part played by John Nichols in perfecting the *Lives of the Poets* was an important one. Nichols was one of the "respectable" booksellers—or, in modern parlance, publishers—who sponsored the edition of the English poets. He was also sole printer of the first edition. With him Johnson corresponded on all matters of detail. To him he turned for information and advice.

One of the duties of the printer, as we have seen, was to supply Johnson with the books on which he drew for materials. Presumably the printer also aided the writer by unearthing bibliographical information concerning Pope's writings. Several notes which seem to have been of this sort have been cut from the proof-sheets in the Hyde collection. There are in the manuscript blanks for the number of subscribers to the Iliad, the number of copies printed, and the amount which Pope received for the translation. These figures are supplied in proof by Nichols, who is probably responsible for uncovering them.

276

Nichols also inserted in the MS similar figures for the Odyssey. When discussing the edition of Shakespeare, Johnson wrote: "of seven hundred and fifty which he printed he sold   at the price proposed. The reputation of that edition indeed sunk afterwards so low, that   were sold at sixteen shillings each." In the existing proof-sheets these blanks are not filled in. Very likely it was Nichols who eventually discovered that 140 copies were sold at the low price, but the first blank could not be filled. The passage was therefore altered to read: "he dispersed a great number."

Such assistance might be expected from a man who was antiquary as well as printer and publisher. But Nichols contributed more than this. He was a careful proof-reader. The order to "Revise" on the first page of each gathering is in his hand, and he queried many of Johnson's statements.

When Johnson wrote that a picture of Betterton, said to be by Pope, "was in the possession of Lord Mansfield," Nichols asked "is it not yet there?" "I believe," replied Johnson in the margin, "it was burnt in the riot." Describing the Gordon riot to Mrs. Thrale in the previous June, Johnson had told of the mob's pulling down Lord Mansfield's town house, "and as for his goods, they totally burnt them." Nichols, it happened, was correct. The picture had been at Caen Wood and therefore survived. But Johnson did not bother to alter his sentence.

A number of times the eye of Nichols caught inconsistencies. Pars. 137 and 138 were an afterthought and were written at some time after par. 139, which originally began: "In the following year" . . . The reference had been perfectly clear. Johnson had mentioned the year 1725 (par. 135) and was now relating an incident that occurred in 1726, but after the interpolation of the paragraphs dealing with Spence, "the following year" was no longer valid.

Another example of changes caused by Nichols deserves to

be recorded, since it illustrates Johnson's attitude towards details he considered unessential. Par. 277 originally began: "One of his favourite topicks is contempt of his own poetry. For this he was modestly reproved in his life-time by Mrs. Cockburne, and in this he was certainly not sincere." Nichols, thinking Johnson would be more accurate if he said that the lady "intended to reprove" the poet, queried: "Did Pope ever *see* the reproof?" Johnson's hand does not appear on this page of the proof-sheets, but in the first edition the second sentence reads: "For this, if it had been real, he would deserve no commendation, and in this he was certainly not sincere."

What Johnson had in mind was a letter to Pope from Mrs. Catharine Cockburn, at the end of which she wrote: "Now I have dipped into your letters, Sir, I cannot forbear taking notice of some reflections I find in them, which much alarm me, as what I apprehend may tend both to your own and to the public loss, if such a train of thinking be pursued. You frequently talk of the finest performances of wit and genius, as mere trifles, of no service at all to a man's real happiness." This letter was never sent to Pope. Hence the query by Nichols. It was published in a life of her by Thomas Birch prefixed to an edition of her works in 1751. Johnson could have made this clear by adding a short clause. That he chose to omit her name altogether suggests that he was not sure of his facts and that he considered the matter too unimportant to verify.

Such annoying matters as spelling, capitalization, and punctuation were left entirely to the printer. Johnson, like Boswell, normally wrote *Emperour, authour, inferiour, errour*. Most of these spellings were modernized by the type-setter while he was working from the manuscript, but a number of them crept into type in the form employed by Johnson and were corrected in proof—not by Johnson. Boswell would have delivered a lecture to the offending printer; Johnson accepts the corrections

A page of Johnson's *Life of Pope*

without comment. To him *i* and *y* were interchangeable, and *dye* for *die*, *stile* for *style*, *scithe* for *scythe*, *gayety* for *gaiety*, *happyest* for *happiest* caused the printer trouble, for at times these forms were corrected, at others they were not. Even more trouble was caused by proper names. Dr. Hill mentions Johnson's tendency to omit the final consonant of names ending in *ll*.[7] So in the manuscript we find Curl, Cromwel, Caryl, Parnel, Tickel, Jodrel. Bolingbroke is almost always deprived of his *g*, and Philips regularly receives an extra *l*.

Perhaps the most difficult task which was performed by those in the printing-house was that of deciphering the manuscript. Even when he was not writing under pressure, Johnson's hand is often difficult to read. But when he writes hastily many words are illegible, and when his hastiness results in the omission of words or syllables little help is offered by the context.

Johnson's printers were remarkably apt at deciphering his script. Since we have nothing like a full set of the proofs, there is no way of telling how many mistakes were made when the copy was first set up, but there are not many more than a half dozen misreadings in gathering L, which seems to be an early proof, and that perhaps is a normal sample. Crousaz, according to the printer, was eminent for his treatise on *Cogreli*, and without doubt the printer was satisfied that there must have been some scholar of that name. But Johnson had not written *Cogreli*; he had written *logick*! (See first line of illustration.) In like manner there is confusion between *seen* and *soon*, *inference* and *influence*, *revises* and *raises*, *derided* and *divided*, *variety* and *vanity*. The use of the long *s* and the old-fashioned *e* created additional problems that would not bother us today. So we find, among other examples, *left* instead of *lost*.

7. *Letters of Samuel Johnson* (1892), I.xv.

Unusual words naturally caused more trouble. *Lodona* is twice printed *London*, and *Lutrin* appears as *Lubrin*.

When, as frequently happened, a word or two had been omitted in the manuscript, the printer normally used his ingenuity and made the passage make sense. Frequently this was not difficult; the omitted word was obviously a common preposition or pronoun. But there were times when he was forced to leave the gap blank. A notable example of this is seen in par. 180, where a phrase was set up in type as it appeared in the copy: "its flowers caught the eye which did not see what the   concealed." The words which Johnson inserted in proof are "gay foliage"—words that the printer could hardly be expected to supply.

Probably it was an error of this sort to which Boswell refers in an undated anecdote. Finding fault with the way something had been set up in proof, Johnson "refused to read it, and in a passion desired that the compositor might be sent to him. The compositor was Mr. Manning, a decent sensible man, who had composed about one half of his 'Dictionary', when in Mr. Strahan's printing-house; and a great part of his 'Lives of the Poets', when in that of Mr. Nichols. . . . By producing the manuscript, he at once satisfied Dr. Johnson that he was not to blame. Upon which Johnson candidly and earnestly said to him, 'Mr. Compositor, I ask your pardon. Mr. Compositor, I ask your pardon, again and again'."[8]

We may be sure that Johnson did not bother when reading proof to verify his facts and transcriptions. And we have seen that the printer took the liberty of supplying words which were omitted in the copy. A combination of these two factors has resulted in much of the petty inaccuracy that is found in the *Lives of the Poets*. Frequently a word dropped out at the bottom of a page. Johnson, writing hastily, reached for a new

8. *Life*, IV.321.

sheet of paper and in doing so omitted a word. Thus when quoting one of Pope's letters (par. 106) he wrote: "as Addison must be the judge in what regards himself, and seems to have no very just one in regard to me, so I must own to you I expect nothing but civility from him." Johnson was quoting from memory. The central phrase should read "and has seem'd to be no very just one to me." In the manuscript Johnson reached the bottom of a page as he wrote: "seems to have," and the new page begins with the words "no very just one." As printed, the sentence is ungrammatical. I suggest that Johnson intended to write "been" at the bottom of the page and that the omission of this word was noticed neither by the author nor by those in the printing-house. In the manuscript words have been dropped at the bottom of pages 75, 84, 111, 142, 147, and 150.

A careful proof-reader might be expected to have queried such a phrase, but the printer can hardly be blamed for such mistakes. There are, however, instances in which the printer nodded. In this way errors crept in which have been retained in all editions. One such error, curiously enough, was made in the opening sentence. The date of Pope's birth is incorrectly printed as "May 22, 1688." In the manuscript the correct figures (21) are clearly written; in the proof-sheets the mistake is uncorrected.

Another minor error for which the printer must be blamed is in par. 13. Warburton had reported that Pope "prevailed with a friend to carry him to a coffee-house which Dryden frequented." Ruffhead, Johnson's source, wrote that he "procured a friend to introduce him to a coffee-house which Dryden frequented." In the manuscript Johnson wrote: "he persuaded some friend to take him to the coffee-house which Dryden frequented." But the printer made *friend* plural, and the word is so printed in all editions.

Johnson's misspellings of proper names are so numerous that it is worth while to note that he properly spells Oufle (par. 225); it was the printer who doubled the *f*. And Johnson's habit of quoting poetry from memory—a habit which often led him to slight inaccuracies—is so pronounced that it is only just to call attention to one of his so-called errors. A line from the "Essay on Man" (par. 177) is correctly written in the manuscript:

> Expatiate free o'er all this scene of man.

In the proof *all* was accidentally dropped, and the omission was not noticed until after the publication of the first edition. The metrical irregularity was apparent, and someone—almost certainly not Johnson—repaired the damage, so that in the second and all subsequent editions the line incorrectly stands:

> Expatiate freely o'er this scene of man.

Details of this sort did not interest Dr. Johnson. As we shall see, he read his proofs with attention. Indeed, since for the most part he had not reread his manuscript before sending it off to Nichols, this was a highly important part of his work. But he was not concerned with factual matters; these, we have seen, he left to others. His concern was to polish what he had written, and the nature of his revisions demands special consideration.

A glimpse of Johnson at this time is given in the elegant words of Mme. d'Arblay:

> While that charming work, The Lives of the Poets, was in its progress, when only the Thrale family and its nearly adopted guests the two Burneys, were assembled, Dr. Johnson would frequently produce one of its proof sheets to embellish the breakfast table, which was always in the library; and was, certainly, the most sprightly and agreeable meeting of the day. . . . Wit was not flashed with the

keen sting of satire; yet it elicited not less gaiety from
sparkling with an unwounding brilliancy, which brightened, without inflaming, every eye, and charmed, without
tingling, every ear.

She adds that the proof-sheets were read aloud by Mrs. Thrale,
and that the discussions to which they led were "in the highest
degree entertaining."[9] Possibly some of the obvious errors of
the press were corrected by Mrs. Thrale; they are made in a
hand that might be hers and is certainly not that of Johnson or
Nichols. And it is tempting to suggest that some of the verbal
alterations were made after some such discussion as Fanny
describes. In par. 316, for example, Johnson had written that
"nothing is easier than to tell how a tree was once a blooming
virgin, or a rock an obdurate tyrant." In proof the word *tree*
has been changed to *flower*, the sort of alteration that might
have been made after the friendly critics had been heard.

When reading proof, Johnson's concern, as has been said,
was with matters of style. Most numerous among the corrections in proof are those that eliminate careless repetitions
of the same word. Long sentences are broken up, and qualifying words drop out, *probably*, for example, becoming *certainly*.

Apart from what has already been noted, Johnson's main
concern in revising was to improve the cadence of his sentences. There is the constant striving for balance which is
characteristic of his style and which led imitators like Mme.
d'Arblay to such excesses as "brightened, without inflaming,
every eye, and charmed, without tingling, every ear." Speaking of the generous sentiments we all have when it costs us
nothing to have them, Johnson first wrote: "self-love does not
suspect them to be the meteor of fancy." Clearly *them* is not
weighty enough to balance the last four words. In its final form

9. *Memoirs of Dr. Burney* (1832), II.177 f.

the sentence reads: "self-love does not suspect *the gleam of virtue* to be *the meteor of fancy.*"

A number of emendations, made it would seem for sound rather than sense, result in a metre that Pope had perfected and that Johnson had used in his best poetry. Of the "unfortunate lady" Johnson first wrote: "She liked suicide better than suspense." This he changed to: "She liked self-murder better than suspense." The conclusion of par. 223, "He cures those that were never sick," was revised to read: "He cures diseases that were never felt." This echo of the heroic line is frequently discovered in a phrase that ends a sentence. Thus, to return to the lady, Johnson first wrote: "Poetry has not often been worse employed than in dignifying *the suicide of a ma[d] girl.*" For the words italicized he substituted: "the amorous fury of a raving girl." One of the changes noted by Boswell was probably caused by the too frequent repetition of *less* and *trouble*. But the phrase "to write the next with less trouble" becomes "to write the next with more facility."

Johnson was severely criticized for including in his *Life of Pope* so many passages from Homer with the emendations of Pope.[1] The manuscript reveals that he had originally intended to include almost twice as many examples of Pope's revision. He restrained himself, declaring that while some of his readers would naturally desire more examples, "most other readers are already tired." That is a warning that his admirers should heed. How Johnson went about the business of writing has been sufficiently indicated. The copy he sent to the printer was hastily and carelessly written. Not until it was returned to him in proof did he set himself to "amplify, decorate, rectify, and refine"[2] his first thoughts and his first words.

1. For example in J. T. Callander's *Deformities of Dr. Samuel Johnson* (1782), 56, and *Critical Review of Works of Johnson* (1783), 25.
2. *Pope*, par. 299.

Johnson in Parody

S. C. ROBERTS

"Parody," wrote a contributor to the ninth edition of the *Encyclopaedia Britannica*, "may be dismissed as Johnson dismissed pastoral poetry. It is easy, vulgar and therefore disgusting." Such a sweeping definition would be difficult to substantiate. It is true that certain authors invite parody. Every schoolboy has, or used to have, his fling at an imitation of *Horatius* or of *Dolores*; and no doubt Johnson himself threw off:

> Hermit hoar, in solemn cell
>   Wearing out life's evening gray ...

or

>   Who drives fat oxen should himself be fat

with comparative ease.

But parody at its best is something different. It is hard to conceive anything further removed from vulgarity or disgust than Max Beerbohm's *A Christmas Garland* and, for Max, writing involved not ease, but the *limae labor* of the conscious artist.

It was *The Rambler* which provoked the first parody of Johnson's style. Shortly after the last number had been issued, Bonnell Thornton produced in his *Drury Lane Journal* a paper entitled ΓΝΩΘΙ ΣΕΑΥΤΟΝ. Boswell took delight in Bonnell Thornton's "witty sallies," and Johnson himself is said to have been "much diverted" by one of his burlesques. But it is doubtful whether the modern reader will derive entertainment from an imitation which begins:

> While capricious Curiosity persuades the youth of *Great Britain* to relish no scenes but those that are extraneous;

285

while the fashionable practice so extensively prevails of visiting distant countries, and, in short, of cultivating anything but what is truly *British* and domestic; I shall beg leave to look at home and take a survey of what more properly may be said to be our own; accurately to delineate the topography of the human body and enumerate its respective inhabitants.

This is parody at its dullest. On the other hand, Archibald Campbell, author of *Lexiphanes* (1767) fulfils every requirement of vulgarity and disgust. For him Johnson's prose was "a barbarous jargon, attempted to be imposed upon us by a few schoolmasters and Pedants . . . who are equally ignorant of books and men and who think they have done a fine thing when they have tack'd an English termination to a Latin word . . ." Alongside this, Johnson's own apologia in his last *Rambler* may fittingly be recalled:

Whatever shall be the final Sentence of Mankind, I have at least endeavoured to deserve their Kindness; I have laboured to refine our Language to grammatical Purity, and to clear it from colloquial Barbarisms, licentious Idioms, and irregular Combinations. Something, perhaps, I have added to the Elegance of its Construction, and something to the Harmony of its Cadence. When common Words were less pleasing to the Ear, or less distinct in their Signification, I have familiarized the Terms of Philosophy, by applying them to known Objects and popular Ideas, but have rarely admitted any Word, not authorized by former Writers; for I believe, that whoever knows the *English* Tongue in its present Extent, will be able to express all his Thoughts without farther Help from other Nations.

Readers of *The Rambler*—a select class—may be left to choose between the two verdicts.

In the ninth *Rambler*, Johnson contemplated the origins of glass-making:

> Who, when he saw the first Sand or Ashes, by a casual Intenseness of Heat melted into a Metalline Form, rugged with Excrescences, and clouded with Impurities, would have imagined, that in this formless Lump lay concealed so many Conveniencies of Life, as would in time constitute a great Part of the Happiness of the World? Yet by some such fortuitous Liquefaction was Mankind taught to procure a Body at once in a high Degree solid and transparent, which might admit the Light of the Sun, and exclude the Violence of the Wind.

Here, indeed, is good material for a sensitive and skilful parodist, but Campbell, with unbelievable *gaucherie*, fastens upon the phrase "fortuitous liquefaction" and makes Johnson begin a rhapsody thus:

> I shall inchoate with one of it's most delicious morsels of eloquence, and shall at the same time be curt. Perpend, and receive my sayings with a steadfast ear. But I obsecrate that in the interim you would, by a proper secession, facilitate my enjoyment of the light, whilst I, by the fortuitous liquefaction of spectacular lenses, and their concordant adaptation to my poral regions, meliorate and prolong its fruition.

To this mirthless rubbish Campbell appends a footnote in which he labours to explain that the paragraph is a Lexiphanic way of saying that the critic should step aside while the reader puts on his spectacles. Boswell, writing of the innumerable "ludicrous imitators" of Johnson's style, truly remarks that their general method is to accumulate hard words and that the resulting attempts are "totally unlike the original." To illustrate his point he quotes from the imaginary ode to Mrs. Thrale, beginning

Cervisial coctor's viduate dame . . .

and in a footnote records his opinion that there was no foundation for the gossip about Johnson wishing to marry the rich widow. He adds, however, that the report had given occasion to another poem, "not without characteristical merit," entitled *Ode to Mrs Thrale, by Samuel Johnson LL.D on their supposed approaching Nuptials.* In the second edition of the *Life* he expanded his note by quoting the first three stanzas of the Ode. The third stanza runs:

> To rich felicity thus raised,
>> My bosom glows with amorous fire;
> Porter no longer shall be praised,
>> 'Tis I MYSELF am *Thrale's Entire.*

Students of Boswell have long ceased to be surprised or shocked by his autobiographical candour. But it is safe to say that the most hardened reader was staggered by the demonstration that this Ode was written by Boswell himself. "Not without characteristical merit"—to gratify his hunger for self-advertisement, Boswell would discard the last rags of decency.

"No, Sir," said Johnson, "the imitators of my style have not hit it. Miss Aikin has done it the best; for she has imitated the sentiment as well as the diction." Here is praise indeed and it may well have been drawn by the lady's essay *On Romances.*

In *Rambler* 122 we may read:

Of the various Kinds of Speaking or Writing, which serve Necessity or promote Pleasure, none appears so artless or easy as simple Narration; for what should make him that knows the whole Order and Progress of an Affair unable to relate it? Yet we hourly find such as endeavour to entertain or instruct us by Recitals, clouding the Facts which they intend to illustrate, and losing themselves and their Auditors in the Wilds of Digression, or the Mazes of Confusion.

On Romances, by Miss Aikin (afterwards Mrs. Barbauld) begins:

Of all the multifarious productions which the efforts of superior genius, or the labours of scholastic industry, have crowded upon the world, none are perused with more insatiable avidity, or disseminated with more universal applause, than the narrations of feigned events, descriptions of imaginary scenes, and delineations of ideal characters. The celebrity of other authors is confined within very narrow limits. The geometrician and divine, the antiquary and the critic, however distinguished by uncontested excellence, can only hope to please those whom a conformity of disposition has engaged in similar pursuits; and must be content to be regarded by the rest of the world with the smile of frigid indifference or the contemptuous sneer of self-sufficient folly.

Even a comparatively short quotation is sufficient to show the justification for Johnson's praise. But it is significant that the sub-title of Miss Aikin's essay was "An imitation" and the imitation is so close and conscientious that the element of parody is barely discernible. Had Johnson published the essay as a *Rambler* paper, it would have provoked little comment. The regular reader would have remarked that it was very much in the usual style; he would not have been tickled by touches of exaggeration or burlesque, touches which are an essential component of good parody. Parody, in Gray's phrase, should at least totter on the verge of risibility.

Johnson's *Life of Gray* naturally provoked humorous, as well as angry, criticism. *A Criticism of the Elegy written in a Country Churchyard, being a continuation of Dr J———n's Criticisms on the Poems of Gray* was published in 1783. In his preface the anonymous author pretends that the work was Johnson's own and withdrawn at the last moment; the author was in fact John Young, professor of Greek in the University of Glasgow and the work is, in his words, "a methodical criticism upon Gray's *Elegy* . . . executed in a manner somewhat *outré*." Each stanza of the poem is examined with merciless particularity. The following analysis of one famous line is typical:

> When I am told that 'all the air a solemn stillness holds,' I hesitate; and in vain, by the help of the Grammar, or Collocation, endeavour to discover which of the two is the holder and which the held. If it is the air that holds the stillness, too great liberty is taken with the verb; and if it is the stillness that holds the air, the action is too violent for so quiet a personage: but the sound was necessary to assist the bell-wedders to complete the lulling of the 'folds.'

Young's description of his own work is exact; it is what Johnson might have written, "somewhat *outré*." Boswell and Sir Walter Scott placed their fellow-countryman as first among Johnsonian parodists and Horace Walpole declared that the author seemed to wish to be taken by Gray's admirers for a ridiculer of Johnson and by Johnson's admirers for a censurer of Gray.

Another Scotsman who was a good-humoured critic of Johnson was John Maclaurin (afterwards Lord Dreghorn). Johnson was entertained by him at dinner in Edinburgh and when Boswell showed him a bundle of criticisms of his *Journey to the Western Islands*, he picked Maclaurin's as the best, though he was careful to add: "But I could caricature my own style much better myself." He had, in fact, seen Maclaurin's verses on his *Dictionary* when he was in Skye and remarked that he was not answerable for all the words in it.

Maclaurin was a lively versifier and his poem began:

> In love with a pedantic jargon,
> Our poets, now a-days, are far gone;
> Hence he alone can read their songs
> To whom the gift of tongues belongs;
> Or who, to make him understand,
> Keeps Johnson's lexicon at hand. . . .
> Be warn'd, young poet, and take heed
> That Johnson you with caution read;
> Always attentively distinguish
> The Greek and Latin words from English
> And never use such, as 'tis wise
> Not to attempt to nat'ralize.
> Suffice this trifling specimen
> To make the admonition plain:

And here are a few lines from the specimen:

> Riches *desiderate* I never did,
> Ev'n when in mood most *optative*: a farm,
> Little, but *arboreous*, was all I ask'd.
> I, when a rustic, would my *blatant* calves
> Well-pleas'd *ablactate* and delighted tend
> My *gemellip'rous* sheep . . .

There was some shrewd sense behind Maclaurin's doggerel. In a note on Johnson's style, he notes that the adoption of Greek and Latin words with an English termination is largely a matter of caprice. We do not use *Ablactate* because *Wean* is "equally expressive and shorter." But why, he asks, do we use *Omnipotent* and *Dislocate* instead of *All-powerful* and *Displace*?

Of parodies of Johnson's biographical style, one of the best is to be found in Eaton Stannard Barrett's *The Heroine* (1813). Barrett was an Irishman who died at the age of 34 after writing a number of literary and political satires which achieved considerable popularity. Walter Raleigh rescued him from complete neglect by editing *The Heroine* in 1909, and Michael Sadleir re-introduced the book in 1927.

The book is in epistolary form and Letter 10 contains the *Memoirs of James Higginson, By Himself*:

> My parents were reputable tobacconists, and kept me behind the counter, to negociate the titillating dust, and the tranquillizing quid. Of genius, the first spark which I elicited, was reading a ballad in the shop, while the woman who sold it to me was stealing a canister of snuff. This specimen of mental abstraction (a quality which I still preserve) shewed that I would never make a good tradesman; but it also showed that I would make an excellent scholar. A tutor was accordingly appointed for me. . . . My first poetical attempt was an epitaph on the death of my tutor and it was produced at the precocious age of ten.

EPITAPH

Here lies the body of John Tomkins, who
Departed this life, aged fifty-two;

After a long and painful illness, that
He bore with Christian fortitude, though fat.
He died lamented deeply by this poem,
And all who had the happiness to know him.

Here is something more than successful imitation, more than the reproduction of a well-known style, "somewhat outré." In *The Heroine* there is a spirit of fun which is the saving grace of true parody and it has a real kinship with the spirit of Johnson's own burlesques.

In his lifetime it was Johnson's *Rambler* prose that provided most of the material for parodists. The publication of the *Life* opened a wider field, and innumerable aspirants have tried their hand at conversational *pastiches*. Sir Joshua Reynolds in his *Two Dialogues* illustrating Johnson's attitude to Garrick had the advantage of first-hand knowledge; he could amplify conversations which he had actually heard and his amplifications preserve the authentic Johnson.

The Reverend James Beresford writing in *The Looker-On* in 1792 caught the Boswellian atmosphere quite successfully, but his *Dialogue between Boswell and Johnson in the Shades* (1802) is laboured and unconvincing.

Similarly disappointing is Landor's *Imaginary Conversation* between Johnson and Horne Tooke. For the most part, it is a lengthy and somewhat technical discussion of philological and etymological problems and the lion's share of the talk is assigned to Horne Tooke. Occasionally there is a little more cut-and-thrust:

TOOKE: Words, like ciphers and persons, have their value from their place. I am sorry you seem offended.

JOHNSON: It is the nature of the impudent never to be angry.

TOOKE: Impudence, I find, is now for the first time in-
          stalled among the Christian virtues.
JOHNSON: No, Sir: impudence is to virtue what cyni-
          cism is to stoicism: nothing is harder or cruel-
          ler; nothing seems less so.

This is crisp enough, but it does not ring quite true.

It is surprising, perhaps, that neither Johnson nor Boswell
was the recipient of one of Andrew Lang's *Letters to Dead
Authors*, but to a small volume of *Golfing Papers* (1892) Lang
contributed a pleasant piece of Boswellian imitation describing Johnson's introduction to St. Andrews:

> He was now determined to exercise himself at the game
> of Golf, which I explained to him as the Scotch form of
> cricket. Having purchased a ball and club, he threw him-
> self into the correct attitude, as near as he could imitate
> it, and delivered a blow with prodigious force. Chancing
> to strike at the same time both the ball and the ground,
> the head of his club flew off to an immense distance. He
> was pleased with this instance of his prowess, but de-
> clined, on the score of expense, to attempt another ex-
> periment. "Sir" he said "if Goldsmith were here, he
> would try to persuade us that he could urge a sphere to a
> greater distance and elevation than yonder gentleman
> who has just hit over that remote sand-pit." Knowing his
> desire for information, I told him that, in Scotch, a sand-
> pit is called a Bunker. "Sir" said he "I wonder out of what
> *colluvies* of barbarism your people selected the jargon
> which you are pleased to call a language. Sir, you have
> battened on the broken meats of human speech, and have
> carried away the bones. A sand-pit, sir, is a sand-pit."

At the beginning of the present century there was a return

to *The Rambler*. In June 1901 Herbert Vivian produced the first number of what he called "the restored Rambler." It was an elegant piece of "period" printing, and in fact the resemblance to its prototype in format and typography was much closer than in subject matter. Vivian was a Tory and an individualist and used his Rambler to tilt against the literary, social, and political tendencies of his time. The disasters of the South African war, the emergence of the "New Woman," the writings of Rudyard Kipling, and many other burning topics of the period come under the lash of his robust invective, and one of his rare articles of commendation, dated 30 November 1901, retains a certain interest for readers of to-day:

> In an age instinct with ponderous Mediocrity, when the successful Part of Mankind is invariably fashioned in one Mould, and Politicians are content to repeat each other's Cries with a Monotony and Lack of Intelligence that would be deplorable in a well-bred Parrot, a cordial Reception awaits any Man who can think for himself, who has the Courage to say what he thinks, and who completes these Qualities by compelling the Publick to hear what he says: such an one, say I, may command our Forgiveness in Advance for many Indiscretions. I have in mind Mr *Winston Churchill*, who, almost alone among the young Men of Prominence and Promise, has refused to be terrorized or cozened by his Leaders or by their Leaders, the Wire-pullers . . .

From these and many other examples that might be quoted, it would appear that good parodies of Johnson the writer are rare. Slavish imitation on the one hand and exaggerated caricature on the other defeat the true purpose of the parodist.

As may be inferred from Professor Clifford's *Johnsonian*

Studies 1887–1950,[1] the composition of Johnsonian or Boswellian imitations is still a flourishing trade, but the practitioners seldom exhibit parody of the highest quality. It may be regretted that Max Beerbohm, the finest parodist of his generation, never treated Johnson in the way that he treated his contemporaries in *A Christmas Garland*, but his essay *A Clergyman* shows an exquisite sensibility to the atmosphere which surrounded Johnson as the Colossus of a *salon*.

A parodist, in fact, must be something of an actor; he must get into the very skin of the author whose part he is playing—not that the analogy of a player would have appealed to Johnson.

"Sir," we can hear Boswell saying, "you will never allow merit to a parodist."

> JOHNSON: What, Sir, a fellow who claps a "Sir" on the beginning of his sentence and a Latin derivative on the end of it and cries *"I am Doctor Johnson?"*

That is where many parodists fail; they pick up the tricks and the mannerisms, but they do not penetrate to their author's heart.

"No parodist," wrote Walter Raleigh, "is successful who has not at some time fallen deeply under the spell of the literature that he parodies," and parodies of Johnson demand spiritual insight as well as verbal imitation. He mimics best who loveth best.

1. "Dr Johnson in Fiction and Drama," 61–64.

Dr. Johnson and The Contrary Converts

JAMES M. OSBORN

This story begins, like many other pages in literary history, with Edmond Malone. Shakespearean editors and students of the Elizabethan stage have long recognized him to be the scholars' scholar, and appropriately have created the Malone Society in his honor. When Drydenians tackle a problem in Restoration literature they turn automatically to Malone. Johnsonians also "begin with Malone": Boswell himself said of Malone, "he is Johnsonianissimus," and much of the work on the great *Life of Johnson* was done in the "elegant study" of Malone's London residence. After Boswell's death Malone superintended four editions of the *Life,* beginning with the third; he continued to augment the biography with new documents and facts until the sixth edition in 1811. Quite fittingly the sumptuous edition of *The Private Papers of James Boswell from Malahide Castle* is dedicated "TO THE MEMORY OF EDMOND MALONE."

When, in January 1811, Malone was busy preparing the sixth edition of the *Life,* he received a helpful letter from his friend, John Nichols, the venerable editor of the *Gentleman's Magazine.* Now preserved among the Malone MSS in the Bodleian, the letter reads as follows:

January 8, 1811

Dear Sir

Understanding that you are engaged in a new Edition of Boswells Life of Johnson, I think it right that you should know that there is still living (in *Britannia Row,*

Islington) an old Friend and Acquaintance of Dr Johnson; concerning whom *Boswell* is silent—and Hawkins,
(in his *Second* Edition) has greatly blundered.

His name is *Compton,* formerly a Roman Catholic
Divine, and Librarian at a Benedictine Convent in Paris,
in which Johnson sojourned. He renounced the Catholic
Religion, on reading a Number of *The Rambler*;—came
afterwards to London—dissuaded Johnson from *retiring*
to the Convent at Paris—was maintained by *Johnson*—
till he could live by teaching the Languages—was recommended to be Master of St. Paul's School, both by
Johnson and *Lowth*—has several of Johnsons Letters—
and abounds in *Anecdotes* of him.—I think he could
have no Objection to communication if you were to address a Line to him.—He is a Man of Character—has a
Pension of our Government, or at least a Salary for
Preaching—and is a regular Member of the Society for
propagating the Gospel.

Possibly all this may either be already known to you,
or not worth knowing. But it at any rate gives me the
Opportunity of shewing an Inclination to communicate
what might be useful; and of assuring you that, with
every good Wish of the Season, I am Sir

Your much obliged
and faithful Servant
J Nichols[1]

Deferring other details for the moment we may profitably
recall the account of Compton that Sir John Hawkins inserted in the second edition (1787) of his *Life of Johnson,* (pp.
530–31):

---

1. This letter and the other quoted below (Bodley MS Malone 39 f. 154,
156) were first printed in Edward Hart's "The Contributions of John
Nichols to Boswell's *Life of Johnson,*" *PMLA,* LXVII (1952), 391–410.

While he [Dr. Johnson] was at Paris, in a visit to a convent in that city, he met with an Englishman, the librarian thereof, an ecclesiastic of the Romish communion, named Compton, who, with the accustomed civility shewn to strangers by persons in his station, produced to him the books of greatest rarity in his custody, and in many other ways gratified his curiosity, and assisted him in his researches. The person, a short time after, came to England, and renounced the errors of popery; but finding no friends, and being in great distress, communicated his wants to the superior of the monks in London, who for some time supplied them; till, having received instructions from France no longer to patronize an apostate, he was obliged to leave him to his fortunes. In this extremity, Mr. Compton recollected his casual acquaintance at Paris with Johnson, and conceiving a hope of assistance from him, found him out and made him a visit. Johnson, at the first interview, heard this story, and, with the warmest expressions of tenderness and esteem, put into his hand a guinea, assuring him, that he might expect support from him till a provision for him could be found, and which he would make it his business to seek. In pursuance of this promise, Johnson furnished him with decent apparel, and afterwards applied to the present bishop of London, who recognized him as a presbyter of the church of England, and licensed him to preach throughout his diocese. Moreover, he allowed money for his support, till about the beginning of last year, when he got to be morning preacher in the church of Allhallows on the Wall, London, and soon after, upon an attestation to his character for three years back, by two clergymen of reputation, he was chosen lecturer of the united parishes of St. Alban's Wood street, and St. Olave Silver street, London.

Chronologically, the next substantial account of Compton comes from the pen of Mrs. Piozzi, who had met him at the Benedictine convent during the excursion of 1775, when she wrote in her diary on October 26th, "Father Librarian & I had a long Tête a Tête in the Print Room, while Queeney danced in another of the Apartments—Johnson staid there till it was time for the Fryars to go to Bed." Twelve years later she recorded in *Thraliana*, under January 28, 1788, the following:

> Compton the Benedictine Fryar who left his Convent at Paris . . . has prospered surprizingly: he came to see me Yesterday, & said he had by his Industry obtained 600£ a Year, almost in *Spite* of our London Clergy, who gave him a very cold reception, and no Encouragement at all . . . Compton however did not become an Anglican from interested Motives—that's clear; He quitted a certain Income, & a very comfortable Life to become an English Parson, and a Beggar,—for such I left the Man receiving a Guinea ev'ry Monday Morning from dear Dr Johnson's charitable Hand, who lived it seems to see him well established, & Money in his Pocket—

Mrs. Piozzi also commented at length about Compton's action in taking a wife despite his former vow of celibacy, and concluded that because he had not known the woman until recently, and since "She did not bring him a Farthing . . . the Fellow *did act upon Principle.*"

Her account of Compton was unknown to Malone, of course, and to all but a handful of privileged readers until the MS was first published by Miss Balderston in 1942. But Malone did look up the account of Compton in Hawkins' second edition and answered Nichols promptly. His letter is missing, but we have Nichols' reply of 10 January 1811, which reads in part:

I have not the *Second* Hawkins—My Copy being the *Editio Princeps*. But the Blunder is, that Sir John represents Dr Johnson's having taken Mr Compton under his Protection, and not quitting him till he had obtained for him *Two Livings*.—I hope you will be able to *extract* much Information from Mr Compton.—Remember to ask him for *the Reason* why *Mr Boswell* did not wish to consult him—and for the story of *Lady Kenmure's Toast* at a Convent in France, THE KING OF ENGLAND!

Of the toast by Frances, Viscountess Kenmure,[2] no record is now preserved; because of her Jacobite connections it seems likely that when Lady Kenmure toasted the King of England she spoke of the Pretender. Luckily the Boswell Papers at Yale contain Compton's original letter to Boswell, now printed by the kindness of the Boswell Editorial Committee and the McGraw-Hill Book Company:

June. 21st—1790

Sir

On hearing from Lady Strange that you were on the eve of publishing the life of your respectable friend Dr Samuel Johnson, I conceived a thought, that perhaps I might have the honour of being mentioned among the living monuments of his universal benevolence. I have been mentioned by Sr John Hawkins in his second edition of the Doctor's life in a manner, respectful indeed to me, but false in the relation. If such anecdotes are to be inter-

2. Frances, Viscountess Kenmure, was the only daughter and heiress of William Mackenzie, fifth Earl of Seaforth (d. 1740). Coming from a Jacobite family, she grew up in France (between the ages of four and eighteen) and was educated by the Blue Nuns at Paris. In 1744 she married John Gordon, attainted eighth Viscount Kenmure. Boswell gives a vivid account of her in 1762 as "prodigiously handsome" when they enjoyed a mild flirtation (*Private Papers*, 1.60–64). After the death of her husband she lived in France but returned to die in Edinburgh (1796).

woven in your history, and you choose to hear from my-self the nature of my connexions with my excellent pa-tron, I will either send you an account of them in writing or will meet you any *evening* you please to appoint.

I generally spent five or six hours alone with him every evening of the winter of the year 1784, and I believe it is entirely owing to me, that he did not retire to end his days in the Benedictine convent at Paris. How different was that notion from what he inculcates in his 6ᵗʰ N[umber] of the Rambler. He little thought that what there he mentions of Cowley would one day be the sub-ject of his own Imitation.

But without entering into farther remarks, for fear of seeming importunate, I will defer them untill I hear whether they come too late, or whether you choose to honour them with your attention.

I am

Sir

your humble Servant

N. 12 Astey Row Islington   James Compton

This letter may reach you several days after the date, as I am to wait on Lady Strange to learn your direction.

Here is amazing news indeed—stated twice unequivocally (to Boswell in 1790 and to Malone *via* Nichols in 1811)—that Johnson, the doughty champion of the Church of England, in the loneliness of old age thought seriously of returning to live at the English Benedictine convent in Paris, where nine years earlier the Prior and the monks had been so cordial to him.

The wonder diminishes somewhat, however, when one re-views the circumstances. His reception at the convent had been so warm that he wrote to Robert Levet, "I am very kindly used by the English Benedictine Friars" (22 October 1775).

A few days later—in fact his last day in Paris—Dr. Johnson revisited the convent. Though he found the dinner of herrings, eels and fried fish "tasteless," he recorded in his diary, "I parted very tenderly from the Prior and Friar Wilkes."[3] On his return to London Johnson told Boswell, "And, Sir, I was very kindly treated by the English Benedictines, and have a cell appropriated to me in their convent" (*Life*, ii.402). Friar Wilks (jokingly called "No. 45" by the other Benedictines) visited Johnson the next year and Johnson gave him a letter of introduction to the Master of Pembroke College, Dr. Adams, saying: "The Gentleman who brings this is a learned Benedictine, in whose monastery I was treated at Paris with all the civilities, which the Society had means or opportunity of showing. I dined in their refectory, and studied in their library, and had the favour of their company to other places, as curiosity led me" (May 29, 1776).

During the following summer Prior Cowley was a guest at Streatham whence Mrs. Thrale reported to Johnson, "I have got some news that will please you now. Here is an agreeable friend come from Paris, whom you were very fond of when we were there—the Prior of our English Benedictine Convent, Mr. Cowley . . . He enquires much for you . . . A cell is always

3. *Life*, ii.399. William Cowley became a monk of St. Laurence's, Dieulewart in 1749, taking the name Dom Gregory, and became Prior in 1765. In 1773 he was translated to the convent of St. Edmund the King at Paris where he presided as Prior until the outbreak of the French Revolution in 1789.—Joseph Wilks of Coughton, Warwickshire, took vows at St. Edmund's and the name Dom Cuthbert on 10 Dec 1764.—James Compton of Salisbury, who had been taken to the continent in 1753 at the age of six, became a monk on 16 Oct 1775 at the very time that Dr. Johnson was hobnobbing with the monks in Paris. In 1782 Compton renounced his vows and returned to England, with the consequences delineated in this paper. For factual details see *Chronological Notes on the English Congregation of the Order of St. Benedict*, B. Weldon, 1881, appendix, pp. 14, 17, 20, 23.

kept ready for your use, he tells me; so when your cruel mistress turns you out, no harm will come of it" (18 Sept. 1777).[4]

Johnson answered her, little anticipating that four years later Thrale would be dead and his mistress soon to fly to Italy: "I am glad that the Benedictines found you at last. Father Wilkes, when he was amongst us, took Oxford in his way. I recommended him to Dr Adams, on whom he impressed a high opinion of his Learning: I am glad that my cell is reserved. I may perhaps some time or other visit it . . ." (25 Sept. 1777).

Additional references to the Benedictines occur in Johnson's correspondence and in Boswell, all testifying to the affectionate regard which Johnson had experienced and reciprocated. It is not surprising, in view of these repeated recollections that "a cell is always kept ready," that a few years later when James Compton came to sit with him during the long lonely evenings, the conversation should turn to the security of convent life. By this time Johnson needed care and attention not available in his own weird household. He knew that his health had been considerably better in France, especially since he there enjoyed greater ease in breathing.

The winter of 1783–84 had been especially difficult for Johnson, who was confined indoors for weeks at a time. In February he wrote Boswell that before the next winter threatened "I shall be glad to try a warm climate." Boswell concurred in the plan and applied for an increase in Johnson's pension to permit him to go to Italy, but the application was denied. Even if he had availed himself of a loan offered by Lord Thurlow, there was the question of who would take care of the sick old man. Until recently a warm room at Streatham had always been waiting for him, where the topic of a trip to Italy together recurred frequently. But the estrangement from

4. Hester Lynch Piozzi, *Letters to and from the Late Samuel Johnson* (1788), I.262.

Thrale's widow reached a climax at the end of June when Johnson wrote the harsh words, "Madam . . . you are ignominiously married." He never again saw Mrs. Piozzi, as she had now blissfully become. Under these circumstances it is not surprising that Johnson's thoughts, like those of other valetudinarians, easily turned to contemplating where he would be welcome, to thinking of a hospice where he had been repeatedly assured, "a cell is always ready for your use when your cruel mistress turns you out."

Moreover, convent life might benefit his spiritual as well as his physical well-being. In May he underwent a miraculous experience, here reported in Boswell's words:

> He had shut himself up, and employed a day in particular exercises of religion, fasting, humiliation, and prayer. On a sudden he obtained extraordinary relief, for which he looked up to Heaven with grateful devotion. He made no direct inference from this fact; but from his manner of telling it, I could perceive that it appeared to him as something more than an incident in the common course of events [*Life*, IV.272].

Even the Methodists heard about it, and began to hope for his conversion to their sect, the very name of which had passed as a term of reproach.[5]

5. See Maurice J. Quinlan, "The Rumor of Dr. Johnson's Conversion," in *Review of Religion*, XII (1948), 243–61. Over fifty books and articles on Dr. Johnson and religion are listed in Clifford's *Johnsonian Studies*, among them many on Johnson's attitude towards Roman Catholicism. Much speculation has been based on the phrase in Dr. Johnson's last prayer, written a week before his death, which asked "forgive and accept my late conversion" (*Life*, IV.417, 553); Boswell omitted it when printing the prayer. But a glance at Johnson's *Dictionary* would have saved much ink, for his first two definitions of "conversion" read: "1. Change from one state to another; transmutation . . . 2. Change from reprobation to grace, from a bad to a holy life" (Quinlan, p. 259).

But Johnson's tendencies in the opposite direction were well marked. After a lifetime of high church Anglicanism he followed the common pattern of tending farther to the right in many of his views as he advanced in age. Actually, in earlier years it is notable that in his discussions with Boswell, Johnson usually took the side of the Roman Catholic church, especially in comparison with the Presbyterian and other low denominations. Only once did Boswell record Johnson as being critical of the "old religion," and that occurred on a Sunday evening when the Doctor "was in the humour of opposition" (*Life*, III.407). In his last year, when Johnson's fear of death intensified, his attitude towards the Roman Church grew even more sympathetic. In June he told Boswell, "I would be a Papist if I could. I have fear enough; but an obstinate rationality prevents me. I shall never be a Papist, unless on the near approach of death, of which I have a very great terrour. I wonder that women are not all Papists" [*Life*, IV.289].

This is not to argue that Johnson considered joining the Roman communion and then retiring to the Benedictine convent in Paris. Guests at St. Edmund's were not required to submit to the Roman obedience. But both Johnson's personal situation and his frame of mind in 1784, as well as other known circumstances, are consistent with James Compton's twice-repeated statement that Johnson thought seriously of going to Paris to occupy the accommodation so cordially offered. Had Johnson done so, his eventual conversion might or might not have followed, a matter that Compton undoubtedly had well in mind. But that is now an academic question, for Johnson remained in England and died in his own bed.

Here a word may be in order about Compton's reliability as a witness. Everything that we know about his trustworthiness and reputation favors his credibility: Dr. Johnson recommended him to churchmen and lay friends alike, Nichols speci-

fied him as "a man of character," and Compton's own letters
have a forthright tone. Moreover Compton's regard for accuracy is shown by his zeal in pinpointing errors in both
Hawkins' and Boswell's books. In Compton's testimony about
Johnson, his only questionable claim is that "I believe it is
entirely owing to me" that Johnson did not enter St. Edmund's
convent. Had the matter reached a head, others would have
joined in protesting, but Compton was certainly in the best
position, based on personal experience, to dissuade Johnson
from further consideration of such a step. We should be fortunate if all depositions about Johnson derived from equally
reliable witnesses.

Boswell nowhere mentions Compton, though we know from
John Nichols' second letter to Malone that Boswell answered
Compton's letter of proffered assistance in 1790 saying that he
"did not wish to consult him." The actual reply from Boswell
to Compton is missing, but a rough sketch does appear
scrawled on the back of Compton's letter. Dated seven months
after Compton wrote him, the draft reply reads:

> R[everen]ᵈ Sir
>   I thank you for the offer which you have been pleased
> to make me; but I have reasons for declining to insert in
> my Life of Dʳ Johnson, a narrative of that nature. You
> will therefore be pleased to excuse me. I am R[everen]ᵈ Sir
> your most obedient humble servant
>   London 19 Febry 1791

Here is another mystery: why did Boswell, who badgered
acquaintances for anecdotes and advertised for information,
give the "brush-off" to such a promising prospect as Compton?

The answer depends in part on when Boswell received the
letter. It bears no postmark, so appears to have been delivered

by hand. Since Boswell's usual habit was to acknowledge letters of this sort promptly, the circumstance argues that Lady Strange or some other intermediary was tardy in providing the address and effecting delivery. Had the letter reached Boswell by the end of July, he could easily have inserted information from Compton in the proper place in Volume II, for only the first volume was then in the printer's hands.

But Boswell's personal affairs may have altered his usual habits of correspondence. Midsummer 1790 was a time of crisis in his life—he had assumed the duties of Recorder of Carlisle in consequence of a mixup from which he could not extract himself. The brutal treatment he received from Lord Lonsdale caused Boswell such mortification that he suffered mental shock and promptly resigned. He hurried back to the quiet guidance of Malone, in whose congenial library he buried himself to revise copy and read proof. Soon he became deeply involved in keeping ahead of the printer.

But even if Compton's letter failed to reach Boswell until the time of Boswell's reply (seven months after the date of the letter) there would still have been time to insert some account of Johnson's sponsorship of the ex-Benedictine, and Compton's reports of Johnson's sayings or actions. Was the subject matter one that Boswell wished to avoid because it would tarnish the statue he had created, the apotheosis of Anglican stability?

Undoubtedly many factors, both conscious and unconscious, were involved in Boswell's response, of which the following were probably in conjunction. First of all, Boswell knew about Compton from Hawkins' second edition, and it is even possible that they had met. Hence, the omission of any mention of Compton, whom Hawkins had cited as a prime example of Johnson's constructive habits of charity (as Malone did later, also), a favorite subject with Boswell, suggests that Boswell had some personal reason for his action. Perhaps Compton's letter sounded overly aggressive, as if he aspired to thrust himself into immortality through Boswell's pages: Compton himself considered that a conscious and significant purpose prompted Boswell's conduct, and stressed the point when talking to Nichols.

The most reasonable explanation of Boswell's "declining to insert in my Life of Dr Johnson, a narrative of that nature" seems to be that he considered Compton was exaggerating both his intimacy with his patron and his report of Johnson's attitude towards the possible retreat to the monastery. Boswell had heard the narratives of Langton and others who devoted many hours to sitting with Johnson as the end approached. The Rev. Samuel Hoole supplied a written account, teeming with daily details. The reports of these known witnesses doubt less outweighed the testimony of one whom Boswell may well have considered eccentric in his religious conduct.

Turning now from Compton's rebuff in 1790 to Malone's labors on the sixth edition in 1811, we find that this time Compton received a cordial response. Malone's letters to him are not known to exist, but from a long footnote Malone introduced into the sixth edition (IV.224–27) we learn that a sympathetic meeting of the two Johnsonians took place. In his footnote Malone straightened out the details of the Compton story, and even inserted two of Johnson's letters that Compton offered. Happily, the copy of the fifth edition that Malone corrected and sent to the printer is now in the collection of Professor F. W. Hilles, thanks to whom we can follow the story at first hand. At the top of page 222 of Volume IV Malone wrote a note to the printer:

> Whenever this sheet is composed, Mr. Dillon is requested to send *two* proofs of it to Mr. Malone some days before it may be wanted to be printed off, as he wishes to shew

one of the proofs to the gentleman concerned in the long note who [erasure] does not live in London.

At the proper place in the text Malone indicated where this "long note" was to go, and instructed the printer, "Insert here the long note marked ⚜ ." The paper became separated from the rest of the copy but is now preserved in the William Salt Library at Stafford. It is in Malone's hand and carries his mark ⚜ at the top.[6]

At this stage it is worth while looking at the long note (omitting Johnson's letters and some other details) because Malone admirably summarizes Compton's career and his connections with Johnson.

> The reader will recollect, that in the year 1775, when Dr. Johnson visited France, he was kindly entertained by the English Benedictine Monks at Paris ... One of that body, the Reverend James Compton, in the course of some conversation with him at that time, asked him, if any of them should become converts to the Protestant faith, and should visit England, whether they might hope for a friendly reception from him; to which he warmly replied, "that he should receive such a convert most cordially." In consequence of this conversation, Mr. Compton, a few years afterwards, having some doubts concerning the religion in which he had been bred, was induced, by reading the 110ᵗʰ Number of *The Rambler* (on REPENTANCE),[7] to consider the subject more deeply; and the result of his

6. Professor James L. Clifford called my attention to this document, and kindly made photographs available.

7. Mrs. Thrale's *French Journal* (p. 144) records that on taking leave of the Nuns of Notre Dame she presented a copy of *Rasselas* and of the *Rambler*. It is not impossible that they also left a copy of the *Rambler* with their Benedictine friends, which would have made it readily available to Compton.

inquiries was, a determination to become a protestant. With this view, in the summer of 1782, he returned to his native country, from whence he had been absent from his sixth to his thirty-fifth year; and on his arrival in London, very scantily provided with the means of subsistence; he immediately repaired to Bolt-court, to visit Dr. Johnson; and having informed him of his desire to be admitted into the Church of England, for this purpose solicited his aid to procure for him an introduction to the Bishop of London (Dr. Lowth). At the time of his first visit, Johnson was so much indisposed, that he could allow him only a short conversation of a few minutes; but he desired him to call again in the course of the following week. When Mr Compton visited him a second time, he was perfectly recovered from his indisposition; received him with the utmost cordiality; and not only undertook the management of the business in which his friendly interposition had been requested, but with great kindness exerted himself in this gentleman's favour, with a view to his future subsistence, and immediately supplied him with the means of present support ... Mr. Compton having, by Johnson's advice, quitted Highgate, and settled in London, had now more frequent opportunities of visiting his friend, and profiting by his conversation and advice. Still, however, his means of subsistence being very scanty, Dr. Johnson kindly promised to afford him a decent maintenance, until by his own exertions he should be able to obtain a livelihood; which benevolent offer he accepted, and lived entirely at Johnson's expence till the end of January, 1783; in which month, having previously been introduced to Bishop Lowth, he was received into our communion in St. James's parish-church. In the following April, the place of Under-Master of St. Paul's school having become vacant, his friendly protector did him a more essential service . . . [Dr. Johnson's] letter procured Mr. Compton so many well-wishers in the respectable company of Mercers, that he was honoured, by the favour of several of its members, with more applications to teach Latin and French, than he could find time to attend to.— In 1796, the Reverend Mr. Gilbert, one of his Majesty's French Chaplains, having accepted a living in Guernsey, nominated Mr. Compton as his substitute at the French Chapel of St. James's; which appointment in April 1811, he relinquished for a better in the French Chapel at Bethnal-Green.—By the favour of Dr. Porteus, the late excellent Bishop of London, he was also appointed, in 1802, Chaplain of the Dutch Chapel at St. James's; a station which he still holds.

After Compton received the proof-sheets and had read them attentively, the Johnsonian ardor warmed in his breast. Taking up his quill he dashed off another letter to Malone, going beyond corrections to the proof-sheets to recount a colorful incident of 1783 that is entirely unknown to Johnson's biographers and editors. This letter is now in my collection; for purposes of narration the following transcription is interspersed with commentary:

> Church Lane april 23, 1811
>
> Dear Sir
> I have received your proof sheets this evening and will spend the remaining part of it with you. If it be not too late I will suggest to you the alteration of one word in your narrative of me. Towards the end you say *Dutch church*, had you not better have said *chapel*? It is the very *chapel* in which the *French* service is performed. I think all the rest is correct, and thank you for the honour you have done me in making such mention of me.

> I have read the other pages of your proof-sheets, which have revived many pleasant Ideas in my mind. I several times met Mr Lowe at the Doctor's house. Boswel makes me smile at his account of Lowe's *picture*. It is very inaccurate indeed. But that is unimportant.

Malone, as we have seen, made the correction to Dutch Chapel. "Lowe's picture" refers to Dr. Johnson's intercession with Sir Joshua Reynolds and other Royal Academicians in April 1783, on behalf of Mauritius Lowe, whose canvas was refused by the Academy despite their having granted him a gold medal in 1769 and accepted his pictures in subsequent years. Happily, Johnson's "intercession was too powerful to be resisted," and the painting, "execrable beyond belief" was admitted, though hung by itself in an empty room (*Life*, IV.202). Incidentally, it was only a few days later, on Easter Sunday, that Lowe teamed up with Boswell to pry details of Johnson's sexual history from Mrs. Desmoulins, as recorded in the "Tacenda" passage in Boswell's Journal. But to continue with Compton's letter,

> How happily you have introduced *my* connexion with the Doctor after having mentioned the declaration of Mrs Thrale! Here is an anecdote about Walker for *your* amusement. If you choose to give it to the publick, you may. I will vouch for the truth of it.

This introduces us to John Walker, onetime actor and schoolmaster who later had devoted his considerable energies and analytical ability to the study of elocution and pronunciation, while maintaining his family by giving lectures and taking pupils. Somewhere along the way Walker had been converted from the Presbyterian Church to the Roman Catholic, and became increasingly strict in his observances. Since Walker was well acquainted with Garrick, he may have come to Johnson's attention before 1775 when he published his *Dictionary of the English Language . . . on a Plan . . . Not Hitherto Attempted.* The novelty was that "The whole language is arranged according to its terminations," so that "Wolf" immediately preceded "Gulf," and "Un-Thought-of" preceded "Scarf." Walker's volume concluded with a rhyming dictionary which prompted the *Monthly Review* to remark: "our young sucking poetasters may think themselves much obliged to him for such a grand magazine of hitching terminations, which will leave them nothing to do but to fill up the measure as well as they can. It is indeed an essay toward Dean Swift's ludicrous scheme for composing books mechanically by an engine" (LII.399). The rhyming dictionary soon left the "new plan" behind, and later editions became such a standard tool for poets that Byron confesses in *Beppo* that

> "Not caring as I ought for critics' cavils,"
> [I take] "The first that Walker's Lexicon unravels."

By 1781 Walker knew Johnson well enough to dedicate to him his *Elements of Elocution* in two closely reasoned volumes, illustrated by engraved plates whose curvatious diagrams showed the rise and fall of the voice and other subtleties of his system. The only time that Walker appears in Boswell's *Life* is on Friday, 18 April 1783, when in a lengthy conversation Johnson resisted the idea that clergymen could be taught elocution effectively; Boswell commented, "Here was one of his peculiar prejudices." But Boswell missed out on the dramatic sequel, which occurred a few days later, according to Compton:

> At the latter end of April 83 I called on the Doctor at his house, where I found him alone with Mr Walker. The Doctor seemed to be uncommonly pleased on seeing me enter and most chearfully exclaimed, I must introduce

you two gentlemen to each other.[8] Mr Compton, this gentleman has quitted our Church to embrace that, which you have lately quitted. This is Mr Walker: perhaps you have heard of his book. How do you account for one another's conduct? My intimate acquaintance with the book certainly prevented all coldness natural on the first meeting of such contrary converts. I was glad to meet an author, who I thought had rendered me infinite service.

Here is one of the high moments of Johnsonian delight in inverted antitheses, a counterpoint of transposed ratiocinations.

The conversation ran on continually between him and me about his book. The Doctor was very attentive to everything that we said. I named several Catholick priests, who had read and admired the book. All which was very pleasing to Mr Walker. But, said the Doctor rather warmly, all these either saw Mr Walker personally or received explanations from persons who had seen him. I was surprised at such a remark, and declared positively that I had read the book at Paris alone in my cell, that I had been much delighted and much improved by it. The Doctor appeared to be rather incredulous and asked me if I were sure I understood it. I answered that I certainly understood it as well as Mr Walker himself. Are you willing to be examined? I am Doctor. Mr Walker, examine the gentleman; I will take your word. Mr Walker then proposed several questions to me, which I answered entirely to his satisfaction. He then ordered me to read aloud the three

8. Johnson's letter to Mrs. Thrale, written 26 Dec 1782 (*Letters* 819.1), reported seeing both Compton and Walker; but the above passage shows that they were not with Johnson at the same time.

last verses of the 8ᵗʰ C[hapter] of Sᵗ Paul to the Rom[ans]: I did so: and he declared I read them perfectly according to his rules. I am satisfied, said the Doctor, and taking, I *think*, a guinea out of his pocket he gave it to Mʳ Walker and said *I believe you will never find another*, meaning that he would never find another man to own, that he had profited by the book *without the explanation of a master.* He told me he had some years before laid a wager with Mʳ Walker of that tendency. I never saw Mʳ Walker any more. The Doctor consoled himself and seemed to give full credit to what I said, when I assured him that it cost me as much trouble, to be convinced of my having caught Mʳ Walker's meaning by his curve lines, as to understand the first book of Euclid's elements . . . And now Mʳ Malone, I wish you a good night.

I am

Sir

with the sincerest gratitude

your humble servant

James Compton

To conclude briefly, both of Johnson's contrary converts achieved successful careers, thus fully justifying the Great Doctor's faith and efforts in their behalf. Walker published a number of books, including a *Rhetorical Grammar* in 1785 (dedicated, like the *Elements of Elocution,* to Johnson) and his *Critical Pronouncing Dictionary* in 1791 which reigned as the accepted authority on English pronunciation until superseded by the *Oxford English Dictionary.* Walker taught many famous pupils, including Boswell's son Alexander, and died much bewept by them in 1807.

Compton's career to 1811 we have already followed, and little more can be learned about him, not even the date of his death. That he did succeed in securing a small glimmer of immortality was due to a connection with his "excellent patron," Samuel Johnson. On that October day in 1775 when the newly professed monk showed the treasures of the Benedictine Library to the blinking old Englishman dressed in "brown clothes, black stockings and plain shirt," who shared their dinner of herring, eels, and fried fish, little did he anticipate where it would take him. But that was before he read the 110th number of *The Rambler,* on REPENTANCE.

Dr. Johnson and the Young Burneys

"We shall go down hand in hand to posterity."

JOYCE HEMLOW

Dr. Johnson "was always indulgent to the young, he never attacked the unassuming," and this observation is nowhere better illustrated than in the great man's kindness to Dr. Burney's young family. "I love . . . all of the race which I do know, and some that I do not, and love them for loving each other."[1] And the scribbling race, "Burney's girls," was able to repay his kindness. Nothing—not even the awe in which they had been brought up to regard Dr. Johnson—could curb their fun-loving powers of observation or lay trammels on the secret journal entries, in which Great Sam now appears in a very agreeable light.

They had first seen him in 1777 when he came by invitation to pay an evening visit to St. Martin's Street. When he entered, a little late, "every body rose to do him honour; and he returned the attention with the most formal courtesie." Esther and Susan were in the midst of a duet on the harpsichord, and

1. Unless otherwise identified, quotations derive from the second volume of *The Early Diary of Frances Burney, 1768–1778*, ed. Ellis (1913); the first two volumes of *Diary and Letters of Madame d'Arblay*, ed. Dobson (1904); and the second and third volumes of Mme. d'Arblay's *Memoirs of Doctor Burney* (1832).

For permission to read and to quote from the Burney MSS I wish to make grateful acknowledgements to the New York Public Library, the British Museum, and to Mr. James M. Osborn. Grateful thanks are also owing to Miss Ann Julia Wauchope, former owner of the Barrett Collection (which is now in the British Museum), and to Miss Ellen Thibaudeau for reading and emending the typescript.

his attention had to be drawn to this, said Fanny, for because of tone-deafness he might not otherwise have found it out! But if he was deaf to the tinkling cascades of notes and blind in one eye ("That Rascal has not served me these twenty years"),[2] he had senses still awake to youthful freshness and beauty and, just then, to the flying motion of the four girlish hands on the keyboard. Somewhat baffled by the melodic art, but curious still, he bent his great head and wig so closely over the keys that the performers could scarcely hit the high notes without hitting him or, what was still more difficult, "keep their countenances," an effort by no means assisted by the ogles of Mr. Seward in the background. When the piece was ended Dr. Burney presented his daughters, and first of all, Esther, who long ago had been presented with an *Idler* and who was now rewarded with a loud and hearty "salute." After these marks of respect to Dr. Burney, his art, and his progeny, the great man moved off to the book shelves, "almost brushing them with his eye-lashes from near examination." "At last, fixing upon something that happened to hit his fancy, he took it down, and, standing aloof from the company, which he seemed clean and clear to forget, he began, without further ceremony, and very composedly, to read to himself; and as intently as if he had been alone in his own study."

Dr. Burney and his eldest daughter then played a duet. Obviously there was no hope of hearing anything else—a specimen, for instance, of the famed conversation. Dr. Johnson was now engrossed in a volume of the *British Encyclopaedia*. The "leviathan of literature" read on; Dr. Burney played; and the young Burneys made mental notes for future journal entries. Dr. Johnson was "indeed, very ill-favoured!"

> Yet he has naturally a noble figure; tall, stout, grand, and authoritative: but he stoops horribly; his back is quite

2. Letter (in the Barrett Collection, British Museum) from Charlotte (Burney) Broome to Mme. d'Arblay, 7, 9 Jan [1834].

round: his mouth is continually opening and shutting, as if he were chewing something; he has a singular method of twirling his fingers, and twisting his hands: his vast body is in constant agitation, see-sawing backwards and forwards: his feet are never a moment quiet; and his whole great person looked often as if it were going to roll itself, quite voluntarily, from his chair to the floor.

He had many afflictions and oddities of manner: "He has almost perpetual convulsive movements, either of his hands, lips, feet, or knees, and sometimes of all together." His dress was of sturdy make and has proved indeed a durable part of the "immortal memory": "He had a large, full, bushy wig, a snuff-colour coat, with gold buttons, (or, peradventure, brass,) but no ruffles to his doughty fists; and not, I suppose, to be taken for a Blue, though going to the Blue Queen, he had on very coarse black worsted stockings."

The only irreverent Burney was the youngest—Charlotte Ann: "Dr. Johnson was immensely *smart*, for *him*,—for he had not only a very decent tidy suit of cloathes on, but his hands, face, and linnen were clean, and he treated us with his *worsted wig* which Mr. Thrale made him a present of, because it scarce ever gets out of curl, and he generally diverts himself with laying down just after he has got a fresh wig on." But time brings about curious revenges. With the absent-mindedness of the aged or preoccupied, Dr. Johnson always referred to Susan Burney's sister Charlotte as *Sophy*, from the analogy of *Susan and Sophy* Thrale. "He calls you *Miss Sophy* Mrs Thrale says—being used I suppose to join the names *Susan & Sophy* together."[3] And the youngest and prettiest Burney has

3. Letter (Barrett) from Susan Elizabeth Burney to Charlotte Ann Burney, 22 Sep [1781]. This letter (with other evidence) corrects the identification of "Sophy" attempted by the late Dr. Scholes for Dr. Chapman. See *Letters* 703.1, n. 2, and index.

suffered some anonymity, therefore, in Johnsonian notes and indexes.

The visit ended after all in some very good talk and a few critical pronouncements on Garrick and the flaws in the "fabulosity" of a prologue he had written ("the call of an eagle," commented Johnson, "never yet had much tendency to restore the warbling of a blackbird"). In a post mortem on the evening the young Burneys complained that their father had not warned them sufficiently what to expect. Dr. Burney laughed, recalling his own first impressions, adding, however, that all that was soon forgotten. The Mind and the Conversation of the man were such as to erase all other impressions. The great man had indeed many afflictions, but "the sight of them," concluded Fanny,

> can never excite ridicule, or, indeed, any other than melancholy reflections upon the imperfections of Human Nature; for this, who is the acknowledged First Literary man in this Kingdom, & who has the most extensive knowledge, the clearest understanding, & the greatest abilities of any Living Author,—has a Face the most ugly, a Person the most awkward, & manners the most singular, that ever were, or ever can be seen. But all that is unfortunate in his *exterior*, is so greatly compensated for in his *interior*, that I can only, like Desdemona to Othello, *"see his visage in his Mind."*[4]

Another evening in St. Martin's Street has been inimitably described by Virginia Woolf.[5] This was the evening when Fulke Greville, half dead with the toothache, had posted himself with two or three other gentlemen before the fireplace,

4. Diary MSS (in the Henry W. and Albert A. Berg Collection, the New York Public Library), 703–4.
5. "Dr. Burney's Evening Party," *The Second Common Reader* (1932).

and Dr. Johnson, sunk irretrievably, as everyone thought, in oblivious and impenetrable depths of meditation, had nevertheless come suddenly to the surface with the remark that "if he was not *ashamed* he would keep the fire from the ladies too." The culprits catapulted therewith from the spot, and the haughty Greville too "was obliged to stalk off in spight of his teeth." Very soon thereafter he rang for his carriage, the evening scene was dispersed as if by a bolt from Olympus, and no one "ever asked, or wished for its repetition." It was some time before the Burneys learned that Dr. Johnson would not talk of his own volition. He had to be "summoned forth to distinguish himself"; and if this did not happen, said Fanny, he commonly "wrapt himself up in his own thoughts . . . completely absorbed in silent rumination: sustaining, nevertheless, a grave and composed demeanour, with an air by no means wanting in dignity any more than in urbanity."

Susan, however, could tell of a happier, more normal evening in 1780 when

> Dr. Johnson & Mrs Williams came an hour before dinner —at 3 o clock—but he was in very good humour & very *charming* all day . . . at about 9 Mr. Greville, Dr. Russel & Mr. Harris came, & the 2 latter infinitely added to the agreeability of the remainder of the Evening, & at Eleven Dr. Johnson s^d to my Father, "When I last look'd at my watch sir it was eight o'clock, & now it is eleven, & I have not perceived how the time has passed."—And yet he was not asleep any part of it!—He was full of wit & brilliancy wth Dr Russel, who alone dared oppose him, on various subjects, but particularly on Politics—& D^r R—defended his opinion wth so much frankness, but gave it up when hard run wth such goodhumour, that he drew out Dr Johnson, & contributed greatly to the amusement of the whole Company— . . . latterly the conversation took a more

learned turn, & D[r] Johnson talk'd upon the Greek & other Languages, chiefly with M[r] Harris . . . & I believe had Mrs Williams been well, D[r] J: w[d] have stay'd to sup wth us, as Mr. Greville did, & *Edward,* who had come by invitation to tea.[6]

"Everybody went away apparently pleased wth this visit" and Susan, too, had had her moments. When she went downstairs with Mrs. Williams, Dr. Johnson detained her.

> *"And how do you live, said he, without Fanny?*—Very ill I told him—
>
> "Aye, s[d] he, shaking his head & laughing, *I hope she will never come back any more!*" At dinner he invited me to sit by him—*Come here my Love,* s[d] he,—It shall be you & I—" & Ma'am he kiss'd my hand!—should I forget *that?*[6]

Johnson had not devoted all his thoughts to Politics and the Greek; and as James L. Clifford has observed, he was not unsuccessful with women.[7]

Susan had had an earlier triumph on the occasion of her first visit to Streatham. In the summer of 1779 Dr. Burney and this favoured "bantling" had set out for a midsummer jaunt to Chessington, and on the way, it being about eleven in the morning, the Doctor determined to call at Streatham and give Queeney Thrale her music lesson. "As a *place,*" said Susan, "it surpassed all my expectations. The avenue to the house, plantations, &c. are beautiful . . . a little Paradise, I think. Cattle, poultry, dogs, all running freely about, without annoying each other." Inside, in the library, "sat Mrs. Thrale and Dr. Johnson, the latter finishing his breakfast upon peaches." When

6. Journal-Letter (Barrett) from Susan Elizabeth Burney to Fanny Burney, 20 Apr [1780].

7. *Young Sam Johnson* (1955), 153, 317.

Mrs. Thrale went to fetch some burlesque verses composed the evening before, Dr. Johnson invited Susan to take the vacated seat near him.

> "Come, come here, my little dear," said he, with great kindness, and took my hand as I sat down, I took then courage to deliver your [Fanny's] respects.
> "Aye.—Why don't she come among us?" said he.
> I said you . . . were very sorry to be away.
> "A rogue!" said he, laughing. "She don't mind *me*!"

While Dr. Burney and Queeney were engaged in the music room, Mrs. Thrale showed Susan over the house—the bedrooms and dressing-rooms, Fanny's room and desk, the dining-parlour, and, outside, the "sweet plantations" and summerhouses. When they came in, Miss Thrale sang *In te spero,* and Susan, when called upon, *Poveri affetti,* because she thought the words might please Mrs. Thrale. While Dr. Burney was playing over some songs from the *Olimpiade,* Dr. Johnson entered the music room with a book in his hand intending to show him some passage, but finding him engaged,

> he put his arm round me, and smiling very good-humouredly, said,
> "Now you don't expect that I shall ever love you so well as I do your sister?"
> "Oh, no, Sir," said I—"I have no such hopes—I am not so presumptious."
> "I am glad you are so *modest,*" said he, laughing,—and so encouraged by his good-humour, (and he kept *see-sawing* me backwards and forwards in his arms, as if he had taken me for *you*) that I told him I must make an interest with him *through you.* He again said he was glad I was so *modest,* and added—"but I believe *you're* a good

little creature—I think one should love *you*, too, *if one did but know you!*"

Mr. Thrale also behaved with the utmost gallantry, making complaint that he too *"had not had fair play about that Miss Susan."* There was then, to conclude, Dr. Johnson's "very good-natured farewell—'*Goodbye, my little love!*' " "There's for you!" rejoiced Susan; "I assure you I shall set this little conversation down among my first honours. It put me in good humour and spirits for the rest of the day!"

If it had not been for Dr. Burney's thinking it such nonsense in his daughters to write long journal-letters to someone who would be seen within a few days, we should know more about the Old Philosopher's visit to Chessington, when he came with the Thrales in a coach-and-four over the dusty summer roads to pay his respects to Mr. Crisp. Susan, Fanny, and other guests in the picturesque old boarding-house of the Hamiltons had been peering for hours over the common with a telescope, but just as all hope failed, the coach was espied. Dr. Burney and Fanny went out to receive the visitors, and Susan, contriving to be much in the way, "received such a Salute from Dr Johnson after he had kissed Fanny, that I was half afraid he had pull'd down all my hair, for he put his two great hands [on] each side of my head to draw me towards him in a very awkward but very goodnatured manner—Mr Thrale too . . . but with somewhat more Gentleness." There was much prowling about the curious old mansion, but at four when the guests were departing, Susan was singled out again. *"Goodbye Susey,* cried Dr Johnson *twice* to me—how comically goodnatured!"[8]

There are many anecdotes reflecting Johnson's kindness, and if his notice was sometimes a little awkward, sometimes a

8. Letter (Barrett) from Susan Elizabeth Burney to Charlotte Ann Burney, 22 Sep [1781].

little abstracted, it was always, it may be said, "improving." And there was a wide variety of youthful recipients: the little bride at Streatham whom he invited forth to see the swans and the Kamchatka dog, but whom he absent-mindedly deserted in the stableyard to make her way back alone;[9] the printers' urchins and schoolboys to whom he gave free but impressive pieces of advice along with the last piece of silver in his pocket;[1] and his godchild, Bennet Langton's little daughter Jane, to whom he sometimes sent letters. One letter addressed to "My dearest Miss Jenny" was "written in a plain hand and worded so that a child of eight years old could understand every syllable." "I am glad, my Dear, to see that you write so well, and hope that you mind your pen, your book, and your needle."[2]

No kindness, however, struck the Burneys with more heartfelt gratitude than Johnson's countenance of the wild young Charles, later to become a Greek scholar of eminence and a Divine. In the days when the Burneys were painfully sensitive about his disgrace at Cambridge, the gay irresponsibilities of his career at Aberdeen, his levity, and the refusal of the Bishop of London to ordain him, Johnson often gave Dr. Burney helpful advice about the boy and often invited Charles himself to come to Bolt Court to talk about philology. The kindness of the old Grecians, Twining, Parr, and Johnson, to the gay and gifted but volatile young Burney is in itself a chapter in humane letters.[3]

After the publication of *Evelina* in 1778, when Fanny lived,

9. A holograph (Barrett), signed H.S. Printed in Joyce Hemlow, *The History of Fanny Burney* (1958), 115.

1. E.g., *Life*, III.223.

2. *Letters* 959. This letter, "framed & glazed" and in the possession of Miss Langton in 1836, was shown around Brighton as "a treasure and a curiosity." "King William sent for her & the letter to the Pavilion." See letter (Barrett) from Charlotte Barrett to Mme. d'Arblay, 22 June [1836].

3. The Twining-Burney Correspondence, 1777–83 (British Museum).

like Johnson himself, as something of a permanent guest at Streatham, she came to know the great man very well. The Old Philosopher and the young novelist alike had wit, a sense of fun, a keen perception of the ridiculous, and imagination. On the Old Wit's part at least, there were astute psychological insights into the deeps of human nature,[4] and the young witling was at least a keen observer, detecting ludicrous shams and pretences with unerring vision. Nothing amused them more than to build up imaginary superstructures in ridiculous human behaviour based on the detection of some flaw or weakness in the springs of action. Johnson's peals of laughter at his own images of Bennet Langton's complacent acts and speech after making his will seem still to echo around Temple-gate.[5] At Streatham he used often to amuse the company with these fancies. On one occasion, in an imaginary reconstruction of Cumberland's chagrin at his daughters being hissed from the theatre because of the height of their feathers, Johnson assumed the part of the "provoking condoler":

> "Mr. Cumberland (I should say), how monstrously ill-bred is a playhouse mob! How I pitied poor Miss Cumberlands about that affair!"
>
> "What affair?" cries he, for he has tried to forget it.
>
> "Why," says I, "that unlucky accident they met with some time ago."
>
> "Accident? what accident, sir?"
>
> "Why, you know, when they were hissed out of the play-

4. For Johnson's analytical comment on one of the Burney catastrophes see *Letters* 557 and index (under Burneys). The runaway daughter in question, however, was not Maria Allen, who eloped with Martin Folkes Rishton in 1772, but a second daughter, Elizabeth, who eloped with an adventurer, Mr. Meeke, in 1777.

5. *Life*, II.262; see also W. J. Bate, *The Achievement of Samuel Johnson* (1955), 116–18.

house—you remember the time—oh, the English mob is most insufferable! they are boors, and have no manner of taste!"

In social discourse wit ruled the day. It was not uncommon for the Doctor to laugh so heartily "as to almost shake his seat as well as his sides." Fanny was amazed at "the gaiety of his ideas!" "How little did I expect, at a distance, from this Lexiphanes, this great & dreaded Lord of English literature, a turn so comic & diverting for burlesque humour!"[6]

But if there was gaiety, there was also "feeling," this being the eighteenth century; and the Victorian editors of the Streatham journals often felt forced to curtail champagne parties, moonlight strolls on the grounds, and comfortable tête à-têtes in the soft darkness of the summer evenings, "for we have no Candles at Streatham till we go to the Library."

> "I was afraid, sir," cried I, "you did not intend to know me again, for you have not spoken to me before since your return from town."
>
> "My dear," cried he, taking both my hands, "I was not sure of you, I am so near-sighted, and I apprehended making some mistake."
>
> [Then the great man, drawing her unexpectedly towards him, kissed her.]

And apropos of Mrs. Thrale's and Murphy's insistence that Fanny undertake a comedy: "I wish you success! I wish you well! my dear little Burney! . . . There is none like you, my dear little Burney! there is none like you!—good-night, my darling!" On another occasion,

6. Diary MSS (Berg), 754. For extempore verses, see Joyce Hemlow, "Dr. Johnson and Fanny Burney—Some Additions to the Record," *Bulletin of the New York Public Library*, LV (1951), 55–65, and *The History of Fanny Burney*, 114–15.

this dear Doctor Johnson came to the back of my chair: &
I told him I hoped he was better than when I saw him
last?—

"Ah, cried he . . . you hope nothing about the matter,—
but have you seen the Print I have brought you?"

"No, where is it?"

"In the Library." Up I *hoisted* . . . & Dr. Johnson, taking
one of the candles, said, "I'll light you." (To be sure the
Pitches did not giggle—nor Mr. Beresford stare, & to be
sure Sir Philip will never again be jocose about my sweetheart!)

The Print is as like him as it can look, & I am sure I
shall ever value it among things most precious to me.

When I had received & thanked him for it, he would
not let me return to the company, but desired me to stay
where I was,—& so, most sociably, we seated ourselves to
a very comfortable Tete à Tete & talked over matters,
things & Persons without *reserve or favour* & we stayed
together till the Ladies & Mr. Beresford departed & the
rest of the family came to eat Brawn.[7]

If wit, talents, and modesty, together with being their
father's daughters, purchased an immunity for the young
Burneys, there were other young ladies by no means so fortunate. The good-humoured Miss Brown with the "wild, careless, giddy manner" and the soft and languishing Sophy
Streatfield alike "were in fevers in [Johnson's] presence, from
apprehension."

"Do you remember, sir," said Mrs. Thrale, "how you
tormented poor Miss Brown about reading?"

7. Letter (Barrett) from Fanny Burney to Susan Elizabeth Burney, 25
Mar 1782. This print is in the collection of James M. Osborn (see illustration). It is annotated by Fanny: "Given to F.B. by Dr. Johnson, Feb.
17.—82."

Samuel Johnson (after Trotter's engraving, 1782)

"She might soon be tormented, madam," answered he, "for I am not yet quite clear she knows what a book is."

"Dr. Johnson has more fun, and comical humour, and love of nonsense about him, than almost anybody I ever saw: I mean with those he likes," emended Fanny, "for otherwise, he can be as severe and as bitter as report relates him."

Mental and physical suffering must sometimes find a vent, and Johnson's strokes of wit, as everyone knew, were often harsh and cruel. "Oh, sometimes I think I shall die no other death," said Mrs. Thrale, "than hearing the bitter things he says to others." "Dr. Johnson says indeed that no one person feels more for the Danger of another than does the Horse when the Cow miscarries, but I cannot think that true."[8] No one venerated Johnson's "Giant Talents & virtues" more than did Dr. Burney, but he too deplored the noisy violence of both Burke and Johnson, "who were both impatient of control & sometimes so violent as to treat [even the gentle Sir Joshua Reynolds, for instance] harshly & unworthily." Although Sir Joshua sometimes complained to Dr. Burney, he had such respect for the two great men and "knew their value so much to exceed their imperfections, that he never let them know how much they wounded his feelings by their loud voice & unguarded expressions."[9] Few escaped; and Dr. Burney tells another story about an evening in the theatre when Dr. Johnson and Dr. Sumner sat "talking & laughing loud," and the young David Garrick, in the midst of a tragic part, not unnaturally complained that they "destroyed his feeling." In his youth, Garrick had an inexhaustible, if not impudent, flow of spirits. "He c^d put off tragedy and put on comedy, like a gar-

8. Letter (Berg) from Hester Lynch Thrale to Fanny Burney, 29 Nov 1783.

9. Charles Burney (Mus. Doc.), extant fragments of his Memoirs (Berg).

ment," and this may in part explain the severity of Johnson's rejoinder: "No, no, Davy. Punch never feels!"[1]

Fanny knew that there were dinner guests who considered Dr. Johnson "as amusing as a fit of the toothache"; and so Mr. Pepys must have felt on the occasion of "the grand Battle upon the Life of Lyttelton." "I never saw Dr. Johnson really in a passion but then," said Fanny, "and dreadful, indeed, it was to see!"

> "It was a frightful scene. *He* so red, poor Mr. Pepys so pale!"
>
> "But how did it begin? What did he say?"
>
> "Oh, Dr. Johnson came to the point without much ceremony! He called out aloud, before a large company, at Dinner. 'What have you to say, sir, *to* me or *of* me? Come forth, man! I hear you object to my *Life of Lord Lyttelton*. What are your objections? If you have anything to say, let's hear it. Come forth, man, when I call you!' "
>
> "What a *call*, indeed!—why then he fairly bullyed him into a quarrel?"[2]

Mr. Pepys would have liked to avoid a fall with "so tremendous a literary athlete," and in spite of the respect that Fanny had for his prowess, she had to admit that on this occasion at least the giant appeared but *mortal* and, to own the truth, "unreasonably furious and grossly severe." "His long-excited wrath," said Fanny, "now burst forth with a vehemence and bitterness almost incredible." Mrs. Thrale, perhaps, might have interfered,

> but a very provoking accident happened to herself. She had called for a Tumbler of water, & the Butler, by mistake, gave her a Tumbler of champagne; but she drank

1. *Ibid.*
2. Diary MSS (Berg), 1843–7.

it entirely off without finding out what she was about. For she does every thing with that sort of impetuosity,—but the moment she had finished, she called out what is it you have given me?—& she grew so extremely frightened when she found it was champagne, that she did nothing but terrify herself, & swallow water, Glass after Glass, all Dinner Time. And that occupied her so entirely, that she could attend to nothing at all else. Otherwise *she* might perhaps have had power to call them to order.[3]

Fanny was not so alarmed, however, as to miss the "one happy circumstance" of the quarrel—namely, the presence of Mr. Cator. This gentleman, "who would by no means be prevented talking himself, either by reverence for Dr. Johnson, or ignorance of the subject in question . . . gave his opinion, quite uncalled, upon everything that was said by either party, and that with an importance and pomposity, yet with an emptiness and verbosity, that rendered the whole dispute, when in his hands, nothing more than ridiculous, and compelled even the disputants themselves, all inflamed as they were, to laugh."

"As to this here question of Lord Lyttelton, I can't speak to it to the purpose, as I have not read his *Life*! for I have only read the *Life of Pope*; I have got the books though, for I sent for them last week, and they came to me on Wednesday, and then I began them; but I have not yet read *Lord Lyttelton*. *Pope* I have begun, and that is what I am now reading. But what I have to say about Lord Lyttelton is this here: Mr. Seward says that Lord Lyttelton's steward dunned Mr. Shenstone for his rent, by which I understand he was a tenant of Lord Lyttelton's. Well, if he was a tenant of Lord Lyttelton's, why should he not pay his rent?"

3. *Ibid.*

"Who could contradict this?" said Fanny. And she goes on: "When dinner was quite over, and we left the men to their wine, we hoped they would finish the affair . . . [but] when they were all summoned to tea, they entered still warm and violent." Mr. Cator had now begun to read the "Life of Lyttelton" that he might better understand the cause, "though not a creature," said Fanny, "cared if he had never heard of it." Dr. Johnson still "harangued and attacked . . . with a vehemence and continuity that quite concerned both Mrs. Thrale and myself, and that made Mr. Pepys, at last, resolutely silent, however called upon." "This now grew more unpleasant than ever," reported Miss Burney,

> till Mr. Cator, having some time studied his book, exclaimed,—
>
> "What I am now going to say, as I have not yet read the *Life of Lord Lyttelton* quite through, must be considered as being only said aside, because what I am going to say—"
>
> "I wish, sir," cried Mrs. Thrale, "it had been *all* set aside; here is too much about it, indeed, and I should be very glad to hear no more of it."
>
> This speech, which she made with great spirit and dignity, had an admirable effect. Everybody was silenced. Mr. Cator, thus interrupted in the midst of his proposition, looked quite amazed; Mr. Pepys was much gratified by the interference; and Dr. Johnson, after a pause, said,—
>
> "Well, madam, you *shall* hear no more of it; yet I will defend myself in every part and in every atom!"

So ended the diary entries of 1781; but in 1783 Fanny was again recounting the circumstances of the Battle with the Lytteltonians.

> "It was behaving ill to Mrs. Thrale, certainly, to quarrel in her house."

"Yes; but he never repeated it; though he wished of all things to have gone through just such another scene with Mrs. Montagu, and to refrain was an act of heroic forbearance."

"Why, I rather wonder he did not; for she was the head of the set of Lytteltonians."

"Oh, he knows that; he calls Mr. Pepys only her prime minister."

There was then the Doctor's encounter with Mrs. Montagu, who "had publicly declared—That she would never speak to him more!"

She turned from him very stiffly, & with a most distant air, & without even courtsying to him. . . . However, he went up to her himself, *longing* to begin! & very roughly said "Well, madam, what's become of your fine new House? I hear no more of it?"

"But how did she bear this?"

"Why she was *obliged* to answer him; & she soon grew so frightened—as *every body* does,—that she was as civil as ever!"[4]

When reproved by Mrs. Thrale, the "dear violent Doctor" was "very candid & generous in acknowledging" that he had acted wrongly. He is "a superior Being in all great & essential points," wrote Fanny, and "too noble to adhere to wrong";[4] yet according to her letters to her father from Brighton in 1782, she again found cause to regret Dr. Johnson's belligerence and its effects.

I am quite sorry to see how unmercifully he attacks & riots the people. He has raised such a general alarm, that he is

4. Diary MSS (Berg), 1843–47, 3509.

now omitted in all cards of invitation sent to the rest of us. What pity that he will never curb himself! nor restrain his tongue upon every occasion from such bitter or cruel speeches as eternally come from him! . . . Poor Mr. Pepys has been shook by him almost to Death: & Mr. Coxe, a Brother of the Writer, had so rough a speech from him, the other Day, that he declares it has made him nervous ever since. Dr. Delap confesses himself afraid of coming as usual to the House; & Mr. Selwyn, having yesterday declined meeting him at Mr. Hamilton's, ran away before his return Home, in the utmost terror of being severely reprimanded for his refusal.[5]

In another letter of about the same time we read that "Mr. Pepys was so torn to pieces by [Johnson] the other night, in a party at Home, that he suddenly seized his Hat, & abruptly walked out of the Room in the middle of the discourse."[5]

"Dr. Johnson has his Health wonderfully well," reported Fanny to Dr. Burney in November 1782; yet he does not "spend his time very agreeably,"

for he is dreaded too much to get any conversation, except by accident; & he has had no invitation since my arrival, but to one Dinner, at single speech Hamilton's. He has therefore passed most of his Evenings alone, & much to his dissatisfaction. He has, however, so miserably mauled the few who have ventured to encounter him, that there is little wonder they wave the ceremony of any meetings they can avoid.[5]

In 1783, as we learn from her conversation with Mr. George Cambridge, Fanny thought Dr. Johnson "much softened."

5. Letters (Berg) from Fanny Burney to Charles Burney (Mus. Doc.), 3, 8 Nov 1782.

"Why, I am now," said he, "come to that time when I wish all bitterness and animosity to be at an end." In the last years Dr. Burney too found the old Lion as "good-natured as a family mastiff, whom you may safely pat & stroke at the fireside, without the least fear of his biting you. The utmost he will do if you are a little rough with him is to growl."[6]

As James Fordyce informed the Deity in 1785, "When trouble and anguish came upon thy aged servant [Dr. Johnson] . . . Then it was, that I heard him condemn, with holy self-abasement, the pride of understanding by which he had often trespassed against the laws of courteous demeanour."[7] With the letting of Streatham in 1782, the circle was broken, and troubles and anguish indeed followed fast. Fanny never forgot the painful contortions of Johnson's frame, the furious rolling of his eye, the heavings of his ponderous chest, as from the great fund of his rage and his rhetoric he could produce only the fateful word, "Piozzi!" From Bath Mrs. Thrale wrote sympathetically, "I sent Dr Johnson a Salmon yesterday, how does he poor soul?" She had received "a most ferocious Letter" on the subject of her marriage, but once it had taken place Johnson behaved "with all the Tenderness you can imagine," sending "Prayers and Wishes" for her happiness and for Piozzi's![8] But the old intimate and comfortable scenes could not in the last years be quite what they were, now with Johnson in bachelor's quarters in Bolt Court. Dr. Burney could visit him as usual, but Fanny sometimes found it difficult. "I wanted to call upon Johnson, and it is so disagreeable to me to go to him alone, now poor Mrs. Williams is dead, on account of the quan-

6. Letter (Osborn Collection) from Charles Burney (Mus. Doc.) to the Rev. Thomas Twining, n.d.

7. "On the Death of Dr. Johnson," *Addresses to the Deity* (1813), 162–63.

8. Letters (Berg) from Hester Lynch Thrale to Fanny Burney, 19 Apr and 12 July 1784.

tity of men always visiting him, that I most gladly accepted, and almost asked, his [Mr. Hoole's] 'squireship."

At the close of 1784 those who were left of the Streatham group knew that Dr. Johnson was "going on to death very fast." According to Fanny, the letter of November 17 was the "last writing" of the "Great & Good Man" to her father: "Mr. Johnson who came home last night, sends his respects to dear Doctor Burney, and all the dear Burneys little and great."[9] And Fanny herself, remembering that he had asked her to visit him often when he should be ill, went whenever she could to Bolt Court. "*Priez Dieu pour moi!*" he had enjoined her in November 1783.[1] And a year later he renewed the injunction, "Remember me in your prayers!" If only she had had the temerity, she later confided to Susan, "to ask *him* to remember *me!*" She scarcely needed to hear from her father about Johnson's last precepts—"Do all the good you can"—or his last prayers—"the most pious, humble, eloquent, and touching . . . that mortal man could compose and utter." On 7 December, the day she had gone twice in vain to see him, she wrote to her new friends the Lockes of Norbury Park:

> [My regard for him] is sincere, respectful, & full of admiration; indeed I have always loved him as well as ever I could, & I . . . *wish* I could love him more. Mr. Locke laughed when I said so, but I meant it in earnest; for when I think a character really estimable, I *want* to love it thoroughly.
>
> Will poor Dr. Johnson *see this* where he is going? No matter, for if he sees less than he expected, in finding how far, far more I love you, whom he will regard as a *new acquaintance*, he will see *more* than he expected in find-

9. *Letters*, 1036.
1. Diary MSS (Berg), 3608; Letter (Barrett) from Fanny Burney to Susan Elizabeth Burney, 20 Jan 1783.

ing that, *with truth*, I loved him *at all*; for he perpetually told me, when we lived a good deal together, that I "cared not for him"; in which indeed he much wronged me, though I did not, because I *could* not, care for him as much as he desired; for, with all his partial kindness to *me*, his behaviour to others kept me in continual alarm.[2]

This attempt at self-analysis was somewhat belied by her actions and feelings when the end came. Having received the message "Tell Fanny—I think I shall yet throw the ball at her again," she went on Sunday, 12 December, to Bolt Court and waited for half the day in the little square parlour below, but the great man could not now see her. Fanny Burney had much to recall as she closed the annals for 1784:

Dec 20 — This day was the ever-honoured, ever-lamented Dr. Johnson committed to the earth. Oh, how sad a day to me! My father attended, and so did Charles. I could not keep my eyes dry all day; nor can I now, in the recollecting it; but let me pass over what to mourn is now so vain.

2. Letter (Berg) from Fanny Burney to Mrs. William Locke, 7 Dec 1784. See Diary MSS (Berg), 1933.

Index